DARTMOOR PRISONER OF WAR DEPOT AND CONVICT JAIL

Dedication.

For my ever loving and supportive wife June who has assisted and helped me in every way in the research and preparations for this book.

Photographs from the author's collection unless otherwise acknowledged.

First published in Great Britain in 2002

Copyright © Trevor James 2002

ISBN 1 898964 50 5

Published by Orchard Publications
2 Orchard Close, Chudleigh, Devon TQ13 0LR
Telephone 01626 852714

Printed by
Hedgerow Print
Crediton EX17 1ES

Part One.

DARTMOOR PRISONER OF WAR DEPOT

CONTENTS

FOREWORD

This is a fascinating story of Dartmoor Prison from its origins to the present. The author explains the foundation of Princetown as a village, the creation of the POW camp within double horseshoe walls, the life of the French and American prisoners, and the 'massacre' of 1815. The latter is dealt with thoroughly and is a very balanced account of the sad events.

The second part deals with the Convict Prison from 1850 to its modern role as a low security prison for adult males.

The book is lavishly illustrated and the narrative flows from the talented pen of Trevor James, an ex-journalist with the old 'Tavistock Times'.

This is a book that will enthral you as you glimpse lives in the harshest of conditions. I could not put it down until I reached the end. No book can have a greater recommendation than that.

John Lawrence
Governor Dartmoor Prison
1994-2001

INTRODUCTION

The purpose of this book is to present an accurate account of the events that led to the building of Dartmoor Depot for Prisoners of War (later to become Dartmoor Prison), its turbulent beginnings and the development of Prince Town. This is not a learned treatise however: the tale you are about to read is a more general account of the lives led by the prisoners who were held in the Depot and on the hulks during the wars with France 1803 – 1815 and the United States War of 1812 (fought simultaneously for some of the time).

A narrative of this kind relies heavily on the writings of the prisoners themselves, making allowances for national pride and the bias against us, the enemy. The data and correspondence gleaned from the libraries and Public Record Offices often make dull reading and are limited here to a few examples of special interest. The historical notes are for continuity and to provide a chronological sequence of events.

The more recent convict era is better known and chronicled, yet there remain many misconceptions among the public generally. The savagery of 19th. and 20th. century convict life cannot be disguised, but progress since those days although slow has been relentless. Prison life today is benign by comparison.

ACKNOWLEDGEMENTS.

The author wishes to express special thanks to:

Mr John Lawrence, former Dartmoor Prison Governor for kindly reading the manuscript and providing a Foreword.

Dartmoor Prison Governor Mr Graham Johnson and Governor Mr Roger Brown for their kind assistance in preparing the final chapter of this book.

Mr. Paul Deacon for many of the illustrations.

Mrs. Betty Thomson, Researcher, P.R.O., Kew.

Mr. Ira Dye, Mill Valley, California, U.S.A.

Capt. David Swales, Church Army, Princetown.

Rev. W. Birdwood, Dartmoor Prison Chaplain.

Prison Officer Mike Chamberlain.

Ex-Prison Officer Alec Palmer.

P.C. Simon Dell M.B.E., Tavistock

Monsieur Robert Martin, Versailles, France.

The late Dr .R. Taverver, Exeter.

Mr. William Saxton, Taunton.

The late Mr. James Barber, Plymouth City Museum.

Commander 'Nobby' Clegg, R.N. (Rtd.).

Duchy of Cornwall Office, Princetown (Mr. C. Sturmer and Mrs. R. Waite).

Mr. B. Estill, former Curator Devon & Cornwall Constabulary Museum.

Mr. B. Johnson, Curator, and Miss H. Smith, Dartmoor Prison Museum.

Col. F. Theobold, Moretonhampstead.

The late Mr. Ron Chudley, Exmouth.

Mr. R. Wood, Plymouth City Library.

Mrs. Rosie Oxenham.

Freemasons Hall of Research, Leicester.

United Grand Lodge of England, London.

Devon and Exeter Institution Library (Mrs. S. Stirling and Miss M. Midgley).

Exeter Central Library (Mr.I.Maxted).

Westcountry Studies Library, Exeter.

Plymouth City Museum and Art Gallery (Miss. A. Attrill and Mr. N. Overton).

Public Record Office, Exeter.

West Devon Record Office, Coxside, Plymouth.

Public Record Office, Kew, Surrey.

Devon Library Services Okehampton and Tavistock.

Regimental Museum (Duke of Cornwall Light Infantry), Bodmin.

Archives Office, Diocese of Exeter.

Moretonhampstead History Society (Mrs. A. Simkins).

There are many others too numerous to mention and the author wishes to express his sincere gratitude to them all.

ORIGIN OF PRINCE TOWN.

The author is indebted to Mr. W. Saxton of Taunton for very kindly providing much of the following information:

The nucleus around which the 18th. century developers congregated on Dartmoor was the Two Bridges area, so-called because there were originally two bridges there, one over the Cowsic River and another across the East Dart. Mr. William Crossing, the eminent writer and Dartmoor authority, has suggested it was this part of the moor that was first known as Prince Town before Sir Thomas Tyrwhitt's proud accomplishments materialised and there is evidence to support this assumption. Prince Hall, one of the 'ancient tenements', was already centuries old at that time and had always borne that title. The spelling changed from time to time: thus in 1537 it was recorded as 'Prinshill' and in 1558 'Prynce Hal'. The origins are thought to lie in the Saxon word 'Prin', which in turn was a variant of the word 'Pin', an alternative word for 'Pound' (a walled enclosure for the rounding up of sheep and cattle). Near Dunnabridge Pound, an enclosure which still exists close by the Two Bridges – Ashburton road, there was once an ancient farmstead comprising a farmhouse and some cottages – a little community in close proximity to a 'Prin'. The old men of the moor referred to such a place as a 'Town', although they were not towns at all but merely hamlets. Several 'Towns' survive today – Daveytown, Moortown, and Cudlipptown, among others. So it was that the very first Prince Town was at 'Prins Town', technically the 'Pound Farm' or settlement. The probability is that the name was transferred to the present day township by Sir Thomas Tyrwhitt and whilst not specially created for his friend the Prince of Wales was intended as a tribute to him. As for Prince Hall, the word 'Hall' is a corruption of 'Halh', meaning a mound in the midst of marshes, which description fitted the house admirably. It too is only a short distance from the 'Prin' at Dunnabridge.

Sir Thomas Tyrwhitt (Photo courtesy of Mr.David German. Reproduced by permission of the Governing Body, Christchurch, Oxford.)

A SAD CORNER OF ENGLAND IN THE YEAR 1812

It was a wild winter night on Dartmoor. Rain and sleet embroiled in a roaring gale from the Atlantic Ocean beat against the walls of the Prisoner of War Depot. The swinging oil lamps suspended from each corner of the prison buildings barely relieved the darkness of the night and formed weird shadows that raced to and fro' across the empty yards. The dim light lent a silvery glint to the water that streamed down the outside of the prison blocks. It seeped through every cranny of the stonework and trickled down inside where thousands of prisoners of war, Napoleon's soldiers and sailors, were trying to sleep. The lucky ones were in their hammocks, side by side and one above the other; the rest were on straw mattresses on the concrete floors. The tiny barred windows had wooden shutters but no glass to stop the howling draught; despite this a warm fusty odour permeated the dormitories from the mass of bodies, a poor substitute for the lack of proper heating. At other times the terrible cold froze their breath in layers on the walls.

Outside the sentries were changed and the old guard doubled away to their stone barracks hoping to find something hot to drink as they splashed through the freezing puddles, whilst their comrades on the walls cursed their luck at being on duty on such a night. The wind shrieked around the wooden platforms they occupied, causing the alarm bells, strung on wires around the perimeter walls to warn them of any escape attempt, to jingle continuously. One might think only a madman would venture forth in weather like this, yet one of the most determined (and unsuccessful) escapes ever attempted occurred on just such a night by a group of Frenchmen who hoped the downpour would shield them from the sentries' eyes. In the event they were spotted and recaptured, every one of them, a tribute to the vigilance and stoicism of the Militia soldiers on that occasion.

Inside the prison there was no furniture other than the bedding, and the men of many nations (Napoleon recruited as he conquered) were awake. Some sobbed quietly from hunger and despair, others sought pathetic comfort from one another in embraces of an unnatural kind. Angry men whispered in the darkness, plotting escape or vengeance on the guards, and there were young boys, bold lads by day, trembling and frightened in the night as scavengers prowled silently among their comrades looking to steal an unguarded crust of bread. Hunger and cold and foul air were the cause of killer diseases. In the hospital were men writhing with dysentery and fevers which were the curse of every gaol – typhus for example, known as 'gaol fever'. Others died from exposure, having gambled away their clothing and often their rations too. This was Dartmoor Depot for Prisoners of War, the most dreaded prison in the land.

The sleet turned to hail which rattled against the granite buttresses, startling the horses in the stables. Beyond the prison walls Prince Town folk snuggled into their straw beds and sighed at the noise the storm made outside. Early next morning the supply wagons rumbled through the streets, the Drummers Call roused the troops in the barracks and across the moor cattle and sheep were herded to their doom in the slaughterhouses. The bakeries were already busy.

Many of the prisoners had spent three years here unaware they were only half way through their term of imprisonment. The French Emperor Napoleon reigned supreme in Europe whilst his faithful servants in British prisons, still convinced a French invasion was imminent, eagerly awaited that day and expected to rejoin their comrades in arms. Meanwhile the tiny hamlet that once housed a small band of agricultural workers and their families had prospered with the opening of the prison and was now a thriving township. The story of those times is one of brave endeavour on the part of Sir Thomas Tyrwhitt (pronounced 'Tirrit') who founded a colony on the open moor, and of the braver spirit of Britain's foes who suffered and died to make it possible.

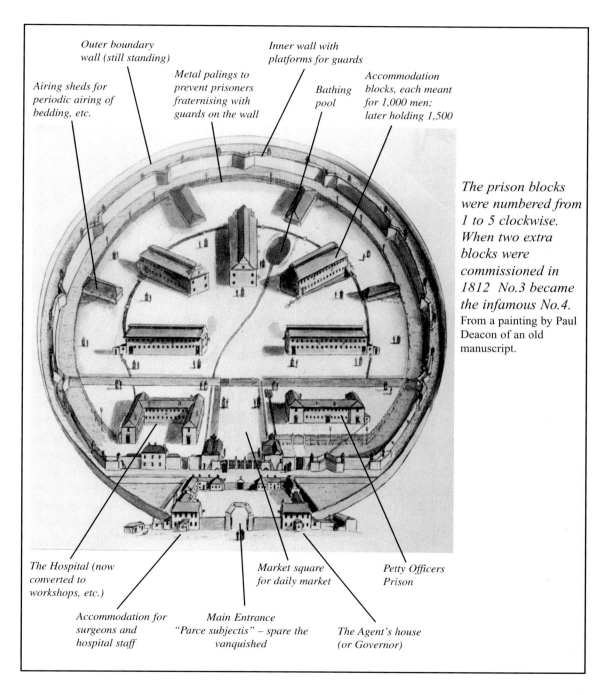

Outer boundary wall (still standing)

Inner wall with platforms for guards

Airing sheds for periodic airing of bedding, etc.

Metal palings to prevent prisoners fraternising with guards on the wall

Bathing pool

Accommodation blocks, each meant for 1,000 men; later holding 1,500

The prison blocks were numbered from 1 to 5 clockwise. When two extra blocks were commissioned in 1812 No.3 became the infamous No.4. From a painting by Paul Deacon of an old manuscript.

The Hospital (now converted to workshops, etc.)

Market square for daily market

Petty Officers Prison

Accommodation for surgeons and hospital staff

Main Entrance "Parce subjectis" – spare the vanquished

The Agent's house (or Governor)

THE SAGA BEGINS

On the Western Quarter of Dartmoor, North Hessary Tor, easily identified by the 700ft. radio mast on its crest, dominates the skyline. From the summit on a fine day the view is breathtaking: beyond the fringes of Dartmoor the rolling Devonshire landscape of fields and river valleys stretches to Plymouth Sound and the pale blue hills of distant Cornwall. The opposite slope faces northeast to the heart of the moor. Take but a few steps and the patchwork scenery behind you is blotted out. In its stead a huge landscape of undulating heath, enclosures, plantations of conifers, rivers and bogs is revealed, surrounded by other distant tors. Below this windswept and isolated spot lies Princetown and close by is H.M. Prison Dartmoor. The grey granite buildings retain a high degree of notoriety from the stark convict days, attracting sightseers like a magnet, most of whom are unaware of its history and beginnings as a prisoner of war depot or the changes that have taken place in modern times.

From the outset of the wars with Napoleon (1803-1815) Britain had the advantage in the number of prisoners taken, mostly sailors. Before long the existing prisons and the hulks (prison ships) were full and a problem then arose as to where to house them. Dartmoor Prison, or Depot as it was called, was one of several specially built for that purpose. In addition to the Frenchmen, it should be remembered there were Dutch and Danish prisoners (although nearly all the Danes were held on board one of the Plymouth hulks), Germans and Italians, in fact men from all the European nations which were either allied to, or had been conquered by France. Americans were here too, again mostly sailors taken at sea during the War of 1812 (often referred to by them as the 'Madison War', or alternatively the 'Second War of Independence'). Among them were large numbers of Negroes. The Depot was opened in 1809 and quickly filled to its capacity of just over 5,000. By 1813, after two extra prison blocks were added, there were nearly 10,000 men imprisoned here. They were guarded by units of the Militia, originally 500 strong, rising to more than 1200 as the prison population swelled, and who must have been almost as cramped in their barracks as the captives in the prison.

Inside the prison walls a legend was in the making and of a most tragic kind. From May 1809 when the first prisoners of war arrived, to February 1816 when the very last of them left for home, disease, self neglect, suicides and the very nature of their confinement – the wet, the cold and the often inadequate clothing – killed more than 1250 French and 271 Americans. Some men were shot or bayoneted whilst trying to escape. In the winter they froze and when Prince Town's fine summer weather prevailed, they endured the baking heat inside the prison walls and the anguish of being forcibly confined on balmy summer days. French and Americans reacted in different ways to their imprisonment. In general, the main body of Frenchmen settled down to make the best of things. They are remembered today for the intricate bone models and ornaments they made, for their many talents in the arts and their ability to entertain themselves. The 'Yankees' on the other hand were defiant and resentful to the end and not without good cause it must be said, because they were neglected by their Government's representative here, unwanted by the French and scorned by their captors.

To understand how Dartmoor Prison came to be built in this unlikely spot it is necessary to consider certain events which preceded it. Up until the final quarter of the 18th. century Dartmoor was a wilderness in every sense. The plantations, stone walls, and fields we see today did not then exist. The moor was a barren, treeless land, over which roamed wild ponies, foxes, badgers and deer, with buzzard hawks circling overhead. Apart from the spoil heaps left by the tinners, the turf-ties of the peat cutters, and a few farmsteads, there was little trace of human activity. The lonely moor was and still is, criss-crossed by ancient tracks along which pack horses (in reality donkeys and ponies), the only means of transport, carried goods like tin ingots and peat to the border towns. The 'clapper' bridges over the rivers and streams can still be seen, the largest of them at Postbridge. News spread slowly in these isolated places and superstition was rife among the farmers and peasants who lived on the moor in harsh conditions. When the winter gales shook the rafters of their tiny cottages at night and the rain swished across the desolate landscape, they kept close to their crackling firesides, barred the doors and went to bed early. Ghosts and pixies were very real to them.

'Dartmoor was a wilderness…'

Then a momentous thing happened. Roads were constructed across the most desolate parts of Dartmoor from Tavistock to Moreton Hampstead and Ashburton. The project was opposed by representatives from Launceston and Okehampton who feared they would lose the trade they relied upon from travellers using the existing highway that passed through the two towns. However the Duke of Bedford, an extensive landowner in the Tavistock area, used his influence to back the scheme and the building of a highway was approved by an Act of 1772.

It changed the face of the moor for ever because in its wake came settlers of a different kind. They were 'improvers', gentlemen of means who saw Dartmoor as a land ripe for exploitation, a fertile country (they thought), ready to be cultivated and make fortunes for them. Alas for their dreams! Working the poor moorland soil has long since given way to grazing cattle and sheep and no fortunes were made. The early settlers included a Mr. Gullet who acquired and improved Prince Hall. He later sold out to (Judge) Sir Francis Buller, who further restored the Hall, planted trees to protect it from winter storms (mostly larch and fir) and built a wayside inn which he named the 'Saracens Head' (a turbaned head forms the top portion of the Buller family's Coat of Arms). It is now the 'Two Bridges Hotel'. The nearby farm named 'Bairdown' was pioneered by Mr. Edward Bray, whose son Edward Atkins Bray was to become the Vicar of Tavistock and whose wife was the well known Mrs. Bray of 'Tavy and Tamar' fame. By 1800 Judge Buller was dead, nearly all the trees at Prince Hall had died and Mr. Bray had relinquished his land to a farmer for a paltry sum for grazing purposes. There were others but one by one they sold up and left, their places being taken by men of humbler status who were prepared to set their sights a little lower and had the practical ability to make the best of what there was to make a living, if not riches.

There was one affluent gentleman farmer though who had a consuming passion to create an agricultural settlement on Dartmoor. Undaunted in the fight against adverse conditions and rightly remembered now as the 'Father of Prince Town', his name was Thomas Tyrwhitt, later to become Sir Thomas. In 1785 he acquired the lease of 2,500 acres of moorland, about two miles south of where the new road passed through a small community known today as Two Bridges. He was twenty three years old, wealthy, influential, and a close friend of the Prince of Wales the future King George IV. The amazing story of the War Depot and the development of Prince Town is entirely due to this man, one of the least known influential figures of his time. He had met the Prince of Wales at Oxford University (where he gained a B.A. Degree and later an M.A.) and they at once became close friends. Being well educated and from a distinguished Lincolnshire family whose members included two Sheriffs of the County and high ranking Ecclesiastics, Thomas Tyrwhitt was high on the list of potentially powerful men in England – a rising star. It was undoubtedly his friendship with the Prince that brought him to Dartmoor and a succession of important posts which included:

1795 Private Secretary to the Prince of Wales.
1796 Auditor and Secretary to the Duchy of Cornwall.
1803 Lord Warden of the Stannaries.
1805 Vice Admiral of the Counties of Devon and Cornwall.
1812 Gentleman Usher of Black Rod (having previously been Knighted).
1812 Keeper (Ranger) of H.M. Little Park at Windsor.

He was also Member of Parliament for Okehampton (1796-1802).
Portarlington (Dec. 1802-Feb. 1806).
Plymouth (March 1806-June 1812).

His dream was to establish a township to be named Prince Town in honour of his friend the Prince and to start with he built a home at Tor Royal, not far from the present day town. The workmen he engaged lived nearby with their families. At first he had some success when he produced a crop of flax to a standard which earned him a medal from the Bath Agricultural Society. A mill was established at Bachelors Hall, not far from Tor Royal, thus laying the foundations for what Mr. Tyrwhitt hoped would be an agricultural community on Dartmoor. The inn he built for his workers and the packhorse drovers was named the 'Prince's Arms' and can still be seen plying its trade in the centre of modern Princetown under its new name 'The Plume of Feathers', a reference to the Prince of Wales' Coat of Arms which is surmounted by a plume of ostrich feathers; it is the oldest building in the town. The tiny cottages that housed the first residents have long since disappeared.

A beginning had been made and Mr. Tyrwhitt, full of optimism, enjoyed happy times at Tor Royal, entertaining many of his friends there. As for the town, a new road was cut from the 'Plume of Feathers' to Rundlestone where it joined the Tavistock to Two Bridges road, thus saving several miles on a journey to Tavistock. It was named 'Tyrwhitt Road' and it was adjacent to this road further development took place including the prison, after which it was named 'Prison Road' (Tavistock Road today). At the commencement of the 19th. century the prison was undreamed of, the intention being to focus every effort on agricultural matters and attract new settlers; but 'Old Dartymoor' brought ruin to many a bold venture and Thomas Tyrwhitt's plans were to be no exception, despite his affluence and enthusiasm. His estate was situated on a cold moor, 1400 ft. above sea level where growth of anything other than ferns and heather is restricted. The soil is acid and stony and by the turn of the century things were not going well at Tor Royal. Because he was absent for long periods on his official duties Mr. Tyrwhitt probably did not realise things were not turning out as he had hoped and that his dreams were beginning to fade. The war with France was to be his salvation.

In 1803 the Treaty of Amiens was terminated when Britain declared war on France after less than two years of peace. Agents had reported French carpenters were working night and day at Calais and Boulogne-sur-Mer building huge barges (more than 2,000 had been planned) to transport a 200,000 strong 'Grand Army' in an invasion of our shores. Like Adolph Hitler, a conqueror of a later date, Napoleon realised his plans for expanding his Empire could only be consolidated by subjugating Britain first and the security of our island now became entirely dependant on the Royal Navy whose job was to blockade French ports, contain her navy (without which the invasion could not take place) and prevent trade. The scale of the Navy's success was reflected in the vast numbers of prisoners taken, especially after the Battle of Trafalgar in 1805, and Britain was faced with the enormous problem of where to confine them. The gaols were full. There were some war prisons from previous wars: Normans Cross near Peterborough, first opened in 1797, could accommodate 7,000 men; Stapleton near Bristol (1782) held 5,000, the oldest being Mill Prison in Plymouth dating from 1695 and capable of containing another 5,000 or so. All three establishments were soon filled. Old castles were then pressed into service; Edinburgh and Forton near Gosport for example, even country houses and dockside warehouses were used for a short while. At Plymouth French prisoners were confined in the Citadel and the China House at Cattedown, Thomas Cookworthy's old porcelain factory (now a popular public house and restaurant). Devonport Dockyard held many hundreds of captives and a brief description may assist the reader in realising how desperate the situation was and how it led to the building of Dartmoor Prison.

Situated in the South Yard at Devonport is the 1,000 ft. long Old Ropery where ropes for British warships were made before Nelson's time. A part of this complex, known as the West Ropery was destroyed by enemy bombing during World War Two, but under the foundations there are more than forty stone 'cells' (formerly storehouses) which were used for the confinement of

Millbay Barracks, Plymouth 1908. This was originally Mill Prison for French prisoners of war.
(Courtesy of Plymouth City Museum and Art Gallery. Ref: Rugg Monk 37.112.24).

French prisoners of war. Each cell is about 20 ft. long and 8 ft. high, the width being about 9 ft. There are no windows so light and ventilation must have been limited to what entered via the barred gates that shut the prisoners in. Altogether these cells held around 1,000 men. The Ropery also has an execution chamber, situated in a room originally used for tarring rope. The lever-operated trap and 'drop' are in perfect working order and the heavy wooden beam from which the noose was suspended is still there. Mounted on the walls are the candle holders which provided light for the grisly business of hanging the 149 men who died in this room between 1793 and 1815. On the stone paved floor below is a lead covered mortuary slab on which the bodies were laid out to enable Plymouth surgeons to remove internal organs (for instruction purposes), after which the remains were thrown into a lime pit outside. Commander 'Nobby' Clegg, R.N., who very kindly showed the author around several years ago, said a nail was knocked into the wall for every victim but only one is still in place, the rest having been removed by an over zealous painter who did not realise their significance. The gallows were erected at the insistence of the French themselves who wanted the ultimate penalty to be available to them for murder and severe breaches of discipline. *'The French acted as arbitrators and judges on their countrymen and probably provided the executioner as well, because the British had nothing to do with it whatsoever'* declared Commander Clegg (although prisoners convicted of capital offences elsewhere were tried and convicted in British courts and hanged in our gaols).

As more prisoners arrived the infamous hulks were commissioned. They had been used in earlier wars and were dreaded by the foe. The hulks were dismasted, derelict men o' war converted to prison ships, where hundreds of men were confined below decks in an atmosphere so fetid that when the ports were opened in the mornings after being battened down for the night the guards often fainted from the stench that exuded from within. The foul air, lack of exercise and poor sanitary arrangements led to outbreaks of fatal diseases and chest complaints. As the war progressed the hulks were used for the confinement of the very worst of men – privateers men and troublemakers from the shore depots. In addition to the problems associated with overcrowding and illness there were several desperate attempts to escape. Holes were cut in the decks and sides through which numbers of men were to emerge, overpower the guards and steal any boats to hand to make a getaway. On at least one occasion fires were deliberately started in the hope of making off in the confusion. A major concern was the possibility of a mass escape which could endanger the huge naval arsenal (ammunition ships filled with gunpowder and shot). Above all the hulks were expensive to run and maintain compared to shore establishments; consequently the time was ripe for another shore prison to be built.

That requirement was about to be met by Thomas Tyrwhitt (referred to from now on as Sir Thomas because he is better known by that title) who saw an opportunity to retrieve a difficult situation at Prince Town. The Prince of Wales (Duke of Cornwall) indicated he was willing to help, being prepared to release a portion of Duchy land on which to build the new Depot. It is not generally realised that the majority of Duchy property lies outside Cornwall, much of it on Dartmoor: all of 'Dartmoor Forest' (forest in this sense meaning Royal hunting ground, with a clearly established boundary around the centre of the moor) is under its direct ownership. In addition to several of the farms and inns on the moor, many properties in Princetown including H.M. Prison at Dartmoor pay an annual leasehold rent to the Duchy.

At this point it should be explained the responsibility for prisoners of war used to lie with the Commissioners of the Sick and Hurt Office whose jurisdiction, as the name implies, was over sick and wounded seafarers. In 1799 this was changed when the Transport Office (or Board) took over the supervision of prisoners. Both these offices were departments of the British Admiralty and subject to its authority. Thus in 1805 the following letter was written to the Admiralty by the Transport Office:

'26 June 1805

Sir;

considering the impropriety of keeping a great body of prisoners in the immediate neighbourhood of the Naval Arsenals, and the very great expense unavoidably attendant on Prison Ships, we have long been desirous of providing as much accommodation as possible in the interior of the country; but having only two inland Depots of Stapleton and Norman Cross, there is still a considerable number of prisoners kept from necessity at Plymouth, occupying six prison ships at a yearly expense of the whole of not less than £18,000. (Author's note: the new prison was expected to incur an annual running cost of less than £3,000).

With a view to reduce this expense, we request you will inform the Right Honourable Lords Commissioners of the Admiralty that we have proposed to erect a prison to contain not less than

5,000 men in the County of Devon at a convenient distance from Plymouth which would save us the expense of 7 or 8 Third Rate Ships. And having judged Dartmoor to be a most eligible and healthy situation for such a purpose, we thought it proper to enquire whether a part of that extensive district could be procured, and in consequence of our application to Mr. Tyrwhitt, the Lord Warden of the Stannaries in Cornwall and Devon has signified to us the entire consent of His Royal Highness the Prince of Wales to our having whatever quantity of the moor we may find necessary for a prison, <u>without any charge to the public other than an Act of Parliament to transfer the property from the Duke of Cornwall to the Crown</u>. (Author's underlining – this was never done, a lease was substituted as previously mentioned).

We now therefore beg leave to submit the matter to their Lordship's consideration and if for the reasons above stated they should approve of the proposed measure being carried into execution we request you will inform us whether it is their Lordship's pleasure that one of the Commissioners of this Board with a surveyor should proceed to Dartmoor for the purpose of selecting a fit situation for the intended buildings in order that we may forthwith procure plans and estimates of the expense to be laid before their Lordships for their ultimate determination.'

The scene was set for building Dartmoor Prisoner of War Depot.

THE PRISON SHIPS.

During the war against Napoleon there were more than forty Prison Ships or 'Pontons', as the French called them, on the South Coast. They included:

At Portsmouth

Prothea	*Suffolk*
Crown	*Assistance*
San Tomaso	*Ave Princessa*
Vigilant	*Kron Princessa*
Guildford	*Waldemar*
San Antonio	*Negro*
Vengeance	*Diamond*
Veteran	

Hospital Ships *Caton, Pegasus, Marengo* and *Princess Sophia*

At Chatham

Cornwall	*Southwick*
Brunswick	*Irresitable*
Buckingham	*Nassau*
Sampson	*Belligueux*

At Chatham (contd.)

Bahama	*Vryheid*
Canada	*Hero*
Bristol	*Eagle*
Glory	*Camperdown*
Crown Prince	*Gelykheid*
Rochester	*Sandwich*

Hospital Ships *Fyen* and *Trusty*

At Plymouth

Royal Oak	*Genereux*
San Raphael	*Hector*
Ganges	*Le Brave*
El Ferme	*St. Isadore*
Bienfaissant	*Ceres*

Hospital Ships: *Europe* and *Renown*

A START IS MADE

Sir Thomas Tyrwhitt was well placed to influence what was intended with regard to a prisoner of war depot on Dartmoor and would have known those persons most influential in making decisions. On 9th. July 1805 the Transport Office, having received approval from the Admiralty to proceed, wrote to Mr. Daniel Alexander the surveyor and architect they had selected and directed:

'that you will be at Mr. Tyrwhitt's Tor Royal between Moreton Hampstead and Tavistock on the 18th. of this month where you will meet with the Hon. E. Bouverie, one of the members of this Board. The intended building at Dartmoor is to be for 5,000 prisoners with an Hospital and the necessary accommodation for the Officers to be employed in the Superintendence of the Prisoners and the Military Guard'.

The 'cat was out of the bag' though as the following report indicates:

Extract from the *Bristol Mirror* 13th. July 1805 (note the date).

'The Prince of Wales is about to erect at his own expense a Chapel at Prince Town in the Forest of Dartmoor under the direction of Thomas Tyrwhitt, Esq., Lord Warden of the Stannaries. Mr. Tyrwhitt has suggested to the government the propriety of erecting a building near the above for depositing such Prisoners of war as may be brought into Plymouth who can without any difficulty be conveyed up the River Tamar and landed a few miles from the spot.'

The article must have been a 'scoop' for the paper as the initial survey on which everything depended had not yet been carried out and the Transport Office had certainly not made a decision about it. Some interesting conclusions may be drawn:

1. Sir Thomas's ambitions for Prince Town and a war prison there were already known about.
2. A settlement was already established, sufficiently large to justify the expense of a chapel (probably at Two Bridges, the area which is now thought to have been named Prince Town first). It so happened the chapel was not completed until 1815, having been built by French and American prisoners of war.
3. The Prince of Wales was aware of developments. It seems the entire project and the location had already been decided.

Five days later the three men, Tyrwhitt, Bouverie and Alexander duly met at Tor Royal and Sir Thomas conducted his visitors to various parts of the moor one of which, the site of the present day prison, was chosen. We can be sure Sir Thomas's opinions were crucial, bearing in mind his position and the fact his companions, who were strangers to Dartmoor, would have relied heavily on his advice. It is generally recognised there were other sites suitable for the War Prison but he was determined it would be built close to his quarries and mills which would fulfil its needs, ensuring a handsome return on his investments as well as furthering his ambitions. Nevertheless it was a wonderful thing that happened. When the War Depot was established the quiet hamlet that had arisen on a bare landscape expanded to form a thriving township. A slaughterhouse was built and two bakeries. All other essential supplies for the thousands of prisoners and the garrison had to be transported by wagon from Plymouth and towns throughout the west. Above the creaking of the cartwheels the ring of the blacksmith's hammer was heard amid the shouts of the drovers and the military in the barracks. The quarries must have been worked to capacity as additions were made to the town and the 'Capital of the Moor' reached its zenith.

Mr. Alexander's expertise should not be overlooked. His task was to assess what could be done with the materials to hand, the manpower that would be required and of course the cost, which had to be kept as low as possible. Daniel Alexander was one of the foremost surveyors of his day and a brilliant designer from early on in his career, his ability having won him a silver medal at the Royal Academy when he was a student there. He was born in London in 1768 and after attending St. Paul's School was apprenticed to Mr. Samuel Robinson, a well known and much sought after builder of warehouses and docks. Young Alexander did so well that on completing his apprenticeship he was immediately hired to build a large house at Highbury Hill (a rapidly growing area of London at that time), an unprecedented event for a recently qualified person. He went on to construct warehouses, harbours and lighthouses for the Admiralty and the London Dock Company and was at the top of his profession when he was chosen to plan and execute the building of Dartmoor Prison.

In many ways the choice of site was ideal. It was seventeen miles from Plymouth and therefore secure, but close enough for reinforcements to be quickly on the scene should the need arise. Most importantly plenty of stone was available on the moor and at the nearby quarries, including Herne Hole, the present day prison quarry (no longer being worked). Wood for building purposes was scarce and expensive (Normans Cross had been built entirely of wood but with the Baltic ports blockaded by Napoleon there were no further imports of timber at that time and in any case most available stocks had been used to construct the Royal Navy's 'wooden walls'). Therefore Britain's most famous prison was built of stone, despite the fact it was intended to be a temporary place of confinement for war prisoners. Another consideration was the enormous quantity of water required for the 5,000 prisoners, the military guards and the workmen. The springs in the locality were inadequate, but ample supplies were at hand from the upper reaches of the River Walkham, from which water was extracted and conveyed by gravity along the contours of the hills via a four mile long prison leat to a reservoir adjacent to the prison. Finally, the climate was judged to be healthy which it certainly was compared to the stinking hulks, but the inspection was made on a summer day in July and experience later revealed (Sir Thomas must have known) that this particular spot is notorious on Dartmoor as being subject to the full fury of winter's icy blasts. Apart from the frightful cold and snowstorms that often occur in winter, there are the thick wet mists which often linger for days, even during the summer months – if there is bad weather about North Hessary will get the worst of it.

The Transport Office was anxious to get the best possible value for its money and for good reason: the war was getting costly and the number of captives to be provided for was an ever increasing burden. Up until 1799 the French and British governments each provided fixed sums for the subsistence of every officer and man held prisoner by the other side, to be used for clothing as well as food. The French then repudiated their commitment, with the express intention of weakening Britain financially by forcing her to provide for the prisoners on both sides. The French were short of funds because of the restrictions on trade brought about by the Royal Navy's blockade, and the fact that Napoleon's vast armies were a tremendous drain on the exchequer. Nevertheless it was a callous decision by the French who abandoned their countrymen to the mercy of the enemy (in Mill Prison at Plymouth for example it was reported the French prisoners were reduced to skeletons who picked out snails to eat from crevices in the walls). The expense of running and maintaining the hulks was worrying too. It was estimated the

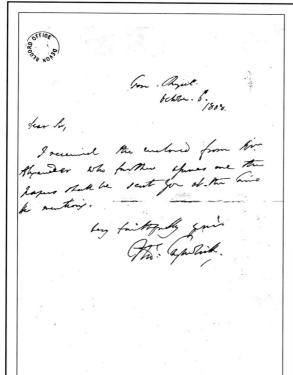
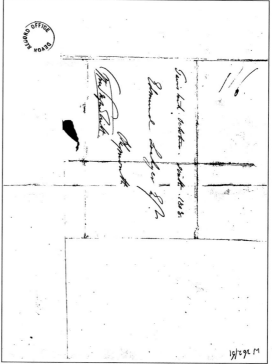

Note written by Sir Thomas Tyrwhitt with reference to Daniel Alexander who designed Dartmoor Prison. The creases are where the letter was folded (no envelopes in those days) and the remains of the sealing wax are clearly visible. (Reproduced by permission of West Devon Records Office, Cattedown, Plymouth. Ref. W362/51).

annual cost of a seventy four gun vessel holding 700 men was £5,869 whereas Dartmoor Depot housing 5,000 men (initially) would cost an estimated £2,600 per annum. Mr. Alexander submitted his first proposals, with costings, on 18th. September, only two months after seeing the ground for the first time. The area allocated for the prison proper was to be twenty three acres with accommodation for 5,282 prisoners, and capable of being enlarged at a later date to house up to 8,370. The total costs were presented as follows:

	£	s.	d.
For 5,282 men	86,423	13	4
Cost of increase to 8,370 men	17,901	3	4
TOTAL =	104,324	16	8

It was not accepted by the Transport Office because, whilst recognising the relatively small cost of increasing the prison's capacity to over 8,000, they felt unable to afford the initial figure of £86,000 plus and called for another plan (yes – it was Plan B). The second plan was approved and is worth recording. From Mr. Alexander's report:

'London Sept. 26 1805
Prison of War Dartmoor.
To the Honourable the Commissioners of the Transport Service, and for the Care and Custody of Prisoners of War.
Honourable Sirs,
in obedience to your direction of the 20th. inst. to see, in what manner, and to what degree, the Plan proposed to your Hon. Board on the 18th. inst. could be reduced, in regard to extent and cost, and so as to be built in the least possible time:
I beg leave further to report that I have made another plan, with accommodation for 5,158 men <u>but without any means of increasing the Depot at any further time</u>: and have reduced the area of ground from 23 acres to 15 acres and a quarter, <u>shortening the length of the boundary walls proportionately</u> (author's underlining; the outer wall still stands, a truly mammoth work approx. one mile long). *The quantity of rough masonry is thus reduced from 29,706 Perches to 18,632 Perches, and the time required to build such a quantity of walling, the only difficulty to be foreseen in the whole work, is consequently shortened. If means are resorted to procure masons from the Moors in Yorkshire, in addition to the Cornish and Devon Moor Men, I think, that the major part of the scheme might be completed by the end of the year 1806 containing 3,374 men, and at an expense of:*

	£	s.	d.
Internal Boundary Wall, water courses, etc	13,756	10	1
Three prison buildings	16,664	18	6
Hospital	7,951	5	1
Cook rooms, etc.	995	18	2
Offices for Management	9,994	5	6
Expense first year: 3,374 men	49,362	17	4

and that the remainder of the prison would be finished in the year 1807 at an expense of:

	£	s.	d.
Barracks for 500 men early in the year	5,004	7	0
Two prison buildings	8,868	5	7
Four sheds	3,070	4	0
Petty Officers Prison	3,107	7	11
External boundary wall	733	8	0
Expense second year	20,783	7	6
TOTAL =	70,146	4	10

I have the Honour to be Gentlemen,
Your Most Obedient and Humble Servant,
Daniel Alexander'.

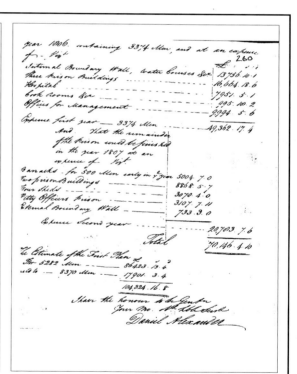

Daniel Alexander's estimate for Dartmoor Depot with letter to the Transport Office
(PRO Kew. Ref ADM 13774).

There are several points worthy of note. The calculations are to the nearest penny, presumably based on an accredited formulae much the same as that used by estimators today (and in much the same way does not always work out in practice!). As always there were unforeseen circumstances which will be considered presently. Note the optimism regarding the timetable – twelve months to complete the first stage (conditions on the moor were vastly different to those in the Capital as Mr. Alexander was soon to discover). As for the masons, in a later communication he said *'the masons in the country are beginning to 'rouze' and by information received at Calstock, Truro, Penryhn, and Helston in the West, that a great many Moor Masons may be procured at prices below what I have estimated'* indicating the Yorkshiremen were no longer needed. Penrhyn was known in those days as the 'Granite Borough' on account of the large quantity of that stone to be found there. Following the stone mason's trade ('always work with your back to the wind') was a family tradition and we know some men from that area did come to Dartmoor to help build the prison (and subsequently went on strike when they realised how poor the pay was). Many of them walked back home.

Both plans were submitted to the Admiralty on 9th.October 1805 by the Transport Office, who had been advised by Mr. Alexander that still further savings could be made by making use of the 'moor stone' lying around on site which would save the time and expense of quarrying. Then a local surveyor engaged by him to examine the place more closely, advised that the layers of peat were not as thick had been thought, and *'could be removed by running off with water'* thus saving on excavation work and that this saving alone would amount to £5,000. As expected Plan B was approved and advertisements appeared in the newspapers in October, including one in the *Exeter Flying Post*, part of which reads:

'buildings and boundary walls will cover about 15 acres; they are to be constructed of moorstone to be broken from scattered rocks on the spot, where there is also fine gravel, sand and water. They are to be floored with timber and slate. Plans and specifications will be laid out at this office and Tor Royal. Tenders are to contain proposals for executing the work, including every trade or for any separate trades with the names of sufficient sureties for fulfilling the contracts'.

It was further stipulated that the contract would at once be cancelled if the war should end.

As it happened the floors were not laid with timber for the reasons previously given and concrete was used instead. Furthermore the quantities of sand and gravel were not as great as had been supposed and ultimately these two items alone added considerably to the final cost. Four tenders were received, all of them from Plymouth and details of three estimates survive:

Messrs. Fowell and Company   £115,377
Messrs. Sheppard and Company   £84,828
Messrs. Isbell Rowe and Company   £66,815

The lowest tender was of course accepted and Mr. Alexander was appointed to personally supervise the work. Far from completing the first phase by the end of the year 1806 with completion the following year, it was to be May 1809 before the first prisoners moved in, by which time the cost had escalated to £135,000 (not only that but in 1811 the capacity of the prison did have to be increased and the Admiralty must have rued the day they turned down Alexander's first plan).

There were problems from the start. As late as 16th. January 1806 the Transport Office advised

Their Lordships that:

'in consequence of a communication from Mr. Tyrwhitt on the part of His Royal Highness the Prince of Wales as Duke of Cornwall, stating that a lease for 99 years of the Ground amounting to 390 acres, being the quantity marked out by the Surveyor upon which the prison is to be built on Dartmoor we request you will transmit to us as early as possible that no hindrance may occur in the prosecution of our works for which we are making the necessary preparations'.

This was a delay not bargained for, but at last all was arranged, the Foundation Stone was laid on 20th. March 1806 by Sir Thomas Tyrwhitt and work commenced. It was to be more than three years before the first prisoners of war were admitted. On 24th. May 1809 nearly 2,500 Frenchmen were marched up to Dartmoor Depot from the Plymouth hulks, many of them from the 'Bienfaissant' which was in such a bad state of repair it was never used as a prison ship again. There were thirty five cart loads of baggage from this ship alone.

THE PRISON IS BUILT

Daniel Alexander the surveyor engaged to design and supervise the building of Dartmoor Depot had written: *'...I think that the major part of the scheme might be completed by the end of the year 1806...'* and *'...the remainder of the prison would be finished in the year 1807...'* (he was referring to Plan B).

How was it that completion was delayed for nearly a year and a half? It was a combination of many factors not the least of which was simply Dartmoor (Hessary Tor) weather. There must have been unimaginable difficulties hewing stone on the open moor in freezing fogs or sleet showers and on soggy ground. Working on Dartmoor in summer heat can be equally trying. No tradesman was prepared to endure such conditions without an adequate reward for his labours and there must have been a large 'turnover' of workmen. Then there was the Transport Office, a parsimonious employer who quibbled over every penny and who must have been appalled when the tender, which was accepted at approximately £3,000 below the estimate, ran to more than twice as much before the job was done. This, together with the fine margins the contractors set themselves, resulted in such hurried and poor workmanship that much of it had to be done again. Another problem arose from the sheer scale of the project. The mighty edifice surpassed anything previously seen in the west and the spectacle attracted a constant stream of official and unofficial visitors, often accompanied by their families and friends, expecting guided tours. It had to be stopped and it was. *Truman's Exeter Post* for 2nd. July 1807 reports:

'...whereas great hindrance and delay is being experienced by the men employed on the works of the said prison in consequence of visitors going through the same: it is ordered that no persons be admitted but such as apply to the Clerk of Works who will give proper directions accordingly, and then none to be admitted on Sundays'.

It had been expected the Depot would receive its first inmates by Christmas 1807, but it was May 1809 before it was ready for occupation, with construction still in progress and only two prison blocks available. Mr. Alexander and his men must have had their patience and endurance tried to the limit. To add to the contractor's difficulties the price of timber (of which some quantity was necessary for the roofing) rose to a level beyond their resources, and the Admiralty were obliged to provide timber from discarded ships at Plymouth dockyard to help out. Some of that wood is still in place.

Here is a description of the prison as it was then and how it later developed. The boundary wall you see now was the outer one of two walls, enclosing an area of roughly fifteen acres. Mounted at intervals on the inner wall were wooden platforms overlooking the interior and manned by armed sentries. The 20ft. wide gap between the walls was known as the Military Walk, a 'no man's land' for potential escapees with guardrooms positioned within for the sentries to rest and take shelter in very bad weather. The inner wall was extended across the diameter of the circular interior leaving a half-moon shaped area on the lower slope (the ground slopes from the front to the rear of the prison) where the main body of prisoners were accommodated in five blocks, each three storeys high and radiating from a common centre in a fan-like formation. This design ensured the maximum amount of light and air between each block as well as giving the guards a wider view of the interior. The ground areas, or yards as they were called, were surrounded by a palisade of iron railings to prevent the inmates from approaching the walls and fraternising with

Dartmoor Prison being built 1807.
(Drawings by Samuel Prout from the Collection of Plymouth City Museum and Art Gallery).

the guards. The yards were lit at night by oil lamps suspended from the corners of each block, and were surfaced with 'macadam', a type of hard surface invented by John Macadam (1756-1836), mainly for use in road building. His method was to use stone broken into small pieces approximately six ounces in weight. When these were compressed and the gaps filled with powder ground from the stones, it formed a solid surface, very strong and enduring. To this day such surfaces are said to be 'macadamised' (not to be confused with 'tarmacadam' which did not appear until after 1869 when Trinidad bitumen was discovered).

The accommodation blocks had granite steps with granite pillars inside to support the concrete floors, no straw or covering of any kind being provided. There was no furniture. Rows of iron posts were installed to enable the prisoners to sling their hammocks one above the other in tiers. At a later stage, as a result of the overcrowding, men slept on the floors as well, a daunting prospect in winter without heating and the two foot square 'windows' having no glass to stop the freezing draught, just wooden shutters which could be closed but which would not have been draught-proof by any means. Each block was designed to accommodate 1,000 men, 500 on each floor. The top floors were laid with wood and were called 'cocklofts', areas where the men could exercise when the weather was bad. Ultimately they were pressed into service as extra dormitories, resulting in 1500 men being crammed into each block, eating and sleeping in hideously cramped conditions. By the year 1812 the number of blocks had increased to seven,

An old photo of one of the original 'French' prison blocks before conversion for convict accommodation.

22

two more having been built by the prisoners themselves, not by forced labour which was forbidden by mutual agreement with the French but by volunteers who were paid a daily rate. These last two blocks had wooden floors throughout made of stout planks caulked and seamed as on board ship; as a result they were warmer and much sought after. Daniel Alexander designed one main kitchen to serve the entire prison population, but by the time the two extra blocks were built, each of the seven had an extension added for that purpose, quaintly marked 'cookeries' on the surviving drawings. Cooks and helpers were recruited from among the prisoners, and received a daily wage.

Three of the seven blocks stand today. One of them is in use for present day inmates who occupy individual cells and unlike the POWs of old, enjoy the benefit of central heating. The roof of this building was restored in the late 1980s, the original wooden rafters made with timber saved from redundant 18th. century men o' war finally showing signs of distress. Of course the entire block has been renovated throughout and proper windows fitted. Another war prison was converted for kitchen use in the 1940s, but is now redundant (a fine new kitchen was commissioned in 1993). The other remaining accommodation block from the War Depot days is referred to by the prison staff as 'The Old Chapel' although it has long ceased to be used for that purpose, alternative premises having been provided. This old building is far from derelict and was the notorious No.4 block about which more will be told later. The building is listed and will be preserved in a practical manner by conversion to a Multi-Faith Chaplaincy greatly helped by the New Start Chapel Project, a fund raising body headed by Lady Georgina Wates. From the outside you can still see the original granite window sills and the outlines of the now blocked up apertures are clearly visible. The roof area (the 'cockloft' of old) is sound, the timbers are dry and a few rusty nails are embedded in the timbers that form the roof supports, some of which may have been used to sling hammocks (although we know from the written accounts of those who lived here that most of them slept on the floor). Many of the overhead beams carry scorch marks, almost certainly the scars left from the candle holders fixed to them at that time. The place has a sombre appearance and an 'atmosphere' very much in keeping with its sad history, for it was in this building two French fencing masters settled a quarrel by duelling with improvised swords, resulting in one of them being 'run through' and killed. It seems this was the place where arguments were concluded, out of sight and earshot of the prison authorities who would certainly have put a stop to such goings on. The despicable 'Romans' were kept in this building, separate from the main body of prisoners. They were degenerate outcasts, so filthy and vice-ridden their fellow prisoners couldn't stand them and in the end they were removed from Dartmoor to finish their captivity on the hulks. American Negroes who were segregated for different reasons afterwards took over No. 4 block.

These were the arrangements for the main body of men. The upper half of the depot was for the supervisory staff, the hospital, and the so-called 'Petty Officers Prison'. Contrary to what the name implies, the last named was a separate enclosed prison specially provided for ships' captains, chaplains, surgeons, army officers, and 'persons of respectability'. The term 'Petty' that was used was probably a corruption by the British of its real title 'Le Petit Cautionnement' which is what the French called it. Among those confined here were the 'Detinues', French civilians who had taken advantage of the period of peace during the Treaty of Amiens (1802- 1803) to visit England. Many Britishers had done the same thing, having travelled to France in large numbers after years of warfare had made such visits impossible. On the very day that war was declared (18th. May 1803) the Royal Navy captured two French warships in the English Channel. This action so angered Napoleon he promptly retaliated by ordering the arrest of all British subjects who happened to be on French territory at the time. Around 1,000 British nationals were detained and this single act was to harden British resolve in the years of conflict that lay ahead. The British reacted by arresting all visitors to this country – hence the presence of 'Detinues' in our war prisons. There were women and children detained on both sides, but not in prisons.

The personnel in the 'Petty Officers Prison' were those who had violated, or refused to take, their parole. Under this system certain officers were permitted to reside in nearby towns in complete freedom, provided they gave their word of honour not to try to escape and to observe the conditions for parole laid down by the authorities. Those who broke these terms or attempted to escape, together with those who refused to accept parole, were held in this separate prison which still stands above and to the right of the main prison blocks (looking from the entrance). The present day chapel, prison hospital and various other offices are integral parts of it now. The hospital for prisoners of war stood opposite and to the left of the entrance to the prison. It was run by a Royal Naval surgeon, a matron, and three attendants, assisted by nurses recruited from the fit and healthy prisoners. This building now houses training workshops and the old (now obsolete) mailbag shop.

Between the 'Petty Officers Prison' and the hospital was an open space called the Market

Wall of the prisoner of war hospital showing the rough moorstone construction.

Square, where a market was held every day from 9.00am until noon (except Sundays) to enable prisoners to buy or barter for food and clothing to supplement what was issued to them. The goods were brought in by country folk from the surrounding farms and traders from Plymouth and Tavistock. Entrance to the square was via two stout gates, one for the prisoners at the lower end, and an upper gate for those coming and going. Also at the higher end of the market square were two roughly circular buildings which were used as storehouses. Originally emergency rations were kept there for when the prison might be cut off by snow during the winter and the daily bread ration was stored here too prior to being issued. These buildings are in use today after extensive renovation work – one is for the reception of inmates' visitors and the other is now an office block.

The Military Walk completed its circuit at the upper gate of the market square. Initially all access to the square and the prisons was through the main entrance, but in 1813, probably for security reasons, a Postern gate was built through the south side of the outer wall. The market people and the military personnel then entered and left by this gate (it was blocked up after the convict prison opened in 1850). The stone pillars and lintel are clearly visible today as is the overhead inscription cut by the French mason who constructed it which reads: *'Henri Prisonniere Journee 1813'*.

The administration and supervisory staff lived in the upper part of the prison near the road.

The old Postern Gateway and overhead inscription 'Henri Prisonnier 1813 Journee Francais'.
(Courtesy of Mr. David German).

The Governor or 'Agent' as he was called (the term indicates he was the agent of the Transport Office whose written orders for the care and supervision of the prisoners he was expected to enforce) lived with his family in the house to the right of the archway, now the Prison Officers Mess. It was also home to the Governors who administered the convict prison in later years. To the left of the arch was the surgeon's house and living quarters for the medical staff and the clerks. Today they are used for offices and stores.

The giant archway, which has become a symbol of Dartmoor prison, is remarkably well preserved as are the words *'PARCERE SUBJECTIS'* ('Spare The Vanquished') engraved overhead. These words are taken from Virgil's *Charge to the Roman People*:

> *'Be These Your Arts:*
> *Pacisque Imponere Morem Parcere Subjectis et Deballare Superbus'*
> (To Impose the Rule of Peace Spare the Vanquished and Abase the Proud).

Thousands of unhappy war prisoners and the convicts who came afterwards have entered into captivity under its grim visage. The sightseers who tend to congregate here on summer days often fail to notice the low stone tower which stands above the wall on the opposite side of the road. This wall encloses part of the reservoir that was supplied by the prison leat and was the source of the water supply to the entire prison. Sluice gates within the tower controlled the flow of water by gravity to the various prison buildings via slate-lined channels. In the prison blocks it first passed through the cookeries, then a washing area before exiting under the latrines (there was a 'foul water' leat that conducted the waste past the Ockery to the wild moorland beyond Tor Royal). At the lower part of the prison compound was a bathing pond described by American prisoner of war John Mellish as *'a plunge bath of great comfort to the prisoners'* which no doubt it was. The water supply sometimes froze solid and during one severe winter the prisoners were compelled to eat snow to alleviate their thirst. One of the principle appointments listed when the Depot first opened was that of 'Navigator' and it has caused much speculation; in fact the post was an essential one. The men who dug Britain's canals were called 'navigators', a colloquial term later shortened to 'navvies' when applied to the manual workers who constructed roads and railways. The navigator's job at Dartmoor was a simple but very necessary one – he maintained the leat and was therefore a key figure who fully merited a mention on the list of staff.

A short distance from the main entrance where the boundary wall curves to the right towards the rear of the prison, there was a stone hut called the 'Dead House' where in the War Depot days corpses were placed prior to burial. There was no consecrated ground for those who died and no religious rites; a shallow pit on the open moor where the prison farm now is was their last resting place. Many hundreds of POWs were interred there and in a manner we would consider callous and inhuman today. All the same it was no different to the way in which British soldiers who died anywhere in the world were simply 'spaded under' and the practice was extended to those in captivity. Over fifty years later the 'cemetery' had become so disturbed by farm animals, the wild moorland creatures and the action of wind and rain, the graves were exposed and the area was littered with human bones. Miss Rachel Evans of Tavistock, whose well known account of *Home Scenes of Tavistock and its Vicinity* was published in 1846 wrote:

'...without the walls of the prison is the burial place of the unfortunate captives, which has of course been sadly neglected; the horses and cattle have broken up the soil and left the bones of the dead to whiten in the sun'.

This shocking state of affairs came about during a period of decline at Princetown between the closing of the war prison in 1816 and the opening of the convict establishment in 1850. In 1866 the Governor of the convict prison, Captain W. Stopford, ordered the bones to be collected and as many of the graves as could be found exhumed. The skeletal remains were then divided, one heap being designated French and the other American. Two communal graves were then dug, each in a separate area and the bones respectfully interred with full religious ceremony. Over the mass graves cairns were built, and on each cairn identical granite obelisks were erected, each bearing the following inscription:

IN MEMORY OF THE AMERICAN (FRENCH) PRISONERS OF WAR WHO DIED BETWEEN THE YEARS 1809 & 1814 AND LIE BURIED HERE

A quotation from the Odes (written by Horace in 23 BC) was added:

'DULCE ET DECORUM EST PRO PATRIA MORI'
('It is Dutiful and Honorable to Die for One's Country')

A discerning observer might question the dates which are identical to each obelisk and honour Americans from the year 1809, three years before the war with America began. This may have been an oversight by the stonemason who inscribed them but technically they are correct, bearing in mind there were American sailors captured whilst serving on French ships who were interned with them. The cemeteries are situated on prison property outside the prison wall and to the rear of the main buildings. They overlook the moors, sheltered from the worst of winter storms and shaded from summer heat by the kindly beech trees that surround them. The view from here has hardly changed since those times and the dead lie in solitude amid birdsong and moorland beauty. Regular visitors here used to be representatives of the National Society of United States Daughters of 1812, an organisation whose members have a direct family connection with the men who fought in that war and are committed to revering their dead and keeping alive the best traditions of that time (their visits have ceased in recent years). They had a replica of the prison archway built, which now serves as a separate entrance to the American graveyard and which bears an inscribed metal Memorial Plaque with the words:

'To the Glory of God and in Loving Memory of the Two Hundred and Eighteen* American Sailors and Soldiers of the War of 1812 Who Died Here. This memorial Gateway is erected by the National Society of United States Daughters of 1812'.

*see Ira Dye (see page 29).

The gateway was dedicated in May 1928 by the then President of the Society Mrs. Samuel E. Shope and the Memorial was unveiled by the then Chairman Mrs. Earle. A circular bronze badge was added by them to their obelisk, which distinguishes it from the French monument at a glance. The badge has the following inscription on it:

'In Honour of Service in the War of 1812'
AMERICANS
N.S.U.S.D. 1812

The French do not visit the cemetery, but their Government did send a message of gratitude to Capt. Stopford for his humanitarian act.

The latest figures obtained by modern research reveal a total of 271 American dead and there may be more. At the time of writing an additional stone memorial, inscribed with the names of the 271 Americans who died at Dartmoor, is being prepared. The cemeteries will then be opened

The French Memorial Obelisk.

The recently renovated American Memorial.

to the public. The foremost authority on the American POWs of the War of 1812 is Mr. Ira Dye, formerly of the University of Virginia (now living in Mill Valley, California) who has devoted many years of enthusiastic research to the subject. He has produced a number of papers containing carefully compiled data and through his generosity several official statistics are quoted here and in the American section of this book. Here in his own words is what he has to say about his countrymen who died at Dartmoor:

'The official British records of American Prisoners of War at Dartmoor show 267 men as having been 'Discharged Dead' (this) may not be an exact number as a few men were transferred to Plymouth and may have died in the hospital there. Dartmoor (and the prison ships at Plymouth and Chatham) were obviously a fertile ground for diseases to spread. However, during the 19 months between early April 1813, when the first Americans arrived at Dartmoor, and October 1814, only 40 Americans died. The next ten months were the killer months, from October until the last Americans left in July 1815. About 225 died during this period. It is especially tragic that about 160 of these men died after the signing of the Peace Treaty in Ghent on 24 December 1814. During that Fall and the winter of 1814/15 there was a smallpox epidemic in the prison, and typhus, and a malignant version of measles. These diseases plus colds that turned to pneumonia, accounted for most of the deaths, of which 236 were rated as Seamen'.

This initial look at the prison concludes with mention of the 'Cachot', which means 'Dungeon' in French but cannot be considered as such in the English context because it was situated above ground. The British always called it the 'Black Hole'. It was a place of confinement for those prisoners who committed punishable offences, such as selling or buying another man's rations, assaulting the guards, or attempting to escape. The first 'Black Hole' at Dartmoor was near the hospital and was simply a barricaded stone hut where offenders were locked up for periods of up to ten days (the maximum an Agent could award a miscreant). Because there were a number of escapes it was decided to build a more secure place of confinement. This was done by a gang of prisoners who cut and dressed huge granite blocks and transported them to a spot below the hospital, between the inner wall and the metal railings. Here they constructed what can best be described as a stone 'igloo'. It was twenty foot square with stone blocks forming the floor, the walls, and the roof. The heavy door was reinforced with metal plates, leaving a small aperture through which rations could be passed (the punishment included a reduction to two thirds normal rations). Ventilation was via a single grill under the roof measuring a mere six inches by four. Inside this frightful place transgressors (up to a maximum of sixty) lived in almost total darkness, stifling in summer and freezing in the winter months. Many a man was carried from it to the hospital in the final stages of hypothermia. Their suffering can scarcely be imagined and Miss Rachel Evans, who toured the prison in 1845, wrote a vivid description of it, concluding with the words:

'...walls are so thick that the instrument of release could never pierce them: the light comes dimly through a small iron grating, and the doubly plated door closes with a thundering sound which reverberates through the vaulted cell. It would be cold heartless misery to sojourn in such a place, even for a short time'.

THE MILITIA

To appreciate how certain unpleasant events occurred at Dartmoor a short description of the Militia forces and their role may be helpful. When Britain declared war on France in May 1803 our defences were at an all time low having been drastically reduced following the Treaty of Amiens which temporarily ended hostilities. The realisation that Napoleon was planning an invasion called for urgent action, the immediate problem being how to raise a sufficient force in time to defend ourselves.

It took many months to recruit and train Regular soldiers and therefore great reliance was placed upon our reserve forces – the Militia. A proclamation had already been announced to bring their strength up to 75,000 but it was soon realised more would be needed. The Militia were a kind of Territorial Army, with the important difference that whereas our present day 'Terriers' are volunteers, the Militia units were raised by compulsory ballot. In general those who were balloted were expected to drill for twenty days (later increased to twenty eight days) a year. When war came the commitment was for three to five years service later increased to service until the end of the war. Many of the problems that lay ahead were because of the system of substitution whereby for a fee of £10 a man could buy exemption and the money would pay for a substitute to serve in his stead. The sum varied from place to place and got more expensive as the war

progressed so that in less than a year it more than doubled.

As a result most Militia soldiers were recruited from the very poor and illiterate classes who were unable to afford the substitution fees and joined the ranks alongside those who were themselves 'substitutes'. The majority of them, coming as they did from the very lowest level of society, were a mixture of scallywags and alcoholics and in most cases outnumbered those who were balloted or volunteered. Their pay was a pittance from which deductions were made for food and necessary cleaning materials. Uniforms and discipline were much in line with the Regulars – flogging was freely employed as a punishment and death was the penalty for serious offences either by hanging or a firing squad. In addition men were away from home for long periods because the Militia were expected to serve anywhere in Britain and deserters were energetically pursued. As the war went on the increasing number of dead and

A Grenadier 32nd. (Cornwall) Regt. Of Foot 1812. 'Redcoats' like this guarded Dartmoor Depot.
(Picture supplied with permission to publish by the Regimental Museum, Duke of Cornwall's Light Infantry, Bodmin, Cornwall)

wounded required an Act for recruiting direct from the Militia to the Regular Army with a bounty being offered as an inducement. It had the desired effect: the historical records of the Notts. Militia tell us that in May 1805:

'The Regiment was called upon to furnish its quota of volunteers for the Line. The number being stated on Parade by the Commanding Officer, more men than were required at once stepped forward for active service, and this, be it remembered, was at a time when a fierce and bloody war was raging...'.

The bounty payment to those who volunteered was around £12 (an enormous sum for a common man at that time) which soon found its way into the hands of the tavern keepers when the recipients celebrated their new found wealth in drunken sprees. Those who transferred to the Regulars had to be replaced and the resulting manpower shortage starved many counties of sufficient resources for the harvesting. The food shortages that then occurred caused riots which were terrible affairs with looting and murder commonplace. Hunger led to a dramatic increase in stealing and poaching leading to the death penalty being introduced for the latter offence. The Militiamen sympathised with the rioters in many cases and were often reluctant to do their duty.

At first Militia officers were recruited exclusively from the 'landed gentry'. Later in the war the shortage of officer recruits compelled the authorities to accept lower standards. Wounded regulars, ordinary householders and tradesmen were permitted to join the officer ranks with occasional dire consequences. In many cases discipline lapsed because shopkeeper officers could not afford to upset their customers in the ranks. In the Lancashire Militia several officers were indicted for keeping taverns and selling illicit alcohol and there were instances where the county officials actually requested their own men be posted as far away as possible because they were so unreliable and troublesome. The picture that emerges from all this is of a low set of ruffians in uniform calling themselves soldiers, but the problem surely was the brutal quality of the lives they led and being treated like brutes.

During the war against Napoleon the Militia duties were to:

1. Repel an invasion.
2. Act as coastal lookouts.
3. Help control smuggling.
4. Suppress riots.
5. Guard prisoners of war. This was not a popular duty, especially at Dartmoor where conditions were notoriously bad.

When we consider the unsavoury characters who formed the substitutes in the Militia ranks doing guard duty we can appreciate how the temptations afforded through bribery, to assist in an escape for example, was often difficult for them to resist. Callousness and sheer cruelty was widespread, particularly on the hulks where conditions were unbearably hard for them as well as the prisoners. An escape attempt was often a welcome diversion (there are accounts of the guards gleefully taking 'pot shots' at escapees who more than likely would have been recaptured). Unlike the Regular army, whose men were trained and disciplined over long periods, the Militiamen were part time soldiers many of whom lacked basic training because when war broke out they were needed at once for their various tasks. A distressing consequence of all this occurred at Dartmoor Depot twelve years later.

RUNNING THE DEPOT

The centre of Princetown is dominated by a building of almost regal appearance with a long history. It was built at the same time as Dartmoor Depot as living quarters for the officers commanding the military forces. After the wars with France and America it was refurbished to become the 'Duchy Hotel' with a history going back to the mid-1800s when there was a small brewery at the back. Later still when the prison acquired it the Prison Officers Mess occupied the ground floor and there was accommodation for bachelor warders. Since then the place has been extensively refurbished and now accommodates the High Moorland Visitor Centre (opened by HRH Prince Charles in 1990). Its present appearance dates from 1908 when massive alterations were made and the rough stone walls were rendered as you see them now.

The main body of troops lived in the huge barracks nearer the prison and on the other side of the road. One of the principle entrances to the barracks was opposite the church and an aptly named Barrack Road marks the spot where one of the old guardhouses once stood (there used to be seven) a portion of which still remains. Nearby are Grosvenor House once an integral part of the barracks and Dart Cottage which used to be another guardhouse. By 1812 the garrison of 500 officers and men had swollen to more than 1200 as the prison population increased and the 'Petty Officers Prison' was requisitioned to accommodate the extra soldiers. The officer prisoners, much to their disgust, were relegated to the prison blocks to live among their men and they rigged heavy curtains to screen them from the others so as to continue living aloof and in privacy.

Exterior of building in Barrack Road, Princetown, which used to be a Guardhouse for the Barracks.

The county regiments of Militia who were stationed at Dartmoor are household names: Staffordshire, Nottinghamshire, Cheshire, Lancashire, Roscommon (Irish) and many others including some Scottish contingents. Bearing in mind the appalling conditions under which the labouring classes (who formed the bulk of the soldiery) lived at that time, it is not surprising that every man was out to fend for himself by whatever means were to hand. Bribery and corruption was rife among the Militia and many an escapee owed his freedom to their help – at a price of course. It was partly for this reason and because of Dartmoor Depot's remote location that the garrison was changed roughly every three months. The punishments for helping a prisoner to escape were severe. In 1809 four soldiers of the Notts. Militia were charged at Plymouth with aiding the escape of some French prisoners who, when they were recaptured, revealed they had paid the Militiamen eight guineas each for their assistance. The culprits were Court Martialled and two of them were shot. The honour of the Nottingham men was redressed the following year when, on October 10th., their unit arrived at Dartmoor to take over guard duties from the Shropshire Militia. The French assumed their new guards would not at first be as vigilant or effective and planned an escape for the following night. Under cover of a heavy rainstorm they gained the outside of the walls before being discovered, but the sentries were so prompt in turning out, some of them clad only in breeches and shirtsleeves, every prisoner was caught and detained.

The prison's position on a bleak moor was deterrent enough for most men contemplating escape. If they did manage to get away, the population were only too glad to earn a reward for apprehending them. The Agents were authorised to pay a reward of one guinea over and above expenses to anyone capturing and returning an escaped prisoner, the fugitive being 'rewarded' with a spell in the 'Black Hole'. Add to this the cold and mists so prevalent on the moor and one can appreciate a prisoner on the run was in for a hard time.

Prince Town's prosperity and that of the various suppliers of goods relied on the continuance of the war and the War Depot. The ultimate cost was at the expense of Britain's captive foes who languished in their stone prison for years, making do on their meagre rations and whatever they could scrounge, barter or buy. The Agents of the Depots everywhere were mostly volunteers and the commanding officers of some Militia units actually applied for guard duties at these establishments. On the hulks, which were commanded by Royal Navy lieutenants, there was a waiting list of applicants and it became necessary to limit them to officers with at least ten years service (Dartmoor Depot's first Agent was Captain Isaac Cotgrave, R.N., a Post Captain with ten years seniority). The reasons were simple: nearly everyone was

INSTRUCTIONS

FOR

A G E N T S

UNDER

The Commissioners for conducting His Majesty's Transport Service, for taking Care of Sick and Wounded Seamen, and for the Care and Custody of Prisoners of War,

RESPECTING THE

MANAGEMENT OF PRISONERS OF WAR

AT HOME;

AS PROPOSED BY

The Commissioners appointed for Revising the Civil Affairs of His Majesty's Navy,

AND ESTABLISHED BY

HIS MAJESTY'S ORDER IN COUNCIL,

Dated the 14th of September, 1808.

'on the make' at the expense of the prisoners. There were honest officials of course, but the temptations were strong and in all too many cases contracts were awarded to suppliers of food and clothing in return for hidden favours. 'Corruption in disguise' was an accepted practice in high and low places in Georgian times, when family connections and wealth were essential qualifications for advancement. The going rate for Members of Parliament buying votes for example was £100 per vote, openly bought and paid for. Commissions in the Army were purchased by men of 'gentle birth' regardless of their suitability for command and Royal Navy Captains relied heavily on prize money to supplement their pay, when the salvage value of captured enemy ships was shared among officers and crew.

It is not difficult to see how the confinement of thousands of prisoners presented an opportunity not to be missed by unscrupulous men whose duty it was to administer and provide for them. In 1812 a newspaper article alleged that certain high ranking officials entrusted with large amounts of money invested it in short term speculations on the stock markets instead of forwarding it at once to the Depots. Likewise private sums advanced by friends and relatives to prisoners of war were often delayed for the same reason and there were cases where local Agents charged a 'commission' for delivering sums of money to officers living on parole. There is a ring of truth in all this because the instructions issued to their Agents by the Transport Office specifically stated:

'...if money be remitted for a prisoner to you for his use you are to take charge of it and deliver it to him without any charge for commission'.

It is obvious the practice of illegally taking a 'commission' was known about and officially forbidden. Consider the clothing allowance which stipulated prisoner's clothing should be renewed every eighteen months but which very often was not. With the vast number of prisoners to be catered for the potential gain from fraudulent practices was colossal. The standard of clothing and bedding was often very poor – accounts of Depot life mention blankets so thin they were almost transparent and shoes that fell to pieces in weeks. As for the food, the quality laid down in the regulations was not always observed by the contractors – if it had been the men at the Depot would have fared better because their rations, the scale of which was based on those laid down for the Royal Navy, would have been very good and not of the dubious quality they sometimes got.

From the *West Briton* 10th. June 1814 :

'...owing to the general shortage of flour, adulteration with foreign matter in order to increase its bulk was not uncommon. The first case of this kind in Cornwall (was) discovered a few weeks earlier at the Treyew Grist Mills, Truro, where china clay was being incorporated with the flour produced. Its consumption had caused illness, not only in Cornwall but also amongst the French prisoners at Dartmoor, and Wellington's Peninsula Army'.

Feeding thousands of Dartmoor prisoners must have been a tremendous task and to learn that flour was brought from so far away indicates how great that task was (and how one of the 'tricks of the trade' worked). The regulations which were drawn up for the proper treatment of prisoners of war were precise and very fair, but of course their implementation was entirely in the hands of those in charge. Happily, there was another side to the coin. There were Americans at the Depot who, prior to the War of 1812, had served in the Royal Navy and were entitled to prize money. These men had aroused the Navy's wrath because they elected to go to prison rather than fight against their countrymen yet their back pay and prize money was paid to them in full during their captivity.

French and American Prisoners of War – Table of Daily Ration

Days	Bread	Beef	Codfish	Herrings	Potatoes	Greens	Scotch Barley	Onions	Salt
	lb.	lb.	lb.	lb.	lb.	lb.	oz.	oz.	oz
Sunday	1.5	0.5	~	~	~	0.5	1.0	qtr	third
Monday	1.5	0.5	~	~	~	0.5	1.0	qtr	third
Tuesday	1.5	0.5	~	~	~	0.5	1.0	qtr	third
Wednesday	1.5	~	~	1.0	1.0	~	~	~	~
Thursday	1.5	0.5	~	~	~	0.5	1.0	qtr	third
Friday	1.5	~	1.0	~	1.0	~	~	~	~
Saturday	1.5	0.5	~	~	~	0.5	1.0	qtr	third
TOTAL	10.5	2.5	1.0	1.0	2.0	2.5	5.0	$1^{1}/_{4}$	$1^{2}/_{3}$

N.B. Bread. To be made of Wheaten Meal, wherein the whole Grain is to be reserved, except such Part as will not pass through the London and Bristol Seam Cloth No. 7, usually called an Eleven Shilling Cloth, or what is considered equal to No. 6 of the Patent Cloth of Fifteen Shillings Price.

Beef. To be good and wholesome fresh Beef, not Bull Beef, and delivered in clean Quarters, a Fore and Hind Quarter alternately.

Cod-Fish. To be the produce of the Fishery at Newfoundland, or the Coast of Labrador; and to be delivered in whole Fish.

Herrings. To be good and sound; and Red and White Herrings to be issued alternately.

Potatoes, Greens, Turnips, and Onions* To be good in their respective Kinds. The Greens to be stripped of outside Leaves, and fit for the Copper.

* When Greens or Turnips, or Onions, cannot be procured, the following are the Substitutions to be made:

For Half a Pound of Greens, or Turnips – Two Ounces of Scotch Barley.

For One Quarter of an Ounce of Onions – Three Eighths of an Ounce of Leeks.

(But no Substitution whatever is to be made without the Special Order of the Board).

LIFE INSIDE THE WAR DEPOT

Most accounts of the prisoner's way of life at Dartmoor Depot divide them into specific groups according to the mode of living they adopted. With the exception of the officers in the 'Petit Cautionnement' and the 'Romans' who were the lowest form of Depot life, they will be examined collectively here.

The rule of the Emperor Napoleon was dominated by continuous warfare, not always of his making but all the same calling for ever increasing numbers of soldiers and sailors. Some of them were raised by ballot, others by conscription and of course there were volunteers, not only in France but from every nation under French rule and from all manner of men – craftsmen, writers, artists, as well as professional soldiers. The 'Grand Army' was probably the first 'citizen's army' (the British only employed the lower classes in the ranks), hence the diversity of men in the Depots, on the hulks and on parole.

At Dartmoor the prisoners soon formed individual groups to which other like-minded men gravitated, a process of natural selection which can be observed in every society. The 'aristocracy' were those who lived in the 'Petit Cautionnement' and were referred to as 'Les Lordes'. The better off ones regularly received money sent by relatives and friends from France, enabling them to buy everything they needed to live in style. Not for them the humble rations provided by the Transport Office; they bought fresh vegetables at the market, poultry, coffee, tobacco, fruit, and succulent delicacies to suit their discerning palates. Furthermore they were permitted to employ servants from the ordinary prisoners to cook and wait upon them and launder their clothes. Tailors maintained their wardrobes and provided them with new outfits made from materials bought at market. Among these privileged ranks were professors of music, fencing masters, language experts and artists, to name but a few. It comes as a surprise to many people to learn of the many artistic activities they engaged in. The French are renowned as a cultured people, yet to discover that among the internees of a war prison there were theatricals, fencing lessons, art classes and music performed to the highest standards taught by experts, is truly remarkable.

For the majority things were not so cosy. As the war progressed and more prisoners arrived they were crammed into their stone prisons and left to cope as best they could with rough conditions, scanty clothing and a boring diet. The official scale of rations (illustrated) yielded approximately 2,400 calories a day per man, probably less after allowing for the bone content of the meat. Yet at a later date one American prisoner declared the Dartmoor ration was better than what he'd received on board ship and it was certainly better fare than that of the average British worker. The exception as far as the 'Yankees' were concerned was the Scotch Barley which was issued. They called it 'burgoo' and because they fed it only to animals at home considered it an insult to be expected to eat it themselves. The prisoners' rations were surrendered to the cooks who prepared the beef and vegetables in communal cauldrons and served it up in wooden bowls as soup, to be collected by representatives from each mess of six men. The bread was baked and issued by contractors in 9lb. loaves, one for each mess per day, one and a half pounds per man. The authorities, recognising the hardships resulting from a restricted diet, allowed an extra 5lb. per cwt. of beef and 2lb. per cwt. of bread to compensate for the wastage in dividing it (exactly how this was done is uncertain).

The hospital diet, more generous and sustaining, was shared by the prisoner nurses and helpers, a welcome perk in addition to the 6d. a day they were paid ('in money' to quote the official phrase). Helpers included washermen, cleaners, etc., all of whom were chosen by the Depot Surgeon from the fit and healthy men. Attention was also paid by him to the well-being of all the prisoners, it being stipulated for example that their bedding should be regularly aired and that the men should stow their hammocks, etc. when absent from their prison blocks so as to permit maximum circulation of fresh air within. Bedding was supposed to be inspected regularly and renewed every two years although it is now known this was not always done. On admission to the Depot every man was issued with a palliasse with straw (the straw to be 'regularly changed') and damages or losses were the responsibility of each prisoner; the punishment for any loss was to be put on two thirds rations until the value was made good. Loss of clothing was more seriously dealt with. For this offence the culprits were placed in the Black Hole and on two thirds rations until the Transport Office decided otherwise. At first the men were given a woollen or straw hat, jacket, trousers, two shirts, two pairs of stockings, and canvas shoes with wooden soles, all of which were supposed to last eighteen months. The rising cost of the war forced the authorities to trim back on expenses; consequently at a later stage all incoming prisoners were examined and a list made of their clothing needs with the exception of what they already possessed. Then a 'ticket' was handed to them signed by the Agent or his Deputy, listing the articles they were given. No article was replaced unless the prisoner produced his 'ticket' and everything he was issued with had to be returned when he was either transferred or released. The severity with which these rules were enforced was cruelly illustrated in 1814 when the French war ended and men were being released, in some cases after eleven years in captivity. A Frenchman who could not produce his bedding intact was prevented from joining his comrades for the march home and killed himself by cutting his own throat in despair.

An old prisoner of war block after conversion for modern day use. (Courtesy Mr. M. Chamberlain).

Try and imagine what it must have been like to be taken prisoner and to find yourself confined within grey stone walls, without heat or light and with nothing to do. The loss of personal freedom has a devastating effect on some men; this is borne out by the surgeons in the Depots and more especially on the hulks, who in their reports concerning chest infections and the like said death was often brought about by moral despair as much as the foul air and conditions generally. Nevertheless the first prisoners to arrive at Dartmoor soon settled in and the talented ones quickly found ways to earn a little money with which to improve their lot. The mass of Frenchmen certainly tried to make the best of things and there was no shortage of men willing to work. As a result money began to circulate inside the prison in a variety of ways. In addition to those who served 'Les Lordes' there were men paid by the authorities for working as cleaners, cooks and barbers, these last being employed to save the expense (not to mention the hazards) of issuing the prisoners with scissors or razors of their own. By the time the Americans began arriving in 1813 there were more than 500 men in work. The cash that was earned soon passed into other hands, mainly through gambling, the curse of every Depot and which was referred to as the 'French disease' (an unkind phrase when in fact British captives in France were equally addicted because there was nothing to do). The problem was worse on the hulks where there was not even a market held.

In the market, many prisoners, probably those without money, traded or sold models of ships, wooden cabinets, workboxes, ornaments and all kinds of novelties in return for little luxuries. There soon developed a huge demand for these articles which were manufactured to a high degree of perfection from left over meat bones and odds and ends. Examples of the Frenchmen's skill can be seen today in museums all over Britain, exquisitely made and beautiful to behold. It is interesting to note that the guards, besides checking for fair prices, were expected to prevent 'bad books' and obscene toys from being exchanged. Straw hats and articles made of wool by prisoners were also forbidden on the grounds it would have encouraged the men to tear up their blankets and extract straw from their bedding, leaving them vulnerable during the winter months. More important still, a large cottage industry was operated in country districts by women and children who made woollen gloves and straw hats to sell. In most cases their very livelihood depended on this extra income and this was recognised by the magistrates who could be relied upon to issue Forbidden Notices where necessary.

However, illicit dealings of another kind took place in the market square under the noses of the authorities. Some clever Frenchmen who were expert forgers used their expertise to manufacture coins and banknotes to such perfection that local banks were compelled to send officials to the Depots to examine and initial their firm's notes before exchange. Eventually things got so bad the death penalty was introduced for any British person participating in this offence. At Dartmoor a Militiaman who got involved in an escape attempt and was paid in forged notes was condemned to death after attempting to spend the money at market. Yet these misdemeanours continued to be committed. In February 1812 Captain Cotgrave closed the market to drive home the point that forgery would not be tolerated and was supported by the Transport Office who wrote:

'...the market is now to be opened but you are to apprize (the prisoners) and not to put notices in writing, that if any forged notes or counterfeit coin should be again discovered to be issued in the prison, the market will be shut and not again opened on any account whatsoever'.

Again it made no difference and the threat was never carried out. As late as January 1814, when the French war was all but won, Captain Shortland received a letter from the Transport Office advising him:

'...that prisoner D'Orangi who is confined in the Cachot for having uttered forged notes must remain where he is until further orders as the Board do not consider two months confinement a sufficient punishment for a crime which in a British subject would have been punished with Death'.

Exquisite bone models attributed to French prisoners at Dartmoor.
(Photos from the Collection of Plymouth Museum and Art Gallery)

With the commerce and regular money coming in from wage earners, the scene was set for trade to evolve among the prisoners themselves. Enterprising men set up coffee stalls using ingredients bought at market and doubtless a few secret additives of their own; others used their ingenuity selling popular snacks manufactured from market produce; there were shoe repairers and tailors at work and one man had a stall selling second-hand clothes acquired from the officers. There gradually developed a busy township within the prison walls where every level of society, culture, and trade was represented. Within this milling mass of toilers were many who possessed no ability whatsoever and of these the lucky ones found paid jobs doing the menial work in the prison, sweeping and cleaning for example – but there were not vacancies for them all. Many of the unemployed men sat about all day in utter despair, finally sinking into a stupor. Then there were scoundrels who were determined not to work at all and battened on to those who did, begging or stealing from them. There were quarrels (an inevitable consequence of keeping sturdy young men in close confinement) which often ended in fights and the occasional murder. Among the hierarchy, the officers and gentlemen who lived in the 'Petit Cautionnement', such matters were settled in the approved manner – by duelling. Their weapons were home made swords fashioned from wooden staves with knives, razors, or compass points attached to them. In skilled hands they could inflict terrible injuries and there were several fatalities. There were quarrels up to the end of their captivity and as late as May 1814, by which time the French war was over and the prisoners were about to be repatriated, a duel took place between Jean Vigneaux and Michael Frappin in which the latter was killed. In August, by which time all his comrades had left for home, M.Vigneaux still languished in Exeter gaol awaiting trial for murder. The other ranks settled their differences with improvised knives made of glass or nails embedded in wooden handles, with equally serious consequences. In 1810 the Plymouth Coroner complained that in four months of that year he had conducted more inquests than in the previous ten years, some indication perhaps of the peacefulness of rural Devon before the Frenchmen came (although not all fatalities were the result of duelling of course, because every death at the Depot, from whatever cause, was investigated). The Coroner spoke on behalf of the farmers and trades people who were called upon to act as jurors, with the result they were granted an extra 4d. a day for expenses.

The most common cause of dissent among the prisoners was the gambling. With so little to do and so much spare time on their hands, even for those who worked, gambling provided the main diversion and to some it became an obsession to the point where they gambled and lost everything they had, including their clothes and bedding. This was to court death in the winter months yet it spread like an epidemic, robbing men of their senses as well as their belongings. They played a form of 'Pitch and Toss', and 'Vingt-et-un' (literally translated as 'Twenty One' or as we would know it, Pontoon). There were races too with rats as runners when morsels of food were strategically placed to entice them into the open at which time someone would shout or whistle loudly to startle them and send them scampering to their hidey holes. The speed with which they achieved this decided the winners and bets were made on these creatures, some of whom came to be known and affectionately named. Confirmed gambling addicts were said to have bet on ridiculous events such as the number of turns a sentry might make in a given time, or on the lengths of straw plucked at random from someone's bedding. When possessions clothes and bedding were lost some poor wretches staked their rations, the losers handing over perhaps several days rations, a gamble with death when they sacrificed their subsistence to unscrupulous comrades. It is a terrible fact that some men did die as a result. Those in charge of the Depot did what they could to stop this vile practice but to no avail. The maximum punishment Agents were empowered to mete out under the regulations was ten days in the Black Hole on two thirds rations, and they did not hesitate in awarding it to evil men, some of whom even traded on their winnings by setting up shop selling rations. The Transport Office gave the Agent their full support at all times and a letter to Captain Cotgrave in April 1812 directed him *'to keep the prisoners who have been detected in purchasing clothing and provisions of their fellow prisoners in the Cachot, on short allowance, until further orders'*. He later threatened to close the market and the prisoner's stalls as well, which had the effect of terminating the practice for a short while but there were always men who could not resist the lure of the gambling tables and were prepared to put themselves at the mercy of the operators to indulge their whims.

Looking back from the relative comfort of our modern world we can scarcely conceive the way of life the French prisoners had to endure. The war dragged on and they were marooned on a stone island in a wild part of England exposed to storms that often buffeted around the Depot in winter such that a man could hardly stand. Showers of rain and sleet battered them, penetrating their clothing in an instant should they venture outside their prison blocks and there was no way of drying their clothes or getting warm. Shipboard life was hard but it was also active and kept the men fit and able to shrug off hardships; in the Depot there was little or no physical activity and consequently they fell easy prey to disease. We should remember the majority of the French came from homes in a milder sunny climate; consequently they suffered a miserable existence on the moor. The delightful summer interludes served only to extend their misery, trapped as they were inside the high stone walls year on year. Our wildest imaginings therefore would not conjure up an accurate vision of the life the 'Romans' lived. They represented the lowest extremes of life within the prison. These horrible creatures are forever cursed by the name accorded to them in grim jest because their antisocial habits caused them to be banished to the Cockloft of No. 4 block (which they called 'Le Capitole' – hence the title 'Romans'). Other prisoners labelled them 'Kaiserlics' because their leader regarded himself as 'Emperor' – a self appointed 'general' who ruled them with the help of a few picked henchmen.. Their status was that of men who had lost or gambled away everything they had, including their self respect. As a result they went about naked as the day they were born all the year round, starving curs who spent their days fighting and scrabbling over scraps of offal and filth often plucked from the drains. They sold their rations as they sold everything else that came into their possession and roamed the yards scavenging or stealing, always on the prowl for cast offs or leavings. So repulsive and dangerous were they the authorities forcibly moved them to No. 4 block (as previously mentioned) around which a wall was built to separate them from the other men. Riddled with vermin, filthy in mind and body, practising every conceivable form of vice, they somehow survived the way of life they had chosen. They survived the epidemics too (the weaker ones probably died quickly), leaving the survivors to form what was probably the most reviled community in any prison anywhere in the world. On more than one occasion they were forcibly scrubbed and clothed in an effort to get them to accept decent standards but in vain. Everything they were given was soon lost and they resumed their revolting style of living, unwanted and shunned. It is recorded their only form of covering when they ventured out was a kind of 'poncho' made from old blankets with a hole in the middle for their heads (even this attire was shared). Finally their guardians came to the conclusion they were beyond redemption or help. On 16th. October 1813, following a nasty incident when they fought the American prisoners who had been interned with them, the four hundred and more 'Romans' were marched to Plymouth under heavy guard and confined aboard the hulks until the war ended. They were the very worst of men and it is amazing to learn that some of them found fame and fortune at home after the war. Francis Abell, *Prisoners of War in Britain 1756-1815*, tells us at least one entered the Priesthood and others entered into government service, reaching high rank. Here surely is a wealth of material for psychiatrists to study!

Examples of Offences for which Prisoners of War were placed in the 'Black Hole' in 1812

24 February.	Louis Constant and Olivier de Camp, for striking a Sentinel on duty.
20 May	Jean Delchambre for throwing a stone at a Sentinel and severely cutting his head.
14 June	F. Rousseau, for striking Mr. Bennet, the storekeeper, when visiting the prisoners.
15 August	A. Creville, for drawing a knife on the hospital Turnkey.
25 August	A. Hourra, for attempting to stab Willaim Norris, one of the Turnkeys, with a knife.
24 September	S. Schamond, for throwing down a Sentinel and attempting to take away his bayonet.
16 October	G. Massieu, for attempting to stab one of the Turnkeys.
23 October	B. Marie, for knocking down a Turnkey and attempting to seize the arms of a Sentinel.
30 November	N. Moulle and B. Saluberry, for having daggers concealed on their persons,

And In 1813

13 March	P. Boissard, for striking a Turnkey and threatening to murder him at the first opportunity.
23 March	F. Bilat, for striking a prisoner named B. Marie, who died shortly afterwards, and taking away his provisions by force.
28 March	J. Beauclaire, for threatening to stab Mr. Moore, because he could not procure employment for him on the buildings.
6 April	F. Le Jeune, for being one of the principal provision buyers in the prison, and for repeatedly writing blood-thirsty and threatening letters.
10 April	M. Girandi and A. Moine, for being guilty of infamous vices.

FRENCH FREEMASONS AT DARTMOOR.

A Freemasons Lodge was established in Dartmoor Prison by the first French prisoners to arrive there in 1809. It was named 'De la Reunion' and was active up to 1814. Freemasonry was widespread among the French forces (as it was with the British) and of course many of them were captured. Their Lodges operated by 'ambulatory discretion', a term signifying they retained their identity and validity wherever they happened to be. The first Lodge in the French army was 'La Parfait Union' which was founded in 1759. By 1787 there were more than seventy with many more to follow.

How was it possible for French prisoners at Dartmoor to operate a Lodge inside the Depot, record their activities and retain the privacy they required for their meetings? Determination, enthusiasm and a strong sense of Brotherhood would not have sufficed – help was needed which could only have come from the Brothers among the British who guarded them. The concept of Freemasonry advocated by and practiced under United Grand Lodge of England (founded in 1717) which administers Lodges in England and Wales, as well as many more overseas, allows a great deal of flexibility to its members on condition that (among other things):

1. They regard their first duty to be a good citizen and to obey the laws of the country they live and work in.
2. Membership is open to all races and creeds, providing they believe in a Supreme Being by whatever name that Being may be called.
3. Religion and politics are not discussed in the Lodge.

Within these guidelines some assistance to French prisoners everywhere was possible without breaking any civil or moral law. There are several recorded instances when French officers living on parole were welcomed into English Lodges and Englishmen were admitted to French Lodges including the one at Dartmoor Depot. (The author acknowledges the invaluable help he received from the Leicester Lodge of Research at Freemasons Hall, Leicester, who not only assisted in every way, but kindly gave permission to use material from *French Prisoners Lodges* by the late W. Bro. John T. Thorp, a Founder Member of the Lodge).

The foremost authority on the French prisoner's Lodges in this country, the late W. Brother John T. Thorp of Leicester, spent most of his adult life researching them both at home and in France. He died in 1932 and bequeathed his fine collection of certificates to the Leicester Lodge of Research at Freemason's Hall, Leicester. He was assisted in his work by Bro. F. J. W. Crowe formerly of Ashburton who later moved to Torquay. Together they succeeded in tracing more than fifty Lodges founded by French prisoners of war. Among them were the following:

Dartmoor Prison   'De la Reunion' ('Reunited')
Plymouth hulks (Bienfaissant)   'De la Reunion' ('Reunited')

It is truly amazing that on 24th. June 1809, just one month after the first batch of French prisoners were admitted to Dartmoor Depot a meeting of Lodge 'De la Reunion' was held within its walls. The explanation is a simple one however. Among the first prisoners to be transferred to Dartmoor from the Plymouth hulks were men from the hulk 'Bienfaissant' and there was a Lodge on that vessel also called 'De la Reunion'. It is no coincidence that the Dartmoor Lodge bore the same name for they were one and the same. In a book entitled *A History of Freemasonry in Normandy* by Bro.H. de Loucelles, published in 1875, the author describes the formation of the

Lodge on board the 'Bienfaissant' on 18th. June 1804. He obtained his information from the Minute Books of the Lodge which contained detailed accounts of their activities. The final meeting on board the hulk is mentioned. It took place on 21st. May 1809 when a resolution was passed that the activities of the Lodge *'be suspended in consequence of the removal of its members and that the Minutes and list of members be packed up and sealed with the seal of the Lodge; and that the W. Master (Le Corps) be requested to take charge of them and on his arrival in France to deposit them in the archives of his Mother Lodge, "Amitie" of Havre'.*

It would seem the prisoners expected to be exchanged but they were mistaken. Instead they were transferred to Dartmoor and it was to be another three years, 27th. December 1812 to be precise, before M. Le Corps was able to fulfill his obligation to deposit the records of the Lodge in his home Lodge at Havre where they were located more than 100 years later by two associates of Mr. Thorp. They told him they were *'so saturated and damaged by damp as to be quite illegible and useless'*. Such was not the case though, because they were retrieved at a still later date (after Mr. Thorp's death) by W. Bro. Lionel Vibert who reported the writing was faded but legible, enabling him to read every word of it. What emerged was startling for among the pages of the books he found a loose sheet on which were written details of a meeting on 24th. June 1809. This was a month after the evacuation of the 'Bienfaissant', and therefore could only have been an account of the first meeting of Lodge 'De la Reunion' at Dartmoor. M. Vibert wrote:

'...there can be no question that this meeting, with its eighteen visitors and thirteen candidates was in fact the inauguration of a new Lodge "La Reunion of the Orient of Dartmoor"...'.

The opening words of the actual minutes (translated) read:

'Under the auspices of the Grand Orient of France the members of the regular Lodge "La Reunion" held on board the hulk "Bienfaissant", floating prison at Plymouth, <u>having re-assembled at Dartmoor</u>, have opened a Lodge in the usual manner...' (author's underlining).

The following nine listed members, who signed the Minutes of the inaugural meeting at Dartmoor, also attended the last meeting that was held on the hulk. They were:

Le Corps (F)	Anquetil
Moutardier (F)	Gilles
L'Amy (F)	Ange Colas
Du Temple (F)	Cordonnier
Mee	Lassalle
Pagalet	

(Those marked (F) were founder members on the 'Bienfaissant').

A number of certificates issued by the prisoners' Lodges have been found. Mr. Thorp said there were at least forty four and he possessed twenty four of them (all of which he bequeathed to the Leicester Lodge). He also indicated they were not Certificates in the true sense that Masons understand them, which are documents confirming a member's rank and Masonic origin signed and sealed with an official seal. They were, he said:

'A Clearance or Travelling Certificate, only issued by a private Lodge to which a brother belongs, and only when he is leaving the Lodge temporarily or permanently; it is a certificate of character and letter of recommendation signed, not by an official who had never seen him, but by the Brethren among whom he had lived and worked'.

They were therefore a kind of passport.

One of the most beautiful of these documents was issued at Dartmoor Depot to the captain of a French merchant ship Marc Guillaume Becot on 6th. July 1810 a year after his attendance at the inaugural meeting and it has been the author's privilege to examine this certificate. The material is a kind of fine linen which has ensured its wonderful state of preservation – all the more remarkable when we consider that such a document would have been kept about Captain Becot's person at the Depot, on the march to the coast after being released and during his voyage home. Among the signatures on his certificate are those of five men who were together on the 'Bienfaissant'.

Certificate issued at Dartmoor to Captain Marc Guillaume Becot in 1810.
(With acknowledgements to Freemasons Hall, Leicester).

On 20th. September 1812 another certificate was issued at Dartmoor of exceptional interest because it was given to an Englishman. It is not mentioned by Mr. Thorp and we can only conclude it was one of those he predicted might one day be found. It is in the Library of United Grand Lodge, London, who most kindly located it and provided the copy reproduced here. The author is grateful to the late Mr. Ron Chudley for drawing his attention to it and for providing a possible explanation for the unusual circumstances surrounding it. The document relates to William Samuel Winkworth, who is referred to as 'Surgeon' although there is no evidence to confirm this other than a reference to 'Mr. Winkworth's House' on a map of the Depot by John Wethams dated 1812. We can be fairly sure he was on the medical staff as he was important enough to merit this mention and the house in question is among those which were allocated to the doctors. Mr. Chudley surmised he may have been apprenticed to a local doctor, in which case he would not have needed formal qualifications in order to practice. This would explain his absence from the records. How did an Englishman come to be initiated into a French prisoner of war Lodge? The only inference to be drawn is that he rendered some kind of service to his French patients which were above the call of duty, and that this was a gesture of appreciation. The wording on the English half of his certificate is as follows:

'We the Master, Wardens and Members of the Worshipful Lodge of St. John, under the distinctive title of the Reunion regularly established at the Orient of Plymouth, in the year 1804 on board the prison ship Bienfaissant, now sitting at the Orient of Dartmoor to all the Fraternity around the globe:

Do certify and affirm by these presents signed by us and countersigned and sealed with our seal that our beloved brother William Samuel Winkworth, native of London, 28 years old, Surgeon, dwelling at Dartmoor, near Tavistock, Devonshire, in England, of the Protestant religion, has been initiated in the symbolical degrees of apprentice, companion, and Master Mason, with all the formalities required and that we have made him set his signature on the margin ne varieteur and consequently we request all the worshipful Lodges that will see these presents to acknowledge him as a true and faithful freemason'.

This transcript further affirms the connection between the 'Bienfaissant' and Dartmoor Lodges. Nearly three months later M. De Corps was home in France where he fulfilled his promise to deposit the Minutes with his home Lodge at Havre. There were three books in all with a register of members names, including those of twenty four merchant captains, fifty Naval officers, and six medical officers. The Lodge at Dartmoor continued its activities up to at least 1814, as is proved by the certificate which was issued in June that year to Jean Felix Lefort, Sgt. Major of the 2nd. Marine Artillery. This document was discovered by Mr. Crowe. Part of the transcript reads:

'...true testimony to the Masonic qualities, to the agreeable character, and to the social virtues of our dear Brother Jn. Felix Lefort, native of Troismereux, Dept. of Oise'.

One of the signatories to this certificate was Gilles (Guardian of the Seals) who was initiated into the Lodge in June 1805 and had therefore been a prisoner for nine years at least, and was probably its longest serving member.

It may be deduced that the majority of Freemasons among the prisoners were officers who would have had a degree of comfort and privacy denied their men who were herded into overcrowded Depots with no parole opportunities. In the parole towns it must have been easy to set up and operate a Lodge*. This was certainly not the case on the hulks (in any case the officers in general were not kept on prison ships) but bearing in mind most of them had private funds on which they were allowed to draw, any lack of assistance from their guards could almost certainly been overcome by a bribe or two. In any case their activities were often commendable; for example it is recorded that when the charity box was passed at the end of every meeting the proceeds were used to alleviate the sufferings of their comrades whether Masons or not.

* For a more comprehensive account of Freemason prisoners on parole see *Prisoners of War in Dartmoor Towns* by Trevor James (£3-95) Orchard Publications (ISBN 898964 39 4).

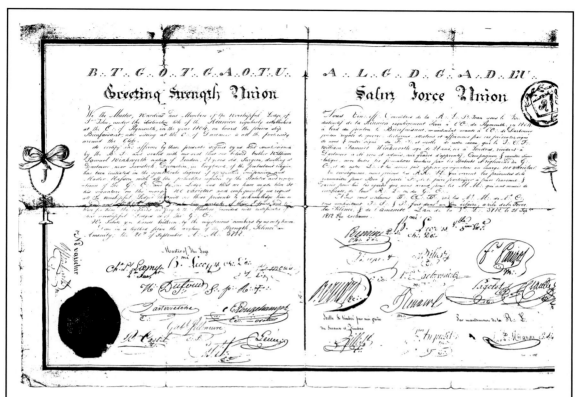

Copy of certificate issued by the French Lodge at Dartmoor to English Surgeon Samuel Winkworth. (Supplied with permission to publish by the Library and Museum of Freemasonry, London).

WAYS OUT OF DARTMOOR AND THE HULKS

There were only four ways of getting out of Dartmoor or any other war prison. The General Entry Books which were used to register the personal details of every prisoner on entry also recorded the method of his departure. The particulars were arranged in columns which recorded the prisoner's name, rank, unit, where captured, etc. and the date of his departure under one of these four headings:

E = Exchanged.	There was a system of prisoner exchange whereby prisoners were repatriated in return for a corresponding number of our men of equal rank.
D = Discharged.	During hostilities this meant being transferred either to another Depot or to the hulks. Troublemakers and recaptured escapees were prime candidates for transfers. When the wars ended a 'discharge' entry in the book meant repatriation, followed by the name of a port and final destination.
R = Run (escaped).	There were several escapes from Dartmoor, the hulks, and by officers on parole.
DD = Discharged Dead.	The number of dead and their burials have already been noted for Dartmoor.

Dartmoor Depot was run by captains of the Royal Navy and the style of the entries shown above is similar to the records kept aboard ship and by the military. Every prisoner was allocated a number and in addition to his personal details very precise note was taken as to where he was captured, what ship or army unit he was serving in at the time, together with dates. Name and rank were supplemented by details of appearance:

Person.	This referred to a man's build, i.e. tall, short, thin, slender, heavy, stout, etc.
Visage.	The prisoner's facial characteristics, i.e. round, long, oval, sharp, etc.
Complexion.	Could be sallow, pale, fresh, weather beaten, black.
Marks.	Tattoos and scars are obvious features here but a record was also made of birth marks, genetic defects (hare lip for example), moles and freckles, and the marks left by disease (i.e. pock marks).

Every man therefore had a 'word picture' on record and many of their descendants, through the Public Record Offices, have obtained a very accurate description of their ancestors which in many cases bear a strong resemblance to themselves. This information was extremely useful in tracking down escapees and deserters. Many men 'went over the wall' from Dartmoor often in groups, having bribed the sentries to help them or simply taking a chance and 'running'. It should be remembered a great number of prisoners who were captured prior to Wellington's Peninsula campaign were privateersmen, semi-pirates, who would not hesitate to kill anyone who got in their way and there were occasions when murder was committed during escape bids. One cannot but admire those civilians who apprehended them and earned every penny of their reward for doing so. Some men with escape in mind bided their time and cultivated acquaintances on the 'outside' – the market traders for example. It was through them that several prisoners managed to obtain a change of clothing, often smuggled in to them out of affection or misguided sympathy, making it possible for a prisoner to merge with them on their departure and be miles away before

Roll Call. A Dartmoor farmer called Palmer was detected giving just such a disguise to a Frenchman and was brought before the local magistrates who promptly awarded him a year in gaol and fined him £5. One famous incident of this kind involved a French navy officer called Louis Vanhille who was sent to Dartmoor for breaking the terms of his parole in Launceston. He was supplied with civilian clothes by a market trader from Tavistock called Mary Ellis and got clean away. With the help of friends he had made in Launceston he spent several months on the run before making his way to Bristol where he embarked on a ship bound for Jamaica, hoping to make his way from there to the United States (a neutral country) and thence to France. Unfortunately for him, when the ship docked at Jamaica his identity was discovered and he was sent back to England to spend the rest of the war confined on board a Chatham hulk.

There are numerous romantic stories about these escapades but in fact escape was not easy. Severe punishments were meted out to soldiers found to have helped in an escape; six hundred lashes was a common sentence in the British Army at that time and serious cases were concluded by a firing squad. In the Depots there were roll calls every day and twice a week they took place in the presence of the Agent when each man personally answered to his name. When the Americans took up work outside the prison they discovered that an escape brought retribution to the entire group and everyone forfeited their accumulated pay (they were paid three months in arrears) which in itself was a very effective deterrent. For a prisoner who did escape there was the problem of finding his way in an alien land, obtaining food, evading capture and being brave enough to take any risk in order to get home. Even then there was a good chance of being wounded or captured again in the next engagement with the enemy.

For most prisoners the one hope that sustained them was the possibility of being exchanged and they dreamed about the day their turn would come. Throughout the wars with France men on both sides were exchanged at intervals on the basis of equal numbers and rank. The conditions varied from time to time, usually as a result of real or imagined breaches of the terms. During the Napoleonic wars the system allowed grade for grade and man for man. Problems then arose because Britain held by far the greater number of captives. During the Peninsula Campaign Napoleon tried (unsuccessfully) to negotiate the return of 3,000 Frenchmen for 1,000 British, the balance to be made up of Spanish and Portuguese prisoners because he was afraid once we got all our men back we would terminate the agreement. There was so much distrust on both sides the Duke of Wellington, when fighting in the Peninsula, was instructed to negotiate exchanges 'man for man' on the spot whenever the opportunity occurred. The British claimed it was because the French and their allies had reneged on the agreements so many times a serious imbalance often occurred, always to the advantage of the enemy. Consequently there was uncertainty and irregularity of exchanges, even its suspension for a time.

The POWs bore the burden of all this in two ways: the lack of exchanges meant we had to keep our prisoners in ever worsening conditions of overcrowding and it prolonged their period of captivity. Loss of their turn of exchange was one of the ways the British used to punish prisoners for misdemeanours (selling their bedding for example) and the rules were often 'bent' to rid the Depots of sick or wounded men who were unlikely to fight again. Some men sold or gambled away their turn of exchange.

Excerpts from the regulations for Prisoners of war in the Depots and on the Hulks, appertaining to Punishment in the 'Black Hole'.

The prisoners are forbidden to strike, menace or insult, an Officer, Turnkey, or other person employed in the prisons or prison Ships, under pain of losing their Turn of Exchange, of being closely confined in the Black Hole, and forfeiting one third of their rations…

…are forbidden to fight, quarrel or excite any Tumult or Disorder in the Prisons or prison Ships, or in the places where they shall be allowed to take the Air, under pain of being confined in the Black Hole and forfeiting one third of their ration for a time proportional to the offence.

Any prisoner who shall be taken *attempting* to escape shall be put in the Black Hole for ten days, and shall lose his Turn of Exchange (author's italics).

…any prisoner who shall be retaken *after having escaped* from the Prison or prison Ships, and shall by this means have occasioned Expense, shall not only lose his Turn of Exchange, and be put in the Black Hole, but shall, *with the whole of the Prisoners kept on the same deck or room from which he has escaped*, be reduced to one third of their Ration until, by such reduction, the Expenses shall be made good, and *even if he should not be retaken*, the whole of the Prisoners in the same manner to reimburse the Expenses of attending such escape (author's italics)

A Market is allowed… but the Prisoners are forbidden to buy or introduce into the prison, Liquor, Knives or Weapons of any kind under pain of being confined in the Black Hole for Ten Days for such offence.

The prisoners are allowed during market hours to sell articles of their own manufacture, except Mittens, Woollen Gloves, Straw Hats, or Bonnets, Shoes, Plaited Straw, Obscene Pictures, or Images, and articles formed of the Prison Stores which are strictly forbidden, and any Prisoner selling or making any of these Articles…shall be confined in the Black Hole, and reduced to two thirds of his Ration for three days…and such Articles shall be destroyed.

Any prisoner who shall have bought, sold, or disposed of his Ration by gambling or otherwise, or shall have sold or made away with any article of clothing, even though such Articles belong to him, shall be confined in the Black Hole, and shall only receive two thirds of his Ration during such time as the Agent may direct, and lose his Turn of Exchange.

These were some of the guidelines upon which the Agents acted to enforce discipline and order in the Establishments under their charge. Examples of actual offences and the relevant punishments are given separately, and are taken from Mr. Basil Thomson's account of the *History of Dartmoor Prison*.

The main ports through which exchanges were made were Portsmouth, Dartmouth and Plymouth, all of which were situated within easy marching distance of the Depots. Morlaix was the predominant French port which was used. The whole business was fraught with danger and abuses, which compelled both sides to draw up strict regulations for the 'Cartel' ships that were hired by the two governments to convey exchanged prisoners across the Channel. The main provisions which in themselves give us an idea of the sort of things that might occur were:

1. The flag of the country of destination as well as the ship's national flag to be flown continuously.
2. Cartels to be unarmed and not to carry weapons or goods.
3. All passengers to be searched for letters or gold coins which were forbidden articles.
4. Ships not permitted to go alongside or their crews allowed ashore.

There was a shortage of gold in France resulting in a lucrative trade in 'Guinea Running'. It was a flourishing sideline, not only for smugglers but for ships' captains and Agents and articles of concealment ranged from hollow walking sticks to shoes with false heels. Probably the most profitable 'trade' was in accepting bribes from escaped prisoners looking for a passage to France, a situation that got so bad the authorities arranged for embarkation to coincide with the tides thereby enabling ships to set sail without delay once their official passengers were on board. Anyone found loitering in dockside areas without good reason were arrested and questioned, which soon put a stop to that particular mode of escape.

The French in general are not remembered for their desperate escape attempts or the dishonour associated with those officers who broke their parole by 'running'. They live on in British history as a brave enemy who in defeat often accepted their fate with dignity despite the hardships of prison life, the worst of which was to be condemned to the hulks or 'pontons' as the French called them. It was as a result of the terrible conditions on board these dreadful floating hovels that Dartmoor Prison came to be built. They were literally carcasses of redundant men o' war, many of them captured enemy ships which had for years been rotting away in half forgotten backwaters and harbours. Necessity brought them into use, as previously indicated, firstly to hold the overwhelming numbers of prisoners and later to confine the troublesome and degraded prisoners from the Depots.

Six prison ships were commissioned at Plymouth on 1805. Some of them were scrapped and replaced after a short time (like the 'Bienfaissant') hence the names of eleven ships appear in the records. They were:

ROYAL OAK	GENEREUX
SAN RAFAEL	EL FERME
GANGES	BIENFAISSANT
HECTOR	LA BRAVE
SAN ISADORE	CERES
SAN SALVADORE (FLAGSHIP)	

There were two hospital ships, EUROPA and RENOWN.

The 'Bienfaissant' was captured from the French at Louisberg in 1758, the 'San Isadore' was Spanish and there were many other foreign vessels among a total of forty four prison ships and eight hospital ships anchored at Chatham and Portsmouth as well as Plymouth. There were hulks at Cape Town, Bermuda, and Nova Scotia too. The suffering endured by their occupants below decks in extremes of cold and tropical heat, without heating or adequate ventilation was acute and the temperate English climate must be the only redeeming feature of the hulks in English harbours.

To refer to the hulks as vessels or ships is to cast a slur on those normally beautiful objects. The prison ships were black, smoky, dirty, smelly and ugly, resembling burnt out wrecks. They degraded the proud names they bore and invoked heavy criticism from our own people (although convicts were held on hulks for years apparently without comment). The prison ships were manned by a Royal Navy lieutenant, masters mate, midshipman, and twenty ordinary sailors, many of whom were wounded veterans. The armed guards were drawn from the Marines at Portsmouth and Chatham but at Plymouth they were mainly Militiamen, each unit having an ensign, corporal, and twenty five privates. At least one Militiaman shared the prisoner's view that *'the naval officers who commanded the hulks were totally unfit for any other kind of service'*, an opinion recorded in a published (anonymous) diary entitled *Marches of the 1st. Devon Militia*. In fact most of the naval officers and crews had seen active service against the French and had little sympathy for them.

A prison ship held between 800 and 1,000 men. The death rate was higher than in the shore prisons and at Portsmouth in 1812 peaked at four per cent, mainly from chest complaints as a result of breathing foul air for long periods below decks. Other contributory factors were the contaminated and evil smelling mud flats exposed at low tides. Try and imagine the orlop deck of the 'Brunswick', which was acknowledged to be one of the better vessels. The decks measured 120ft. by 40ft. and was a mere 4ft.10 inches high so that few men could stand upright. Crammed into this space were 460 men, living in hideous conditions with hammocks slung so close together many of them had to make do on the deck. For security reasons only a few men were permitted on the main deck at any one time for exercise, in fact the only real exercise they got was the physical work involved in hoisting aboard fresh water and provisions from the supply boats. These were strictly monitored and only came alongside after being searched for contraband – liquor, newspapers, candles and so on.

Mental boredom was the biggest burden the prisoners on the hulks had to bear. There was so little to occupy them and with no market or social contact of any kind, gambling inevitably became the main pastime accompanied by the attendant evils of men wagering their clothes and rations, some of them dying as a result. The naval surgeons allocated to these floating hovels were expected to live on board, but the vast majority were known to have practices ashore and lived on land with their families; consequently many of their sick patients on board ship were close to death before a doctor even saw them. Then again the scrubbing of the decks and periodic airing of bedding were not always enforced. A number of surgeons were dismissed for neglect of duty and brought shame on a Service universally respected and admired.

There was shame of another kind on the part of officials and contractors who provisioned the ships, namely corruption and fraud. In an advertisement in the *London Gazette* for 17th. March 1814, tenders were invited:

'for the victualling of Prisoners of War at Mill Prison, Plymouth, and on the prison ships. Duration of contract to be six months, each tender to be accompanied by letters from Respectable Persons engaging to become bound in the sum of £500 for the due performance of the contract'.

Perhaps this last was an attempt to stamp out racketeering, it being well known that provisions for our own sailors on board His Majesty's ships were notorious for poor quality and short weight, resulting in (futile) letters of complaint from captains who had not had an opportunity to examine the goods until they were opened for consumption at sea. There was little chance of an honest deal for the prisoners on the hulks. In one incident at Plymouth the French prisoners rioted and threw their provisions overboard, the surface of the sea becoming a mass of floating debris which included whole cheeses, stinking and inedible. A similar event at Chatham on board the 'Samson' ended with the guards opening fire and killing fifteen Frenchmen. A prisoner afterwards wrote: *'I do not believe any Frenchman lives who hates this nation more than I do and all I pray for is that I may be able to revenge myself on it before I die'*.

The dreaded hulks. From a painting by Paul Deacon.

Some time after this terrible indictment, three Frenchmen on the same ship drew lots as to who should kill one of the marine guards. The 'winner' could not bring himself to kill their chosen victim, a sergeant with a family, but the debt was paid all the same by the murder of another marine by stabbing him. All three prisoners involved were tried and executed. The reputation of the hulks was well known to the enemy and many French commanders urged their men to greater effort by reminding them of the fate that awaited them on the prison ships if they lost the day. Before the Battle of Waterloo Napoleon himself addressed his men with these words: *'Soldiers! Let those among you who have been prisoners of the English describe to you the hulks and detail the frightful miseries they have endured'*.

Our own Lord Napier once commented: *'...the annals of civilised nations furnish nothing more inhuman towards captives of war than the prison ships of England'*.

This brief appraisal of conditions on the hulks concludes on a lighter note and concerns the 1st. Devon Militia who were doing guard duty at Plymouth. One of the sentries fell overboard and was rescued by a French prisoner called Masse who was afterwards promised his freedom as a reward. This led to a spate of 'accidental' near drownings when soldiers were invariably saved in the nick of time by a succession of brave Frenchmen. Suspicions were aroused and Colonel Bastard, their commanding officer, ordered an enquiry with the result the first sentry was Court Martialled for complicity in a plot to aid a prisoner. His fate is not recorded but Masse did not get his release and the sentries took greater care not to fall into the sea.

In the light of what we now know about confinement on the hulks, we get some idea of Dartmoor Prison's grim reputation when we read that the American POWs on board two of the Plymouth hulks, on learning they might be moved there, *'drew back with dread at the very mention of the name'*. The American prisoners played a large part in Dartmoor Prison's history and have been sadly neglected in the annals of the Moor. They undoubtedly reacted more strongly than the French to the treatment they had to bear, their very natures having been nurtured on that sublime state we call freedom. What follows is a story of defiance that was the cause of much disruption and frustration for the authorities.

A Private and Officer of
1st. Devon Militia 1812.

THE AMERICANS ARRIVE

The War of 1812 is a little known war that neither side won. It never developed into large scale warfare where whole armies faced each other but there were bitter battles (especially at sea) ferociously fought. The Americans emerged from the war with a feeling of pride, having won a number of land and sea fights over the armed might of Great Britain. It was also the inspiration for their National Anthem the *Star Spangled Banner* (composed in 1813 by a young Georgetown lawyer called Francis Scott Key). One of their most famous victories was at New Orleans when battle-hardened British 'Redcoats' were put to flight by the savage fire power of a concentrated American force. A short account of some events that led to the war will help explain the aggravation and ill feeling felt by the American prisoners of war at Dartmoor.

The war began as a direct result of certain British 'Orders in Council' which decreed all foreign vessels trading with France during the war with Napoleon were liable to a Duty to be paid according to the value of the cargo and to call at a British port to be examined for contraband. These 'Orders' severely restricted America's trading with the continental countries, which had slumped dramatically during the Treaty of Amiens (when British trading was resumed) and increased spectacularly when the war with France recommenced in 1803. By 1807 American trade figures had rocketed from $54,000,000 to more than $108,000,000 and it was resented by the British who maintained that trade closed to neutral countries in time of peace should not be open to them in wartime. With what the Americans regarded as high-handed arrogance the Royal Navy intercepted American ships at sea and searched them for illegal cargoes (arms for example). The naval boarding parties had no scruples about taking advantage of the opportunity to 'press' crew members into their Service which was desperately short of men. Americans were naturally angry and resentful – *'Free Trade and Sailor's Rights!'* was their cry and with some justification. Their expanding merchant fleet had led to a high demand for seamen and many British seafarers, some of them Royal Navy deserters, were happy to oblige in return for better conditions and higher rates of pay. It was the British men the naval search parties looked for but they didn't hesitate to 'press' American crewmen who were unable to prove their national identity (the distinctive American accent we recognise today had not yet developed, and people on both sides of the Atlantic spoke with a British style of pronunciation). Often the ship's master was left with only enough seamen to get his ship safely to port. Consequently as early as 1796 the American Government passed an 'Act for the Relief and Protection of American Seamen' in an effort to prevent them being 'pressed'. Her sailors were issued with Protection Certificates but there was a flaw: the documents, more often than not, were signed by a Customs man or a dockside official, not by a legal representative who would have asked for proof of family and birth. This meant that technically anyone who wanted such a document simply turned up and asked for one and when British sailors took to forging them they became meaningless. It was one of the immediate causes of the War of 1812. The certificate illustrated is typical – note the detailed description on Ignatious Parson's certificate and the proud manner with which it is dated: *'Twenty seventh day of August in the year of Our Lord 1810 and of the Independence of the United States the thirty fifth'*.

That great Irish playwright and philosopher Bernard Shaw once said there would never be a peaceful world so long as there was Nationalism – and how right he was! Here was a 'new nation' having to endure indignities imposed upon it by the very power it had defeated in the War of Independence. It was time for America to assert herself, establish her independence anew and demonstrate her worth once and for all. The Republican Party, for whom things were not going too well at this time, needed a boost and saw the war as a way of arousing national fervour. This would be to their advantage because it would distract attention from domestic problems at home. It was also an opportunity to put a long awaited ambition into effect, namely the conquest of Canada which Americans had always regarded as their territory by right. They wanted her rich farmlands to help feed a swelling population (the great expansion westwards had not yet begun) and the U.S. Government realised that the war would provide some justification in pursuing that claim. As for the British, they were determined nothing would stand in the way of victory over the French and in any case were still smarting after the humiliation of their first defeat at the hands of the 'rebel' colonists. When both sides remained adamant over their 'principles' the Americans finally declared war. It was to last two years and eight months, from 18th June 1812 to 17th. Feb. 1815.

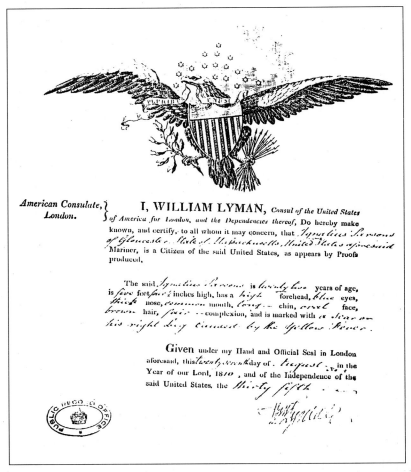

American sailor's Protection Certificate. (PRO, Kew. Ref: ADM 103/465).

The British gained an immediate advantage in the number of prisoners taken when American sailors serving in the Royal Navy declared themselves unwilling to fight against their own country and preferred imprisonment to doing so (an estimated 2,500 Americans, volunteers and pressed men, were on Royal Navy ships at the time and most of them decided to 'declare themselves'). There was outrage in America when it became known these same men were not to be regarded as prisoners of war but as renegade sailors. This was grossly unjust when we remember many of them had served the British for years, much of their time on active service against the French. Their plight now was unusual because they were not eligible for exchange and were destined to remain in custody until the war ended, a cause of much of their unruly behaviour, and who could blame them? In addition every effort was made to induce them to re-enlist either in the Army or the Royal Navy and a number of men did so, mainly to escape the intolerable conditions imposed on them by their captors to 'encourage' them. This tactic had worked to some degree with the French and the British Expeditionary Force later sent to America included a French prisoner of war contingent, the 'Chasseurs Brittanique', who took an active part in the conflict there. As with the French, the fact Britain held the greater number of prisoners caused consternation to the Americans when a shortage of manpower developed in the their armed forces. To help redress the balance and for reasons of national pride, the American Government began paying a 'bounty' of $25 per man to privateers who as a rule preferred to dump prisoners in a neutral country at the first opportunity to save the expense of keeping them on board ship. This payment was later increased to $100 per man.

At the start of the war there were instances (on both sides) when abuses of prisoners occurred and this led to a convention being arranged to draw up rules for the proper treatment of captured men. A fixed scale of rations was established in line with those issued to the French and a strict ban on corporal punishment and forced labour was agreed to.

American prisoners of war marching to Dartmoor, April 1813. From a painting by Paul Deacon
(Reproduced by courtesy of Mr. J. Langton, 'Plume of Feathers', Princetown). Image prepared by Cinnabar, Okehampton.

American prisoners were not the easy-going fatalistic type associated with the French. On the contrary almost to a man they were unrelenting enemies, even the several British among them, one of the reasons being the harsh treatment they received before arriving in this country. Some of those who 'declared themselves' for example were discharged from the Royal Navy with curses ringing in their ears (after having fought at Trafalgar and other notable actions). Some of those who were sent to Plymouth went to Mill Prison, but most of them were put on board the hulks 'Hector', 'Ceres', or 'Le Brave' anchored in the Hamoaze. The officers were sent on parole to Ashburton, Odiham and Dartmouth, the most senior ones going to Reading.

Although life on the hulks was grim, the Americans were aware of Dartmoor Depot's evil reputation and dreaded being sent there. Unfortunately for them their fears were realised on 3rd. April 1813 when 250 of them were landed from the 'Hector' at New Passage (where the Torpoint Ferry now operates from) and marched to Prince Town. On the seventeen mile trek to the moor in pouring rain they passed through Mannamead, then on to Roborough (sometimes referred to as 'Jump') and over the downs. At the Rock, a well known landmark near present day Yelverton, the guards handed them over to soldiers from Dartmoor Depot for the remainder of the journey. As they tramped under heavy escort through Dousland to the windswept Dartmoor hills, they were reminded they would be shot to death if any of them broke ranks. The moor was under a layer of snow as they passed under the cold stone arch at the entrance to the prison and into the inner recesses to join the French already there.

Their reception was not a happy one. All the Depots were overcrowded and Dartmoor was no exception, resulting in the newcomers being resented by the French as intruders. The Americans in turn were angry and there was soon friction. The authorities responded on 1st. May by sending them to No. 4 block to live among the 'Romans'. Now their existence was a tough one indeed as they found themselves cut off from the main prison by high walls and a strongly reinforced gateway. With only the stone walls to look at and the worst of the French for company one cannot but sympathise with their predicament. They had no money, no opportunity for employment and it was to be another ten months before Mr. Reuben Beasley, their Consul and the only American representative in England, was authorised to pay them an allowance. In any case they were barred from the daily market and desperate men resorted to selling their clothes for a little extra food and tobacco.

The Americans described the prisons as worse than 'horse stables' where water continually ran down the walls onto the concrete floors which were as cold as ice. They afterwards related (Charles Andrews *A Prisoner's Memoirs*) how they ate their food huddled on the floor around wooden buckets, each containing the ration for six men every one of whom was armed with a wooden spoon and jostled for his share. The overcrowding was so bad their hammocks were slung as many as five high, one above the other in the gloomy draughty dormitories. On 28th May another 250 of their countrymen joined them from Plymouth and were soon reduced to the same pitiful state with just the daily ration to sustain them. To add to their misery they had to endure continuous harassment from the British officers who did all they could to persuade them to enlist in their service, the Royal Navy in particular. As well as making things intolerable for them in order to encourage enlistment, the authorities offered a bounty as an added inducement. Those who did succumb were instantly segregated from their comrades for their own safety and detained in the guardroom until they could be sent to naval or army establishments. It says much for the stalwart spirit of those early American prisoners that out of the 6,500 or more who passed through Dartmoor during the war less than one hundred took up the offer. The Americans flogged those they caught volunteering but it is nonetheless to their credit that so few did so, an indication of their resolve as well as Dartmoor's unsavoury regime.

YANKEE WAYS.

Despite their initial difficulties the 'Yankees' as they called themselves eventually settled down to make the best of things and in a democratic manner. They elected Committees of twelve men who drew up rules to preserve order and discipline (among the French prisoners a similar system had evolved from the beginning and it seems the authorities were happy for the prisoners to organise themselves – a more convenient and peaceful way of keeping order). Important decisions were made by the prisoners themselves shouting *'Aye!'* or *'No!'* after 'criers' circulated among them with announcements and called for their votes. The Committees organised courts where offenders were tried and punished for disloyalty or acts which were judged to be against the common good. Punishments ranged from being 'sent to Coventry' as we would say to a flogging, usually with hammock cords. The most common offence was stealing which merited twenty four 'stripes'. Benjamin Palmer (a prisoner who witnessed these events and afterwards wrote *Diary of a Privateersman*, an account of his capture and later imprisonment at Dartmoor) related how one man was sentenced to 500 'stripes' (he does not mention the offence) of which he received seventy five before his back was so severely cut he was sent to recover before having the rest administered. On another occasion the cooks were caught 'skimming the pots'* and each of them got twenty five stripes across the back. It was rough justice but who knows what good it did in the long run at a time when brutal treatment was the order of the day. In any case these events cannot fairly be compared to modern day standards.

The cooks boiled the meat or fish and vegetables in nets for each mess. The fat that rose to the surface of the cauldrons congealed when cool to be skimmed off and probably sold to other prisoners to be spread on bread, a highly prized and nourishing addition to their diet. This was a recognised 'perk' for cooks in the Royal Navy at that time but caused much resentment among prisoners of war at Dartmoor.

Here are some of the rules laid down by one of the Committees, written and signed by the afore-mentioned Benjamin Palmer who was a Committee Secretary (spelling taken direct from Mr. Palmer's book):

'Regulations established by the Committee appointed by the Majority of Prisoners

Article 1

Any person or persons who shall be found guilty of Gambling for money or any other thing shall pay 2 Shillings each...

Article 3

Any person or persons who shall be found guilty of Treachery, Theift, or uncleanlyness, shall receive corporal punishment – according to the Nature of the offence – & as the Jury Shall determine.

Article 4

Any person or persons who shall be found guilty of making any neusance (except in the Necessary) shall be made to clean the same and pay one shilling.

Article 5

Any person or persons who shall be found guilty of washing in the well shall pay 1 shilling for every such offence (author's note: this must refer to their drinking water).

Article 9

Any person who shall have cause of Complaint shall make the same Known to the Committee whose decision shall be definitive unless they shall see fit to call a jury.

Article 11

All moneys collected as fines shall be appropriated to defray the expenses of Pens Ink and Paper &c. and to pay the Constables criers for their trouble - & it shall be the duty of the Committee to appoint a person to Keep a regular account of all receipts and disbursements'.

It shall be the duty of the Committee – to appoint 8 men out of the Sd. Committee to attend in the Cook house, and 2 to attend outside and Inspect the provision'.

Article 14

Any one of the Committee who shall be guilty of a breach of any of the foregoing Articles, Shall pay double.

Dartmoor Prison No. 7   *Order of the Committee Oct. 11th. 1814*
                                                                      BENJn. F. PALMER
                                                                               Secty.'

The Transport Office instructions were that the prisoners should be permitted to inspect their provisions before they were issued. On one occasion the entire batch of daily bread was rejected and the contractor heavily fined. It happened in October 1812 after a sample of the bread was

The 'Argus' and HMS 'Pelican' engagement 14th. August 1813. From a painting by Paul Deacon (Reproduced by courtesy of Mr. M. Chamberlain).

sent to the authorities in London; retribution was swift and uncompromising as the following letter from the Transport Office to Captain Cotgrave makes clear:

'I am directed to acknowledge the receipt of your letter of the 29th. instant with the sample of bread therein referred to and to acquaint you that they have ordered (a fine) of £500 to be imposed on Mr. Cock for his breach of contract, and have given him notice that his contract will cease on 31st. January'.

It was during their first months at Dartmoor, when the Americans were forced to endure the worst of conditions and subjected to humiliations heaped on them both by their captors and the French prisoners, that a famous sea battle was fought in British waters. It led to an act of chivalry seldom seen in warfare and years later a barbaric revenge taken on fellow Americans by outraged Dartmoor prisoners of war. The story is of interest, illustrating the best and worst of circumstances when an early 19th. century sea battle was fought and is relevant to certain events that took place at the Depot.

For much of what follows the author is indebted to Mr. Ira Dye of Mill Valley, California, writer, researcher, and author of *The Fatal Cruise of the Argus* (United States Naval Institute, Annapolis, Maryland 1994).

The Saga of the 'Argus' and the 'Pelican'

The battle was fought in the Irish Channel between two naval Brigs – the American 'Argus'(ten guns) and the British 'Pelican' (eleven guns), culminating in victory for the 'Pelican' and an exceptional act of gallantry by the British when the American Commander, Lieutenant William Henry Allen who died of wounds, was given a public funeral in Plymouth with full military honours. His crew ended up at Dartmoor.

The 'Argus' crossed the Atlantic in June 1813 with the American Minister to France on board. After landing him at L'Orient she proceeded to raid shipping in the English Channel, sinking or burning several British merchant ships. The 'Argus' then made her way into the sea lanes in St. George's Channel, continuing to destroy shipping and proving to be such a menace the British Admiralty determined she must be stopped. The 'Argus' ran out of luck on 14th. August when she was intercepted by H.M.S. 'Pelican' under the command of Capt. John Fordyce Maples, R.N. who had been told his quarry had been sighted in that area the previous day. Although the two vessels were fairly evenly matched the 'Argus' was superior in sail and could easily have escaped, but her Captain, Lt. Allen, full of confidence after his recent successes, elected to meet his adversary and fight it out – he actually hove to and waited for him.

The encounter was brief and bloody. After a short exchange of fire at close range the British managed to get alongside the 'Argus' and board her. One of Lt. Allen's legs was shattered by cannon shot at an early stage in the fight and he was out of it five minutes after the first shots were fired. His leg was amputated shortly afterwards. Most of the other officers became casualties too including Midshipman Richard Delphey who lost both legs by cannon fire and died three hours later. Deprived of effective leadership and weary from previous encounters, the Americans were overwhelmed in hand to hand fighting and surrendered forty five minutes after the battle began.

The 'Argus' was taken to Plymouth by a prize crew, arriving there two days later on 16th. August. On 18th. August the Commander of the British Flagship at Plymouth, Capt. Nash, R.N. sent his personal launch with a large cot slung in it to convey Lt. Allen, whose condition was fast deteriorating, to the hospital at Mill Prison. The surgeon there was Dr. George MaGrath, who afterwards transferred to Dartmoor and served with distinction at a critical time (to be described later). He rendered every possible assistance and together with Mr. Inderwick, the 'Argus' surgeon, remained with the patient until the end. William Henry Allen died at 11.00pm that night.

Lt. Allen was already known to the British on account of the kindness he showed to Royal Navy prisoners taken from the 'Macedonian' when she was captured by the U.S. Navy's 'United States', of which he was First Lt. earlier in the war – hence his burial with full military honours which took place on 21st. August 1813. The funeral procession included the Band of the Plymouth Division of Marines, a contingent of British Marines marching with reversed arms, eight British Royal Navy Captains as pallbearers, and of course the surviving officers of the 'Argus'. He was laid to rest alongside Midshipman Delphey in a vault at St. Andrew's Church in the area between the church itself and Prysten House at the rear. Thus a link with those almost forgotten times exists but we do not know exactly where the two Americans lie.

Meanwhile the 'Argus' crew reached Plymouth as prisoners and on 8th. September 1813 they were moved to Dartmoor Depot. The only homicide among the Americans at Dartmoor was committed by the 'Argus' Quartermaster, a seaman called Thomas Hill, already known among his shipmates as a violent man. He and another 'Argus' crewman, James Henry, had a serious argument and decided to settle their differences in the traditional manner – with their fists. The fight took place in the cockloft of the notorious No. 4 block (where the Americans were still confined) and James Henry soon got the worst of it, Hill beating him so savagely he died on the spot. An inquest was held, as was customary with every death at the prison, and a verdict of manslaughter was recorded, resulting in Thomas Hill being sent to Exeter for trial where he was acquitted and returned to Dartmoor.

In America the 'Argus' men were held in high regard because of their successes prior to the encounter with the 'Pelican'. They were also the only U.S.Navy prisoners of war in Dartmoor at that time (the main body of captured Americans so far were privateersmen) and as trained seamen were badly needed for the conflict. The crewmen knew this and waited expectantly for word of their exchange. It came in October 1814 when, together with a small number of other POWs, they were repatriated; but the saga didn't end there. Just weeks after the 'Argus' men went home, six American sailors who had enlisted in the Royal Navy were discharged from the service having decided to 'declare' themselves. They were sent to Dartmoor where some of them were recognised by other Americans. After becoming drunk (drink was regularly smuggled in to the Depot as will be explained later) two of them, who had served aboard the 'Pelican' when the 'Argus' was defeated, began boasting about their exploits to the fury of their fellow prisoners. They paid a terrible price for their indiscretion, when their infuriated listeners vented their anger by forcibly detaining them and holding a court. The majority were for putting them to death, but their lives were spared; instead their faces were branded by tattooing in Indian ink the letters US (United States) on one cheek and T (Traitor) on the other. All six men were later transferred to Plymouth where hospital staff tried to remove the markings by blistering but without success (one of the two marked men died after his wounds became infected).

Such was a Yankee sailor's lot at Dartmoor in 1813, cast among the worst of the French, without access to the daily market, no allowances, despised by their guards. It was an unhappy time and there was worse to come.

MORE TRIBULATIONS AT DARTMOOR – THEN BETTER TIMES

Love of country beat strongly in American hearts and 4th. July (Independence Day) was celebrated by flying improvised flags depicting the Stars and Stripes, making patriotic speeches and singing national songs with musical accompaniment. These activities were actively discouraged by the guards and Independence Day 1813 was marred when one of their flags was confiscated; in the ensuing scuffle shots were fired, wounding two of the prisoners.

All this time their relations with the 'Romans' (which were never cordial) deteriorated, culminating in a fight on 11th. July 1813 when the Frenchmen emerged from their quarters early armed with home made knives, cudgels and stones. When the Americans came out they were set upon and during the ensuing battle at least twenty men on both sides were so badly hurt they had to be taken to the hospital. The authorities now decided to segregate the two factions by building another wall dividing the No.4 yard in two, one for the 'Romans' the other for the 'Yankees' – but not for long. In October the 'Romans' were taken to Plymouth and confined to the hulks as previously related.

Autumn brought more tribulations when an outbreak of smallpox struck the Depot followed by the worst winter in living memory. The disease was a common one for those times but the additional burden of surviving in sub zero temperatures for weeks in the icy cold of the stone built prison blocks must have been hard to bear. The prison leat froze over and water standing in buckets became solid ice overnight, forcing the men to eat snow to alleviate their thirst, never a satisfying substitute for man's most precious need. Snow drifts were recorded as having reached the top of the boundary walls and the guards cowered inside their shelters. The danger now was of hunger and deprivation because the supply wagons were unable to get to Prince Town and salted emergency rations were resorted to for the Military and the town's inhabitants as well as the men inside the Depot (a scenario which has been repeated more than once since Dartmoor became a convict prison in 1850). The continual ill treatment they had suffered up to that time together with the harsh climate prompted one American prisoner to write home describing Dartmoor as '...that accursed place (which) extinguished every impression we formerly entertained of the British Nation as magnanimous, pious, liberal, and honourable or brave'.

In May 1814 another American, Peter Drinkwater wrote to his brother in North Yarmouth (Maine) in vivid terms about the conditions at Dartmoor Depot (author's note: spelling and punctuation unchanged):

'This prison is situated on one of the highest places in England and it either rains or snows the whole year round and is cold enough to wear a great coat the whole time their is 10,000 of us here now but the French are going home, (the French war had ended in April 1814 and the Frenchmen were being repatriated) *I shall send this by A Frenchman that will Leave heir tomorrow for France. This is the first time I was ever deprived of my Liberty and when I sit and think it almost deprives me of my sences for we have nothing else to do but sit and reflect on our present situation which is bad anough god noes for we have but 1lb. of beef and a Little beef tea to drink and all that makes us one meal a Day the rest of the time we have to fast which is hard times fior the Days are very Long heir now I want to get out of heir before the war is over so that I can have the pleasure of killing one Englishman and drinking his blood which I think I coud do with a good will for I think them the worst of all the human race. If these rebels are the bullwark*

of our religion I think That I will never have any. When they called up 500 French men to go away there was one that had been in the prison Nine years and had worn his blankwt out so that he had but half of it to give those rebels and on that account they sent him back and put him on the bottom of the books for exchangeing, the man took it so hard that he cut his throught and was found dead between the prison dores. It is a great misfortune to me to be placed heir in my present situation but I shall bear it with as much fortitude as I am posesed for I scorn to complain to those rebels before I would ask them for a mousel of bread I hold up my head as high as possible and mean to live through it'.

These recriminations indicate very clearly the hardships of Depot life but for the 'Yankees' the turning point was at hand. Capt. Isaac Cotgrave, R.N. resigned on 22nd. December 1813 and the new Agent Capt. Thomas Shortland, R.N. took over. One of his first acts was to permit the Americans the use of the daily market – two of their number were allowed to attend on behalf of them all. They were then issued with proper clothing, albeit in the 'King's Yellow'. Each man received a jacket, waistcoat, pantaloons and a woollen cap. The caps were *'thick and coarser than rope yarn'*, as one man put it and as you might expect few men got outfits that fitted them. An additional stigma as far as they were concerned were the initials 'TO' (Transport Office) stamped on each garment. Even so they were far better than the worn out rags they were now able to throw away. Shirts and wooden soled shoes completed their attire. In February 1814 came the glad news they were to be paid one and one half pence per day with which to buy soap and tobacco (they could, if they had wished, have bought 2lb. potatoes or three 'chews' of tobacco with it). The money was paid by the American Government through their London Agent Mr. Reuben Beasley, who was the only official contact between that government and this country. He must have been a very busy man or a careless one because his lack of communication with the prisoners was to cost him his integrity and good character. The American prisoners thought he was busy lining his own pockets at their expense. This was very likely true of his subordinates who were responsible for the clothing later issued to them from their government because most of it was ill fitting and of poor quality. Mr. Beasley was at fault by not replying to the many letters of complaint he received and took the trouble to visit Dartmoor only once during the whole course of the war. On that occasion, rather than visit the prison blocks to see for himself the basis of their discontent, he summoned a number of men to an office he was assigned and engaged them in casual conversation concerning their homes and families. Whatever his true intentions (he wrote to his superiors after the war in very hurt tones about the injustice of the criticisms made against him) the prisoners saw him as their only hope for fair treatment; when he failed them he became in their eyes a hated figure, neglectful and uncaring.

Happily the Americans' way of life was transformed by the money they now received. It was a boon to them, enabling them to engage in several enterprises when cash began to circulate among them. They could now set up market stalls of their own instead of having to barter with the French at inflated prices. The stallholders stocked clothes, shoes, and little luxuries concocted from ingredients bought or bartered for at the regular market. The latter included fritters, stews, and what the Yankees called *'plumgudgeons'* made from mashed potatoes flavoured with codfish, fried to a crisp brown and sold as small cones. The 'coffee' was manufactured from items such as burnt peas or bread crusts ground to a powder.

Then the gambling started. Charles Andrews (*A Prisoner's Memoires*) tells us gambling was forbidden by the Committees in February 1814, but we know from the Committee rules Benjamin Palmer wrote up in October 1813 it was already banned. That gambling for money and anything else of value went on regardless is therefore certain. Palmer himself wrote in his account of Dartmoor life a description of a typical day: '...daylight comes with the sounds of gamblers who have been up all night – some drunk, fighting, cursing, night comes and there is bedlam, gambling, etc. starts over again'.

Card games were a favourite activity (mainly 'Vingt-et-un' and Brag). Then there was a form of Roulette and Backgammon which was especially popular. Palmer relates how he himself was challenged to an unusual race (for a bet of course) the 'runners' being lice. His opponent kept his 'steed' under his shirt collar but when all was ready the collar was found to be empty – the beast had fled and his owner had to forfeit the bet! He also recounts how, after the French were repatriated in the summer of 1814, those men employed outside the prison (more about this later) found it easy to smuggle in rum and openly distributed it. By this time they had also managed to establish an officially approved beer shop.

Meanwhile the American's energies were concentrated on escape plans and aggravating the British. The latter occupation, which took the form of stone throwing, hurling insults at the guards and jeering about the several defeats the British suffered from time to time, prompted a heartfelt comment from one officer that there was more trouble from 4,000 Americans than from 40,000 Frenchmen! These distractions no doubt contributed to the continual bedlam as Palmer called it, night after night, with the gambling tables in full swing and fights over disputed losses. In January 1815 the gambling tables were destroyed by order of the Committees on the grounds some watches and other personal possessions were allegedly stolen during the proceedings. It appears therefore that the gaming etc., went on all the time and that there were periodic crackdowns by the Committees.

In March 1814 the Americans' fortunes improved still further when the gates to their compound were unlocked leaving them free to roam the prison at will. That same month their spirits were again uplifted by a further money allowance. The news came in a letter from Mr. Beasley which said:

'Fellow Citizens,

in addition to the three halfpence per day which has heretofore been allowed, I shall make remittance to Captain Shortland to enable you to have coffee and sugar twice a week, that is, the days on which your rations consist of fish: my intention at first was to have the articles themselves sent to be distributed, but it being suggested to me by the Committees at other Depots that the value in money would be more serviceable to the prisoners, I have determined to allow three pence halfpenny per man, two days in the week, being the value of those articles and I hope the Committee will find the means to ensure it being applied to the purpose intended'.

The letter was accompanied by the first payment of the additional allowance which must have caused Mr. Beasley's standing with the men to reach an all time high. Every man was now entitled to the equivalent of an extra penny per day in addition to the one and a half pence per day already received. This represented a total of 6s.8d. per man per month. In fact it was paid every 32 days in the form of two £1 notes per six men*. This large injection of money on a regular basis was more than welcome as can be imagined. This was when the men got permission to open a beer shop selling beer at 'twopence halfpenny a pot', but even more gratifying was the instruction to the guards that everyone of them was to have access to the daily market. The enterprising Americans, like the French, manufactured items with which to bargain at market, exchanging carved models made of wood and bone, paintings, ornaments, etc. for tobacco and snuff. A civilised and flourishing community now evolved. For example there were a number of boys held in the prison, mostly ships' boys many of whom were related to members of the crew (it was British policy, and a wise one, not to separate them in the boys' own interests). There were among the Americans at Dartmoor, seven boys under the age of twelve and seventy five under sixteen. Most of them were employed as waiters by the French officers; now a school was established for them where they were taught reading, writing and arithmetic for a fee of 6d. per month. The future looked brighter for the 'Yankees' at last.

*For the benefit of younger readers:
Each man already got one and a half pence per day (x 32) = 48d.
The new allowance = 1d. extra per day (x 32)   = 32d.
Total   80d.
(20 shillings = £1 and 12 pence = 1 shilling)
80d = 6s.8d., which is exactly one third of £1 and therefore £2 per six men = 6s.8d. each.

The French war ends

In the meantime Britain was still engaged in fighting two wars, against France and the United States, but for Napoleon the end was near. A series of defeats found France fighting for survival on French soil and an excerpt from the *Times* of 29th. December 1813 read:

'Christmas Present for the British Nation!

Wellington's Victories, etc.

In one little year Russia, Austria, Prussia, Holland, Petty Sovereignties of the Rhine, Portugal, Spain – all freed from their tyrranic oppressors! Now must Bonaparte humbly sue for the Peace he might have Commanded! A Victorious British Army has entered his Kingdom!'.

By April 1814 the French Emperor was besieged in his Capital, and on 11th. April he abdicated, enabling the Treaty of Paris to be signed on 30th. April 1814. The long French wars were over at last. There were tumultuous scenes all over England – church bells rang out, there were Thanksgiving services, dinners, elaborate parades, and rejoicing in the streets. For the French prisoners of war, some of whom had been prisoners for nearly eleven years, it was a time of wild elation. On Dartmoor some of the local gentry rode over the moor to the War Depot to congratulate the French on their imminent freedom. The officers were presented with a white flag and white cockades (the emblem colour of the Bourbon King who would succeed Bonaparte) but their reaction was not at all what was expected. The flag was burned in front of them in full view of the British officers. *'We would remain prisoners another eleven years before we betrayed our Emperor!'* they declared. Loyalty such as this in the face of defeat is a rare thing and says much for the stature of the man they so faithfully served.

On 16th. May 1814 the Transport Office wrote to Capt. Shortland instructing him:

'that your Depot should be cleared of (French) *prisoners with as little delay as possible'* and *'to acquaint you that Captain Pellowe has been directed to inform you from time to time of the numbers he may be able to receive at Mill Prison and that you will send off the prisoners without*

waiting for particular orders, reporting from time to time the numbers you may have so discharged'.

They were being shipped home as soon as transport became available. Dartmoor Depot was being prepared for a specific purpose – the confinement of all American POWs in this country.

The first 500 French left the Depot on 21st. May, the last of them departing on 20th. June. Among them were some Americans who had served on French vessels and were fluent in the French language, passing themselves off as Frenchmen after observing the British were not too particular in checking identities. Some French sailors who had been captured on American ships were also freed at this time. Preparations for their departure included their various tools and artefacts, market stalls, etc. being eagerly purchased by the Yankees who were now wise to prison ways and saw an opportunity to exploit their own talents in the market place without competition. They were also able to take advantage of the fact they were now the sole occupants thus ending the overcrowding.

At about the time the French were leaving certain American seamen who had served in the Royal Navy received the back pay and prize money that was due to them, an indication of the intended fair treatment of prisoners by the British authorities (there were good and not so good Agents running the Depots who interpreted and applied the regulations as they saw fit, but this would have been an unequivocal directive from the Admiralty). The extra money was soon dispersed within the prison community to the benefit of the gambling element and the market stallholders. As a bonus they were visited by Mr. Beasley's representative, a man called Williams,

who was accompanied by a Jewish trader bearing fresh clothes for them from their own country. No clothing of any kind had been allowed them since 15th. March, almost two months previous, on orders from the Transport Office directing Captain Shortland *'not to issue any more clothing and to transmit lists of such Americans as may have been supplied with any article of clothing since January'.* They had evidently been informed that the United States had assumed responsibility for furnishing their men with clothing and no doubt hoped to claim the cost of what had already been issued. Now jackets, shirts, and trousers in 'Pilot Blue' were handed out together and with the news that from now on they would be supplied by their own government. The Yankees threw away the hated yellow garments and spruced themselves up with pride.

Reservoir and control tower for water supply to War Depot.

DARTMOOR BECOMES AN AMERICAN DEPOT

By the end of June 1814 all the French had gone home, Napoleon was living in exile on the Mediterranean island of Elba and the Americans had Dartmoor Depot to themselves. Roughly fifteen per cent were coloured men – Negroes and Mulattos (half breeds). These unfortunates suffered the most from the effects of climate and disease, accounting for nearly one third of all American deaths at Dartmoor. This was said at the time to be related to their unclean habits and poor sanitary standards which in turn led them to be segregated at the insistence of the whites, who also accused them of persistent stealing. On 22nd. February 1814 the 'Black Jacks' as the Yankee sailors called them, were banished to the top floor of the infamous No. 4 block where they established a community of their own. By September all the white men had abandoned No. 4 and it was occupied exclusively by the coloured men.

Yet for all the contempt in which they were held by the white Americans, their newly established community was very orderly and disciplined. This was due to the iron rule of 'King Dick', a giant Negro six foot three inches in height, whose real name was Richard Crafus. He was a native of Vienna (Chesapeake Bay) and only twenty three years old when he was captured in March 1814 on board a privateer. This powerful individual kept a tight reign on his little kingdom and earned for it a grudging admiration on account of the orderliness he commanded. The proverbial 'iron fist' was much in evidence and he was described by one observer as a king in his own right, wielding a club and wearing a bearskin hat, accompanied everywhere by two white boy attendants. The way of life over which he presided (with the help of a few hard-case associates) commanded the respect not only of his fellow prisoners but the authorities as well. There were boxing matches and other entertainments, including plays and concerts which often attracted the other prisoners, indicating the standards must have been high. They even had a band. Benjamin Palmer tells us about a visit to No. 4 to see a play, with tickets on sale at 6d. each. Mob rule prevailed though and most men simply shoved their way in to a packed house where the performance rendered by the players received no less genuine applause from them than if they'd paid full price for admission!

Sunday was always a special day and was observed by all the Americans as a day of quiet leisure. In No. 4 block church services were held. The style was Evangelical and conducted by Preacher Simon, an apparently very ugly black man who nonetheless attracted good attendances, supported by an all black choir. There came a time however when the black men were forced to accept the worst of prisoners in their midst. For example, in April 1815 three men were severely flogged after being discovered committing homosexual acts, and were banished to No 4 block. They were later joined by the 'Rough Alleys', the name the Yankees bestowed on troublemakers and undesirables about whom more will be said presently. To their credit 'King Dick' and the coloured men generally were not involved to any great extent in the unruly behaviour and turmoil that often occurred at Dartmoor.

On 24th. June 1814 Captain Shortland announced he was empowered to employ masons, carpenters and the like, for work on the church (now Princetown's Parish Church of St. Michael's and All Angels) and the neighbouring parsonage, which the French had largely constructed and left unfinished. In addition labourers were needed as road menders, blacksmiths were wanted, as well as coopers, painters, nurses, etc. There was no shortage of volunteers and more than 150

No. 4 Block cockloft showing scorch marked timbers (almost certainly from candles in the Depot days).

No. 4 Block now known as the 'Old Chapel', a listed building from the Depot days. The former home of the French 'Roman' outcasts and afterwards 'King Dick' Crafus and the American coloured population. (Courtesy Lady Georgina Wates, Founding Patron, New Start Chapel Project).

men were taken on. Charles Andrews recorded the rates of pay for those lucky enough to be employed, and they included the following:

1 Sweeper per 1,000 men	3d.	per day.
1 Cook per 200 men	4¹/₂d	per day.
Barbers	3d.	per day.
Nurses	6d.	per day.
Carpenters	3d.	per day.
Hospital helps (1 to every 10)	6d.	per day.

Those who worked outside the Depot made up to five shillings a day extra by smuggling **out** forbidden items (straw hats for example), and smuggling **in** candles, oil, rum, etc. The prisoners in work took to wearing tin badges in their caps denoting their trade or occupation and their fellow prisoners, who were not lacking in industry, took up the manufacture of articles to barter with at the market – home made shoes, fiddles, tin ware, and model boats were specialities.

From: *Trumans Exeter Post* London 16th. April 1814.

'200 American prisoners passed through Exeter from Stapleton en route to Dartmoor War prison...'

The Transport Office, probably for reasons of security and economy, had decided to confine all American prisoners of war in Britain in one place. Stapleton near Bristol had been the first choice but for reasons not entirely clear (perhaps Sir Thomas Tyrwhitt had a hand in the matter) the Depot at Dartmoor was chosen instead. Besides Stapleton American POWs were moved to

Dartmoor from Normans Cross near Peterborough, Mill Prison and the hulks at Chatham, Portsmouth and Plymouth. The prisoners who came from Stapleton were mainly ex-Royal Navy sailors who had seen active service and naturally were resentful of the treatment they'd endured. At the end of January 1814 there were approximately 1,000 Americans on the moor, rising to 3,000 by August and 5,500 by December. All the same, with the departure of the French and the overcrowding at an end, life in the Depot started to improve.

All was not sweetness and honey though. Much ill feeling was generated by malcontents among the lower classes of seamen prisoners, some of them Britishers who had found employment on American vessels where they were later captured. The bulk of these men were privateersmen, a hotch potch of ruffians, toughs, and sullen rascals of the worst kind whose activities closely resembled that of the notorious 'Romans'. After being recognised for what they were by the decent men they were sent, like all the other undesirables, to No. 4 block to live with the black men. There they became known as the 'Rough Alleys', a title they revelled in and tried to live up to at every opportunity, not bestial and vice ridden like the French outcasts, but certainly incurable troublemakers. Into this mixture of resentful humanity were added a number of bitter ingredients. When the French capitulated a number of British officers swaggered into the Depot, taunting the Americans with exaggerated tales of British valour and the fearful consequences that would befall their folk at home now that the full might of British arms could be employed against them. Another cause of friction and injustice that had long rankled the Yankees was the fate of twenty four of their countrymen who had been captured with the French in 1810. They were ignored by the French and British alike, being recognised as neither French nor American and during all those years had been forced to live by begging from their fellow captives. When the Frenchmen were repatriated they were detained and were not acknowledged by their own government until early 1815 after hostilities had ceased.

For the details concerning the following account of a cruel fate the author is again indebted to Mr. Ira Dye for supplying an extract from Green Hands First Cruise by A Younker (Baltimore 1841).

The most inhuman punishment inflicted on prisoners at Dartmoor Depot was endured by four seamen captured under unusual circumstances. They had shipped aboard the armed schooner 'Surprise' of Baltimore, a privateer which went cruising in the Pacific Ocean looking for enemy merchantmen to capture and loot. There they met up with a fleet of likely prizes and determined to attack and take them one at a time. Their first and only capture was a schooner of little value, but it was decided to put four seamen on board as a prize crew with the intention of transferring captured crewmen from other vessels they hoped to take, who would eventually be left to make their way to a port of their choice. When the Royal Navy man o' war guarding the merchant ships appeared and pursued the 'Surprise' over the horizon, they were left stranded on the prize with very little food or water.

Several days later a brig was sighted whereupon it was decided to fly a distress signal to lure the stranger close enough to engage and hopefully capture her. However the brig became suspicious and hove to at a distance but within range of the schooner's six pounder guns which opened fire. The intended prey made off and easily outsailed her attacker. In their haste the four privateer crew members had carelessly flung aside the burnt matches used to fire the guns, some of which fell into the hold. This was crucial to their later sufferings when later on they were captured by another Royal Navy ship and taken off as prisoners, having been replaced by navy 'tars'. The burnt matches were discovered in the hold close to the powder kegs and it was at once assumed the intention had been to blow up the captured ship. This action would have been against all naval etiquette in time of war, when the victorious officers and crew had the undisputed right to claim a portion of the prize value for distribution among themselves. In fact many officers in the Royal Navy (and other navies too) relied on this 'perk' to supplement their pay. Consequently the four alleged saboteurs, despite their protestations, spent the forty two day voyage back to England in irons and were sent to Dartmoor in August 1814, having been sentenced by the Transport Office to spend their entire captivity in the dreaded Black Hole. There they would have died but for the merciful attention of their jailor who smuggled items of food to them in addition to the two thirds rations allowed to prisoners under punishment. Their American comrades voted to donate a halfpenny per man per month to help with this (and to bribe the jailor?) after their petition to the Transport Office for clemency was rejected. The men who suffered the worst punishment ever inflicted at Dartmoor were:

Elisha Whitten of Massachussets

Simeon Hayes of Baltimore

John Miller, an Englishman

James Ricker (origin unknown)

For nearly eight months they were confined in the stone coffin that was the Cachot, in semi-darkness and (officially) on short rations (the sequel to this unhappy episode will be related in the next chapter). At about the same time, August 1814, a large number of ex- Royal Navy men were shipped by sea from Chatham (where they had been detained on the hulks ever since the war began) to Plymouth and marched up to the Depot. Most of them were those who had chosen to go to prison immediately war was declared rather fight against their homeland. They had fought for Britain in the war against France, something that not only embarrassed the guards but was another cause of the resentment that was carried to the Depots by men who after all were true to the highest of principles – loyalty to one's country.

The main body of Americans had now decided by popular vote on a mass escape attempt. A large tunnelling operation commenced with the intention of burrowing under the boundary walls to the open moor, after which it was planned for as many men as possible to escape under the cover of darkness, each making his own way to freedom once he was clear of the depot. Bibles were obtained and every participant was sworn to secrecy under pain of death. The plan was to dig down about 20ft. from No. 4 block before working outwards under the walls. It was a bold venture and one that very nearly succeeded. Tools (Andrews refers to 'daggers') were smuggled to those digging the tunnels by men who were employed in the blacksmith shop. By September three tunnels were under way (work began from the unoccupied No. 5 and No. 6 blocks as well), each one progressing outwards at the same rate, the idea being that at an arranged time as many men as possible would emerge and make their escape separately.

Their hopes were dashed when Captain Shortland suddenly appeared one day with a search party. It was obvious he knew what was going on because one of the tunnels was quickly found and blocked up with stones. Captain Shortland was evidently unaware of the other two tunnels so when another draft of prisoners arrived (they were the ones from Chatham previously mentioned) and were allocated to 5 and 6 Blocks where excavations had been started, the delighted Americans at once resumed their underground toil. They dug around the stone filled one and resumed work on all three tunnels full of optimism at the good progress they were making. Then there was a final set back, an act of treachery resulting in one of their number being taken away by the guards, never to be seen again. Shortly afterwards all three tunnels were uncovered by a search party and blocked up with stones as before. The entire prison was put on two thirds rations (there wouldn't have been room for all of them in the Black Hole) until the cost of filling them in was recovered and the damage made good. It took ten days. It was as well for the informant he was spirited off, probably on the next Cartel to the United States, because as Charles Andrews wrote: *'they* (his comrades) *would have torn him to atoms!'*.

There were still individual escapes of course, but this would have been a notable episode in the annals of prison escapes and typical of our American cousins who do not do things by halves.

FRUSTRATION AND A NEW REGIME

There now occurred a series of events that culminated in a ghastly tragedy.

From the *Sherbourne and Yeovil Mercury*, Monday 7th. November 1814:

'The 1st. Somerset Regt. of Militia which lately returned into Taunton from Ireland for the purpose of being disembodied, marched in two Divisions on Monday and Tuesday last for the Royal Prison, Dartmoor, to do duty over the American prisoners. The first Division passed through Exeter on Wednesday morning. This fine body of soldiers who have ever been distinguished for the excellence of their Discipline and Good Conduct, marched on this service in the highest spirits'.

No doubt there was a lot of truth in the description of the 'fine body of soldiers' marching to Dartmoor. However, many Militia regiments were being disbanded at this time, including the Devons, and the Somerset men must have felt they too were entitled to go home, having previously served in Ireland and Mill Prison in Plymouth. They were no strangers therefore to prison duty and must have resented the fact their latest assignment meant being posted miles from any town, probably in poor accommodation with very little social life. Nearly all the War Depots were situated in just such locations for security reasons, but the soldiers must have known Dartmoor had the reputation of being the worst of them. Furthermore the task allotted to them would be vastly different from guarding the French. Another newspaper had stated: *'...the Americans are unruly, and refuse to settle down to manufacturing pastimes'.*

The Somerset Militiamen did not yet know it, but there was the pent up passion of desperate men to contend with on the moor, men who felt they had endured more than their fair share of injustices and were ready to revolt.

From *The Times* 13th. November 1814.

'...the American prisoners of war there (Dartmoor) *are far from orderly and quiet – they are constantly trying plans of escape, not occupying themselves as their predecessors the French did in different works to while away the time, and it had been found necessary to have an efficient Militia force there'.*

The impression given is that the Somerset Militia were selected for the role they were to play at Dartmoor on account of their efficiency.

The war with the United States was being fought to a standstill. Both sides were financially drained and ready to seek a compromise. For prisoners of war everywhere the long awaited peace came at an appropriate time – Christmas Eve 1814 when the Treaty of Ghent was signed, effectively ending hostilities. There was a delay however because the Treaty had to be ratified by the United States Government. A fast Royal Navy sloop, the 'Favourite', was dispatched across the Atlantic bearing the precious document, whilst at Dartmoor Depot where the news was received on 29th. December after several false rumours, the 'Yankees' sang with glee. Their elation was still high when they flew their home made flags, boldly painted with the slogan *'Free Trade and Sailors Rights!'* a defiant gesture dating from the first day of the war. It was repeated on New Years Day 1815, with the prisoner's band playing *Yankee Doodle!* This was trying Captain Shortland's patience too far and the celebrations were terminated on his orders, with the comment that hostilities had not yet officially ceased. All the same the excitement and hopes for the future must have dominated the thoughts of every man – but there was to be more suffering before those happier days arrived.

In January 1815 there was an outbreak of smallpox of exceptional virulence, which killed more than 200 Americans. It was referred to as the 'African Pox' and soon reached epidemic proportions, overwhelming the hospital staff who struggled valiantly to contain the disease. Ultimately extra medical assistance was called for and the Chief Surgeon of England was summoned to Dartmoor. He attributed the rapid spread of the disease to the impure air in the dormitories. The very conditions that had for so many years prevented deaths from winter cold was now proving fatal, his opinion being partly confirmed when he took temperature readings both inside and outside the prison blocks on a cold February morning. With the outside temperature standing at thirty eight degrees at 7.30am the readings inside one of the prisons registered fifty six degrees on the first two floors rising to a maximum of sixty six degrees on the top level. The prisoners had evidently acquired stoves for heating because the authorities at once ordered them to be doused and more adequate ventilation provided. We can be certain the inmates blocked up the apertures around the windows to help keep the heat in; this of course led to a shortage of fresh air with all the accompanying bad results. Charles Andrews has left a vivid description of how bodies were removed to the Dead House after being stripped of their clothing and cut open to determine the cause of death. They were then placed naked in rough coffins, after which, when a sufficient number had accumulated, they were buried in communal graves on the moor. The number of dead from the dreaded pox was no reflection on the abilities of the resident surgeon, Dr. George MaGrath, who laboured incessantly despite his own ill health at the time. It was he who summoned the extra help to alleviate the suffering, which was all that could be done in the early stages. The outbreak was finally brought under control by vaccination (still a relatively new cure) which the noble doctor initiated. Many Americans rejected this form of treatment and had to be persuaded by their government who threatened to stop their allowances if they refused.

In February there occurred the first serious confrontation between the Americans and Agent Shortland. He had granted a concession to the four men who had been locked in the Black Hole for so long and were due to be confined there for the whole of their imprisonment. He allowed them to exercise for half an hour every day on the grassy area between the inner wall and the iron railings. When they emerged from the Black Hole the entire prison community were shocked at their appearance, an emotion not easily aroused among tough seafarers in the days of sail. Plans were made and on 13th. February Simeon Hayes, actively encouraged by the onlookers, managed to evade the guard and scale the railings where he was seized by the other prisoners and borne triumphantly away. It only took a few moments to transform Hayes into a 'black jack' sailor using smuts from the cookeries, enabling him to mingle undetected among his comrades, with frequent changes of clothing. When extra roll calls were made and the prison blocks examined by search parties, Hayes was hustled from one block to another among a crowd of men or concealed in a hollow space beneath a stone. In the end Captain Shortland personally led a search for him, only to be confronted by a jubilant mob egged on by the 'Rough Alleys', taunting and jeering. When they found no trace of the wanted man Shortland, in a moment of impotent anger, told them if Hayes was not surrendered he would close the market and if necessary stop the water supply too. This was the spark that turned rough banter to ugly rage and soon stones were flying amid the insults, one of which passed very close to Captain Shortland's cheek. This was too much.

Confronted with an angry mob and outraged by their aggressive behaviour, he halted the soldiers and ordered them to open fire but the Captain of the Guard averted sudden death by striking up the muskets with his sword upon which both sides retreated in sullen silence, it being clear a tragedy had only just been prevented.

Captain Shortland did not stop the water supply – such a course would have had disastrous consequences, but he was determined to stamp his authority on the Depot by stopping the market. As expected, American pride and the goading of the 'Rough Alleys' united them in a fierce resistance. They decided the market would be boycotted for as many days as Shortland kept it closed and anyone caught trading would be liable to corporal punishment. One American stallholder who suggested Hayes should be given up for the common good had his stall smashed up and all his goods confiscated. Another man who was caught selling tobacco at inflated prices, taking advantage of the shortage that resulted from the market being closed, suffered the same fate.

There was one prisoner though who had no regrets about the market and wrote:

'...no longer shall Yankee tars support innumerable shoals of farmers, market women, and Jews... they have fattened on the hard earnings of American prisoners, charging what prices they liked, knowing they had no competition in the market and that prisoners could not be supplied elsewhere'.

If what he said was true, it bears out the assertion that the authorities paid only lip service to the regulations and permitted traders a free hand to extract what they could from their captive customers.

It took almost a week for tempers to cool sufficiently for a compromise to be reached: it was agreed the market would re-open provided a promise was given that 'no Englishman in Captain Shortland's employ would be molested'. This was a strange and weak response by the Agent, and we can only surmise he must have had the Peace Agreement in mind and the thought that he would soon be able to lay down the burden of being responsible for more than 5,000 prisoners impatient for their release. It so happened that Simeon Hayes was recaptured shortly afterwards but he and the others who shared his fate were released from the Cachot when the peace was confirmed.

The Military Walk as it is today.
(Courtesy Mr. M. Chamberlain).

Napoleon returns from Elba

Suddenly other events took place which shook all of Europe, sending tremors to every corner of Britain and all the way to Dartmoor Depot. On the evening of 26th. March 1815 Napoleon sailed from Elba and returned to France. Even this news was overshadowed when it became known many thousands of French soldiers were abandoning the Bourbon King and joining their Emperor (he had retained his rank by agreement at the Treaty of Paris) on his march from the south of France to Paris amid an ecstatic welcome from the people. It was the beginning of what came to be called the 'Hundred Days' (more accurately 136 days) during which time he set about restoring to France the form of government he had abdicated less than twelve months previously. The charisma of the man who once made Europe tremble was undiminished as countless numbers of old comrades hastened to swell the ranks of his re-established army, cheered by the hope they might win back the power and the lost territories of once mighty France.

At Dartmoor Depot there was gloom on the part of the Militia who envisaged more years of service than they'd bargained for, most of them having enlisted to serve until the end of hostilities. The Americans backed 'Old Boney' and taunted them to distraction. Beneath it all the ferment of dissatisfaction and enmity was still simmering, fuelled by rumours that varied almost daily – an inevitable result in a situation where thousands of war weary captives were waiting to be returned to their homeland. Yet there were moments when these hardened veterans displayed compassion of a rare quality. On 4th. March an insane hospital patient ran amok and stabbed a prisoner nurse who later died. The dead man, Jonathan Paul, had an English wife living nearby in poor circumstances and this aroused the sympathy of the Yankees every one of whom voted to go without his fish ration for one day. A contractor bought the lot (twenty five barrels of pickled herrings) for the equivalent of $100, all of which was given to the woman who had lost her man. Truly there is hope for the world when prisoners living in great hardship voluntarily go without their precious dinner to help alleviate personal distress.

On 14th March 1815 the 'Favourite' returned to England with the now ratified Peace Treaty and the American war was officially over. Three days later the news reached Dartmoor Depot where, after the initial rejoicing, there was anger as the men were told their allowances were to cease forthwith, no authority having been given to pay it in peacetime! Then the market stopped – the flow of money having ceased all commerce was stifled. Conditions rapidly deteriorated to practically the same level as when the Americans first arrived on the moor and things were going from bad to worse at a time when they should have got better. The only beneficiaries were the twenty four Yankee sailors who had been captured with the French and were neglected for so long: four days later (and nine years too late) the American Government at last sent clothes for them and formally recognised them as their own.

The Depot seethed with discontent, the brunt of which was borne by the sentries who were subjected to endless insults and the occasional missile from their charges. There was an increase in the number of escapes, many of them successful with the guards actively assisting the escapees over the walls (no doubt for a bribe). Those who got away were not pursued, their only fear being the Royal Navy 'press gangs' who were still active – in fact the menace they presented effectively deterred the faint hearted from even attempting to abscond. The rumours, the uncertainty, the delay in procuring their release, was proving an intolerable strain on prisoners and guards alike.

On the last day of March 1815 Charles Andrews personally counted all the prisoners at

Dartmoor and found there were:

Those discharged from the Royal Navy, etc.	2,200
From privateers and merchant ships	2,243
United States soldiers and navy men	250
Coloured men (various)	1,000
Total:	5,693

Of these 130 were in the hospital.

That same day they were told their Cartels were held up in the Downs by adverse winds. This could have been a ploy to try and calm a situation which was understandably getting out of hand. It so happened Mr. Beasley was doing his best to obtain ships to take the men home, but ship owners generally preferred to wait for more lucrative cargoes which were bound to come their way now the war was over. To their shame both the British and American Governments were bickering over who should bear the cost of repatriating prisoners. The American view was that each nation should charter the number of vessels needed to repatriate the prisoners they held. The British, who as already mentioned held twice as many captives, insisted each country should organise transport for its own men. The fact of the matter was both countries were impoverished by the cost of warfare and whilst British prisoners waited patiently for release from America's shores, the Americans fretted at Dartmoor.

THE PRINCETOWN MASSACRE

With an explosive atmosphere at the Depot and men dying of disease two blunders were made which precipitated the 'Princetown Massacre', an event that marred the reputation of the Militia and brought death to several Americans, all of whom who were fired on at a time when they were no longer prisoners of war but free men waiting to go home.

On 4th. April 1815 Captain Shortland left the Depot to attend to some business in Plymouth. It was widely known that the prisoners at Dartmoor were not only restive but threatening to break out if they were not released soon and a prudent Agent would surely have remained at his post. In his absence another, worse error of judgment was made when it became known the bread ration for that day was to be stopped (allegedly on orders from the Transport Office) and 'hard bread' or 'biscuit' which was kept in store for emergencies issued instead (this would have been the notorious ship's biscuit, baked in small rectangles and hard as iron). Moreover the quantity was reduced from one and a half pounds per man to one pound which in itself would arouse the prisoner's anger. With hostilities at an end perhaps it was decided to wind down the emergency supplies, but more than one prison riot has been triggered by a dispute over the food and this was to be no exception.

The American 'criers' received a roar of approval when it was put to them the substitute biscuit should be rejected. Loud and uncompromising demands were made for their rightful ration of 'soft' bread and by nightfall the position was critical. The contractor responsible maintained fresh bread could not be obtained until the next day but the Americans, who knew the storehouses contained their proper rations were in no mood to be fobbed off with feeble excuses. By evening hunger and frustration drove them to a dramatic course of action: it was resolved to force the gates leading to the market square and the storehouses, disarm the soldiers and help themselves to their rightful bread allowance whatever the consequences might be. At dusk, when they were summoned to their respective prisons for the night, everyone congregated at the gates after ignoring the order. At a prearranged signal the gates were forced open and there was a rush for the storehouses. The few sentries on duty together with the Turnkeys hurriedly retreated to the guardhouse. Within minutes the drummers were beating *'To Arms'* and the alarm bell was rung; a party of soldiers soon appeared with bayonets fixed and advanced to within yards of the prisoners. Bloodshed seemed inevitable. To the remonstrances of the officers the Americans declared unless their bread was issued they would level the storehouses to the ground and every man would march out of the Depot. Furthermore, if the troops charged them or opened fire, they must take the consequences. At this point the contractor intervened, saying that provided they withdrew to the main prison yard, their proper issue of bread would be given out. The men agreed but only on condition they took one of the clerks with them as a hostage until they were satisfied he meant what he said. This was done and at midnight the 'soft' bread they were entitled to was issued.

The noise and shouts had alerted the neighbourhood, and (according to Charles Andrews) at the sound of the alarm some of the women at the Depot fled in terror, afraid the prisoners would wreak (an imaginary) revenge upon them all should there be a mass break out. For weeks it had been expected that sooner or later the discontent at Dartmoor would spill over into open revolt and families in Prince Town thought that moment had come. The haste with which the guard had

The Market Square at Dartmoor Depot. (From a painting by an unknown Dartmoor Prison inmate.)

The Market Square as it is today – little has changed..

turned out was evident by their dishevelled appearance – some were in shirtsleeves, others without their breeches, all of which induced much hilarity and aggressive banter from the 'Rough Alleys'. Fortunately the officers managed to maintain discipline. Nobody wanted a head on confrontation – yet this was the very thing the rowdier elements among the prisoners regarded as a weakness, making their feelings known with hoots of derision.

The compromise which had been reached solved an immediate problem but a deep feeling of resentment was planted in the soldier's minds. Not only that: the incident prompted Major Jolliffe, the Military Commander at Dartmoor to write to Major General Brown, Officer Commanding the Plymouth Garrison *'...for instructions as to ordering the troops to fire in case of necessity and received very proper directions'*. The author has been unable to ascertain what those 'directions' were but the fact that guidance was sought and given indicates very strongly the scale of agitation brewing among the prisoners and the growing alarm in the minds of those responsible for the security of the Depot.

Captain Shortland got news of the affair from a messenger who had been dispatched to Plymouth at the first sign of trouble. He lost no time in obtaining reinforcements from the Plymouth Citadel and arrived back at Dartmoor Depot early the next morning with 200 extra soldiers only to find everything quiet and peaceful. A nasty incident had only just been avoided and the Agent realised this for he lost no time in summoning the prisoners and apologising for what had happened (Charles Andrews). Whilst the garrison and civilian population of Prince Town got the fright of their lives (perhaps Shortland too had been unnerved) the 'Rough Alleys' considered they had won a victory and felt a glow of satisfaction at having got the better of their captors. It was an error of judgment for which a high price would be paid.

Thursday 6th. April 1815 will forever be a bleak day in the history of the 1st. Somerset Militia and the Derbyshire Militia, the two units guarding the Depot at that time. The embarrassment lies in the fact the victims were prisoners in name only, peace having been declared several weeks earlier. What happened in the market square and the vicinity that day is shrouded in confusion, inaccuracy, and the biased evidence of those who were present, depending on which side they were on. Every account admits confusion on one vital point: who gave the order to shoot. An on the spot Inquiry failed to get at the truth of the matter and a further international inquiry, under the direction of one British and one American representative, was unable to resolve the question as to why British troops shot and killed unarmed Americans.

The massacre

It had been a warm sunny day. The Americans were in cheerful mood, revelling in the evening sunshine, with games being played and a lot of 'skylarking' going on. The Turnkeys, who were responsible for the men being locked up each night, had signalled, by the sounding of a horn (other accounts say the Turnkeys always hallooed 'Turn in! Turn in!) it was time for the men to retire to their respective prison blocks. Most of them were already inside and all but one door to each block had been locked in anticipation of a normal conclusion to the day. Only some stragglers lingering outside were still to be accounted for. It was 6.00pm.

A few minutes later Captain Shortland was informed a hole had been made by the prisoners in one of the retaining walls in close proximity to the 'Petty Officers Prison' (which, it will be remembered, had been commandeered and converted to a barracks for the troops). The hole was near to where the muskets were stored, but a great deal of the evidence given at the subsequent inquiry indicated the small hole already there (which soldiers must have been aware of) had merely been enlarged. The aperture was now large enough for a man to pass through and a number of Americans were congregating there which probably gave the impression an escape attempt was about to take place. The Americans later argued why should they attempt a break out when deliverance was close at hand? Their assertion that the hole had been made by some of the boy prisoners for the sole purpose of retrieving a ball they'd been playing with seems a plausible explanation. From the soldier's point of view, bearing in mind the events of 4th. April the day of the bread dispute, it is understandable the Agent ordered the alarm bell to be rung for the second time in three days. Some accounts accuse Captain Shortland of panic but the orders he gave merit a kinder judgment. He was a seasoned officer of the Royal Navy who had seen active service. Hot blooded he may have been but his actions so far were fully justified and as so often happens, the officer on the spot has but a minute or two to assess a situation before acting on the information he receives. His critics more often than not reach their conclusions after long deliberation over written reports.

Unfortunately it was the sounding of the alarm bell that proved to be the critical factor leading to what followed. It aroused the curiosity of the men already in the prisons who came tumbling out in hundreds to find out what was going on and who assembled around the entrance to the market square. Whether by force or because of the sheer weight of numbers straining to see what was happening the gates gave way and a confused jostling crowd spilled into the square just as Captain Shortland appeared at the head of about one hundred soldiers. He was accompanied by two of the Guard Commanders, Lt. Fortyne and Lt. Aveline, whilst another officer (Ensign White) had taken his men to the breach in the wall to prevent any prisoners breaking out through it. It was dinner time for the officers and those present were the only ones on duty when the alarm was raised. The Americans claim Captain Shortland took full charge and that the officers relinquished their commands, an assertion which was confirmed by the officers themselves at the subsequent inquiry. Certainly he was very quick in sizing up the situation and noting a large body of Americans in the forbidden area of the market square gave the order for the soldiers to form an extended line across the square to contain them. It is equally certain he and Dr. MaGrath, the highly respected surgeon, remonstrated with the Americans; the Doctor afterwards testified how they had both tried to reason with the men but because of the heaving mass of bodies it was impossible for those in front to go back owing to the pressure of those behind them pushing to see what was going on. The 'Rough Alleys' were hooting, yelling, and taunting the guards, openly daring them to take action. After winning a 'show down' two days previously they probably felt they could get away with anything short of actual revolt.

This time though the authorities were determined not to back down. Captain Shortland and his men faced a potentially dangerous situation with hundreds of prisoners advancing towards them in a menacing manner in a forbidden area with the gates open for others to follow. At the same time the bread wagon was being unloaded and if the contractor were to leave and the upper gates to the square opened for him, there would be just a line of soldiers between the unruly crowd and the outside world. When the now hostile mob showed no sign of retreating the soldiers were ordered to the 'charge' (i.e. to level their muskets and advance at the point of the bayonet) but it was impossible for all of them to do so because of the close proximity of the foremost prisoners who were still under pressure from those behind them. There was then some scuffling and throwing of stones. Some of the soldiers later said there were attempts to snatch their muskets whilst other prisoners defied them to fire, all of which was denied by the Americans who maintained they were by this time *'hurrying and flying in terrible flight'*. By their own account however they had stood firm in the 'bread crisis' and it is difficult to believe they ran away so soon on this occasion. What is undisputed is that someone shouted *'Fire!'*. The response was an erratic burst of fire, mainly over the prisoner's heads, the soldiers finding it almost impossible to take aim in the melee.

'...there was some scuffling and attempts to snatch the soldier's muskets...'
From a drawing by Paul Deacon. (Image prepared by Cinnabar, Okehampton).

The prisoners said it was Captain Shortland who gave this order; all other evidence is to the contrary and that someone else gave it. Furthermore, Captain Shortland in his written statement to the Inquiry that followed said it was Major Jolliffe who gave the order to open fire. This was vigorously denied by the Major and with justification, for he was at dinner a quarter of a mile away in Princetown when the alarm was raised and by the time he arrived on the scene with a body of Grenadiers the shooting had already started. One of the conclusions reached by the Inquiry was that if all the officers had been present, the shooting and bayoneting would most likely have been stopped sooner and the soldiers prevented from pursuing the prisoners to the doors of their prison blocks.

The Americans finally realised the serious intent of the military and there was a general retreat to the prison yards. A few defiant men, noting there were no casualties, yelled *'blank cartridges!'*

upon which a large number of them halted their flight. It should be borne in mind most of these men were no strangers to a fight – they were captured on active service and did not scare easily. All the same it is an undisputed fact they were all inside the prison yards when the shooting resumed. Dead and wounded men fell, causing panic on the part of those who had not regained their prison blocks. The Turnkeys it will be remembered had already locked some of the doors, consequently access to the blocks was restricted as crowds of struggling men were trying to gain entry. The musket fire now was sporadic and continuous.

The tension at Dartmoor had finally snapped and the soldier's tempers with it. For months they had endured insults, taunts, and stone throwing; now the time had come when once the first shots were fired, the troops were out for bloody revenge. One brave American, a U.S. Navy Warrant Officer named James Greenlaw, ignored the whizzing musket balls and actually advanced towards them, pleading with the soldiery to desist. He was taken no notice of (the Americans claimed Captain Shortland called him *'a damned rascal'* and that he *'would listen to nothing'*). The more credible evidence is that seeing matters had got out of hand the Agent was at this time trying to stop the shooting, but it was to no avail. The soldiers in the market square were joined by the sentries on the walls in executing a terrible cross fire on the mass of men below. Other soldiers broke ranks and pursued the prisoners to the very doors of their prisons, shooting and bayoneting as they went, firing into doorways at close quarters. This was later verified by an examination of the pock-marked interior walls.

The entire episode was over in minutes. Captain Shortland and the Militiamen finally left the scene leaving the indomitable Dr. MaGrath and his helpers to collect the dead and succor the living. The doctor recognised at once the serious condition of the wounded and sent to the nearest town (almost certainly Tavistock) for help. It says a great deal about his integrity and the respect he commanded among the Americans that he was allowed into the prison blocks to see if there were further casualties who might need treatment. A frightful price had been paid for what was most likely a misunderstanding on both sides. Accounts vary as to the exact number of casualties but Mr. Whiteford, the coroner for the district, held inquests on six men who were killed on the spot and three of the badly wounded who died later, bringing the total number of dead to nine. The Americans at first said there were sixty three dead and injured, claiming there had been victims who were buried secretly so as to minimize the official number killed (this was refuted by Charles Andrews who checked the victims names against the hospital records). The true casualty figure will never be known because apart from the thirty seriously hurt a large number of wounded men retired to their dormitories and stayed there, too frightened to come out even to receive medical attention. Several others had holes in their hats and clothing from bayonet thrusts or musket balls. The condition of the casualties can scarcely be imagined – the bone crushing musket shot inflicted injuries of a horrifying nature; looking back from our modern world we can hardly begin to conceive the agonies of undergoing surgery without anesthetics or pain killing drugs.

Most significant of all was the prisoners' knowledge they had been attacked at a time when they were technically free men by troops of a now 'friendly' nation. One individual alone was singled out for blame: Captain Shortland. The Militia officers, perhaps unnerved by events, were quick to deny responsibility. Lt. Aveline for example later testified *'...the soldiers did not fire by my order. I considered myself under Captain Shortland's orders'* (but he also said if he had been in command he would have ordered the troops to fire sooner than they did). Lt. Fortyne said *'My guard took up the firing from the others without my orders'*. The Americans branded the Agent *'a Nero and an inhuman monster'*. One has to sympathise with them but as their individual testimony afterwards revealed, and as any police officer would tell you today, events are seen and interpreted quite differently by different observers. One incident that occurred is to the everlasting credit of the Americans. When the shooting began and the prisoners ran for safety a lamplighter from the very regiment engaged in killing their comrades was caught in the rush and carried bodily inside one of the prisons. There the Americans could have taken their revenge but good sense prevailed: after some consultation the man was freed *'that the whole world might distinguish the difference between unprovoked British soldiers and the injured and provoked American seamen'*.

At 9.00am the next morning the American flag was hoisted and flown at half mast from every prison block. A colonel arrived from Plymouth with a body of troops and assumed command of the Depot. He met and talked with prisoners at the gate, informing them an inquest would be held on the dead the next day and that *'a strict investigation would be held'*. This was confirmed later in the day by Rear Admiral Sir J. Rowley, Bart., K.G.B. who also met and talked to them. The admiral was sympathetic and conciliatory in his manner, which encouraged the Americans to believe their account of the affair would be accepted.

Meanwhile some of the prisoners, including Charles Andrews, visited the hospital and were appalled at what they saw. The tables were still littered with amputated limbs and the groans of the wounded men, together with the sight of their injuries *'was enough to freeze the blood of the most hardened parricide'* (Andrews). The horrors of the wards revealed all the dead had been killed by musket shot and every one of the wounded suffered from both musket shot or bayonet wounds, in some cases both. Several men had been wounded up to five times. When account is taken of those who declined to seek medical attention and the number of near misses, the savagery of the attack is convincingly apparent.

A jury of twelve Dartmoor farmers under Coroner Joseph Whiteford spent nearly two days taking evidence from all concerned and on the evening of the second day (9th. April) they returned a verdict of *'Justifiable Homicide'*. Now the dead could be buried and this was done in the usual manner without any ceremony. No-one was permitted to attend the burials, something which only served to deepen the bitter feelings of their fellow prisoners.

Those killed were:

John Haywood, a coloured man from Virginia	shot in the chest.
Thomas Jackson from New York, a boy of fourteen	shot in the belly.
John Washington from Maryland	shot through the heart.
James Mann from Boston	shot in the chest.
Joseph Toker Johnson from Connecticut	shot in the chest.
William Laverage from New York	shot in the chest.
James Campbell from New York	shot in the eye.

The first six of these were killed on the spot on 6th. April; James Campbell died on the 8th. The Coroner's verdict described John Haywood as *'an American prisoner who was killed by the military in attempting to break prison'*. The others were referred to individually as *'another American prisoner also killed by the military'*. This was not the end of this unsavoury incident, for among the wounded were two men who died several days later and for whom Mr. Whiteford was obliged to arrange further inquests. The details are as follows:

John Grey: Wounded in the left arm (his arm had to be amputated); died 26th. April. Inquest on the 30th

Verdict: *'Killed by the military firing on the prisoners to prevent their escape'*.

John Roberts Wounded twice in the thigh (hit by musket shot). Died 12th. April. Inquest 16th. May.

Verdict: *'An American killed by the military firing to prevent the escape of prisoners'*

All the spellings of the dead men's names (except Grey and Roberts) are taken from Charles Andrews' account. To this day the impression held by the British is that either a mutiny or a mass escape attempt was the cause of the massacre.

Hatred and revulsion festered among the Americans:

'Your whole nation is involved as a black accomplice to your monstrous guilt' wrote Charles Andrews, *'the blood of my unfortunate countrymen, shed by your base hand, must ever remain a stain on the character of your nation'*. Benjamin Palmer's reaction was more blunt: *'We cry for vengeance!'*.

American outrage and anger lasted for more than a generation.

The Americans' sentiments were expressed by an anonymous poet who penned a graphic account in rhyme entitled *'Horrid Massacre at Dartmoor Prison, England'*, too long to be included in full but which concludes:

'Give us redress, let Shortland swing, or meet our swords again.
Old George beware! If you again the contest shall renew
We'll show you that the Yankee lads have better pluck than you!
Revenge is sweet, and on the Book of Heav'n now stands enrolled
Your hellish deeds, your murd'rous acts, your bribery with your gold,
Look to Yourself, for should again the veng'ful sword be drawn
The setting sun of England's pride should hail Columbia's dawn.
The Stripes and Stars should proudly wave, that Neptune from his car
Would yield to us his Tridents up to hurl the bolts of war!
Your haughty Ensign by our own tars from your tall masts be torn,
Your red Coats dread to see True Blue, on swiftest pinions borne.
So for the present, fare ye well, your long lost fame regain
And when we settle up accounts – we'll call on you again'.

THE INQUIRIES INTO THE 'MELANCHOLY OCCURRENCE'

Captain Shortland reported the tragedy to the Royal Navy Commander in Chief at Plymouth, Admiral Sir John Duckworth, Bart., K.G.C.B. who received the news late at night on the day it happened. He at once ordered an Inquiry and in a letter dated 7th. April instructed Rear Admiral Sir J. Rowley to proceed immediately to the prison at Dartmoor taking with him Capt. A.W. Schomberg of H.M.S. 'York' the Senior Captain at Plymouth. After indicating what form the questioning should take his letter goes on: *'You will then address the prisoners and will use every argument that may suggest itself to you to conciliate them, to tranquilize their minds, and to prevail upon them cheerfully to look forward to their speedy return to their own country. You will explain to them they ought not to feel as Prisoners but as Passengers waiting for conveyance...'.*

This was the speech previously referred to which caused the Americans to think their version of events would be believed. The army held a separate Military Court of Inquiry on the orders of Major General Brown, Officer Commanding the Plymouth Garrison (the details of this Inquiry were not made known at the time having been forwarded to the Horse Guards but were made available for the consideration of those who conducted the second, International Inquiry). The Naval Inquiry was prompt but brief and was completed in a day (it did not take account of the soldiers' statements they said *'...not feeling ourselves authorised to carry our investigation into the transactions of the Military'*).

Four of the statements taken were:

1. **Captain Shortland**. After describing the events leading up to the shooting he mentions the efforts made by Dr. MaGrath and himself to *'induce them* (the Americans) *not to go on in their attempt, which I looked upon to be to surround the guard and disarm them. Upon them still advancing close to the military they* (the soldiers) *charged and fired, but not before the prisoners attempted to wrest the muskets out of some of their hands. My advanced situation at the time of firing would have made it an imprudent act of mine to have directed the Military to fire. The reason of the present riot I have not been able to ascertain further than that general dissatisfaction prevails at being detained in England'.*

2. **Lt. Aveline, 1st. Somerset Militia**. Described Captain Shortland's unsuccessful attempt to remonstrate with the prisoners who were advancing when: *'...a shot was fired from a soldier, when the guard fired ...it is my opinion that if the guard had not acted in that manner they would have been endangered ...the prisoners had hold of the musket of the soldier who fired so that he was obliged to fire in his own defence. I understand that some of the Military thought that Captain Shortland had given the order to fire, but this morning contradicted it'.*

3. **Surgeon George Magrath**. Described his and Captain Shortland's exhortations to the prisoners (then) *'I heard some person say "Charge" and I was then driven at the point of the bayonet towards the lower part of the square, and when I was endeavouring to get in the rear a discharge of musketry took place. I then immediately left the place to make preparation for the expected wounded'.*

4. **Lt. (Ensign) White, 1st Somerset Militia**. Told how he went with the West Guard to the breach in the wall which was *'...a considerable hole... I repeatedly desired the prisoners to desist but they continued throwing stones and behaved in a most insulting manner'*. He and his men stayed there until half past eight so were unable to help further in the inquiry.

In the report submitted to Admiral Duckworth and dated 7th. April, Rear Admiral Rowley and Captain Schomberg affirmed they had assembled all the American prisoners at Dartmoor and asked them whether they had any complaint as to their treatment in the prison.

'...they answered they had none whatsoever. They had complained a few days ago of the alteration of their allowance of biscuit in lieu of soft bread but this had been remedied. They repeatedly and unanimously declared that they did not attribute their protracted confinement to any fault of the British Government but from their own not having sent conveyance for their removal'.

Having examined the breach in the wall and heard related by the officers of the Depot an account of the riotous behaviour of the prisoners the Americans were asked to give an explanation.

'...they denied everything relative to any riot and said the hole had been made by some of their boys at play'. The report concluded: *'but as a powerful force of men was found at the breach at the time of the riot, ready to force their way through it, it is clear that the breach was intended as a part of the attack upon the Depot. We are of the opinion that there had been no ostensible cause for the riot and can only attribute it to a strong desire on their part to escape from confinement at any risk notwithstanding their assurance to us of the contrary'.*

The Americans were stunned. They had thought their evidence to be irrefutable and their anger was further inflamed by a newspaper report which referred to their actions on that fateful day as a 'mutiny'. There was a glowing account of how the valiant Captain Shortland faced the mob alone and unarmed (the same report said twelve men were shot to death, thereby refuelling rumours about secret burials).

By this time several prisoners were leaving the Depot ahead of the rest having volunteered (in response to requests by American agents) to man a number of vessels in European ports under American command. Most of these men passed through London and made it their business to deposit sworn statements with the authorities there which contradicted the outcome of the Inquiry and the inquest verdicts.

Extract from the Transport Office letter to Captain Shortland 18th. April 1815:
'Sir,

It having been represented to His Majesty's Government that the cause of the late riot among the Prisoners at Dartmoor was very different from what has been reported to us, and it being expedient that in an Affair of such importance there should be no misapprehension, we acquaint you that Mr. King has been appointed on the part of the American Government and Mr. Larpent by His Majesty's Government to proceed to Dartmoor for the purpose of investigating the causes of the Melancholy Occurrence, and we desire that the greatest attention be paid to these gentlemen'.

Mr. Francis Seymour Larpent was an ideal choice for this delicate task having had wide experience as Judge Advocate to the Duke of Wellington in the Peninsula from 1812 to 1814. In 1813 he was taken prisoner by the French but was quickly released on exchange. All the same the experience must have enabled him to play his part with some sympathy and he was probably the most fair-minded person available on the British side. Mr. Charles King was an eminent businessman from the State of New York, merchant, editor, and 9th. President of Columbia University. He had also served as captain of an American Militia Regiment despite the fact he was privately opposed to the war. He happened to be in England on business when he was asked to participate in the Inquiry. Charming, handsome, dignified, with a reputation for impartiality, he was considered an ideal choice, but when the findings were made known his summing up was thought by the Americans to be far too magnanimous. Mr. King and his father were afterwards ostracised at home by politicians and businessmen alike. This second Inquiry was to be the final and most exhaustive one with evidence taken from Americans in Plymouth who had been released and were on the point of sailing for home (some of them were from the Cartel ships, among them the 'Maria Christiana' where Charles Andrews was one of the passengers).

The Transport Office sent the following letter to the Lord Mayor of Plymouth:

'Whitehall 18th. April 1815

Sir,

I have Lord Sidmouth's (Ex-Prime Minister Henry Addington now Home Secretary) directions to acquaint you that Mr. Seymour Larpent and Mr. Charles King have been appointed on behalf of the British and American Governments respectively to proceed forthwith to Dartmoor for the purpose of investigating the late unfortunate event in the prison at that place. For the purpose of executing their commission it will be necessary that these gentlemen should have the assistance of the Civil Authorities of that District for the purpose of calling witnesses and administering oaths. I am therefore to request that you would take the trouble of attending the enquiry above alluded to, and of rendering such assistance to the Gentlemen above mentioned as may be necessary in the course of their investigation, and that you would solicit some other Magistrate to accompany you on this important occasion for the same purpose.

I have the Honour to be, Sir,
Your Most Obedient and Humble Servant,
J.Becket'.

The proceedings were conducted in the City Hall at Plymouth and, as the mayor was unable to attend, Mr. Woolcombe a City Magistrate officiated assisted by Mr. Hawker, a County Magistrate and former American Consul. Several members of the American Committee at Dartmoor* who had been released and were in Plymouth at the time were invited to enquire around the city and on the Cartels for any of their countrymen who were prepared to give evidence. A number of soldiers of the 1st. Somerset Militia who had been present in the market square were selected to appear and the depositions made at the Military Court of Inquiry were made available by Major General Brown. The investigation then removed to the Depot for three days where other members of the American Committee who had not yet been released together with any other prisoners willing to attend were questioned. This was followed by an examination of the prison blocks. It was a very thorough inquiry where statements from a total of seventy two witnesses were scrutinised.

* The prisoners appointed a committee of ten men to prepare a summary of their version of events, taken from statements made by those who were involved.

The American Committee report said there was no intention on their part to attempt an escape. They refuted claims that they had thrown stones or harassed the soldiers and intimated the whole episode had been planned by Captain Shortland in order to punish them for not being compliant captives and in revenge for what happened two days previously when they demanded (and got) their bread ration instead of the biscuits. They claimed he was heard to say *'I'll teach the damned rascals directly!'* before sending soldiers to man the walls in readiness for what followed and that he was intoxicated (this assertion was refuted by Surgeon MaGrath who said in evidence: *'that there was not the least pretence for this accusation as he was most perfectly sober and that in his mode of living and domestic habits* (he) *was in every respect particularly abstemious'*). They said a soldier had warned them they *'would be charged upon directly'*. The most serious and controversial allegation they made, after admitting a number of prisoners had invaded the market square, was that:

'Captain Shortland ordered the soldiers to charge upon them; which orders the soldiers were reluctant in obeying, as the prisoners used no violence; but on the order being repeated, they made a charge, and the prisoners retreated out of the square into their respective yards and shut the gates after them. Captain Shortland himself opened the gates, and ordered the soldiers to fire in among the prisoners who were retreating in different directions towards their respective prisons... there was some hesitation in the minds of the officers whether or not it was proper to fire upon the prisoners. Shortland seized a musket out of the hands of a soldier, which he fired'.

Prisoner witnesses who gave evidence before Mr. Larpent and Mr. King swore two prisoners were cornered by soldiers outside their prisons and were shot to death whilst pleading for mercy. The rest of the evidence given by the prisoners was just as biassed, either glossing over the stone throwing and abuse hurled at the military by their comrades or simply leaving out anything that might incriminate them.

The soldiers' testimony was equally one sided. Almost every one of them who was called said there were stones thrown at them (one of them was hit in the head and had his cap knocked off by another missile), that the Americans persisted in trying to push past them, that some of them tried to get hold of their muskets, and that they were (most of them) unsure about how the firing commenced, only that someone had given the order to do so. A turnkey, William Wakeline, described how a prisoner called Reeves *'was very violent and opened his breast and challenged them to fire saying "fire you bastards fire!"'* giving credence to a suggestion by the investigators that it could have been one of the prisoners shouting that caused the shooting to begin.

Lt. Aveline confirmed Captain Shortland had pleaded with the prisoners to return to their prisons and that in ignoring his pleas *'they were pressing on the left where the line did not go close to the walls* (this would have been the wall by the hospital), *the men fell back that the prisoners might not get too near them* (it was noted by Captain Shortland who cried *'for God's sake soldiers, keep your ground!'*) *that his men finally charged, and he was with them. It was not by his order or he would have charged before or indeed have fired before, judging that this was necessary from the threatening manner of the prisoners who could have surrounded his guard'.*

Captain Shortland himself made a statement later judged to be a confused one. He described being told about the breach in the wall and going to examine it. After remonstrating with prisoners who were attempting to enlarge it he heard someone call the lower gates to the market square were being forced and saw prisoners in the square. He ordered the alarm bell to be sounded and led one of the guards under Lt. Aveline to the market square where he estimated there were between four and five hundred prisoners. He described the soldiers forming a line across the square and how he was trying to reason with the prisoners when the shooting started – a musket ball actually grazed his temple he said. He then claimed Major Jolliffe must have given an order to fire, having just seen him appear at the scene (the Major arrived after the firing began and all the evidence is that his first act was to order it to stop). Shortland's evidence concluded with: *'I did not hear any orders to fire. It must be understood that I was with the prisoners who were making a great noise, hurrahing and rioting at the time... taking into consideration the apparent temper and resolution of the prisoners, and my remonstrances having no effect, I do not think they could have been driven back without firing'.*

Here are some of the more important findings of the Inquiry:

1. Since the Ratification of the Treaty of Ghent the prisoner's impatience for release did lead to a threat to break out of the Depot.
2. The 'bread riot' was resolved without the use of force.
3. The breach in the wall was large enough for a man to pass through. At the time of day when the men should be returning to their prisons a large body of men had congregated adjacent to the hole (in the area between the wall and the railings) which in itself was against the regulations as well as giving cause for alarm.
4. Arms were kept in the Armoury adjacent to the hole but although there was no evidence to suggest this was the motive in making the hole it was further cause for suspicion and alarm.
5. Captain Shortland had sufficient grounds for sounding the alarm
6. It was confirmed the gates were forced. There was no evidence that a planned escape was about to take place but the only inference to be drawn from the number of prisoners in the market square was that it might be attempted. It was confirmed the bread wagon was due and that the outer gates might be opened at about this time, giving the prisoners an escape opportunity if they got past the line of soldiers drawn up across the square. (The bread wagon had arrived already and was being unloaded.)
7. When firing commenced there was an unruly group still in the gateway. As to who it was gave the order to shoot, Captain Shortland was an unlikely suspect because, as was pointed out, he was standing in front of the soldiers at the time.
8. The stone throwing, the pressing of large numbers of men pushing against those in front and the remonstrances of the Agent and Surgeon MaGrath were all confirmed by the evidence given. As for Captain Shortland and the question of who did give an order to fire, the inference drawn by the Inquiry was concisely expressed by Mr. Larpent in the final remarks he made in a separate report to Viscount Castlereagh:

'...Captain Shortland had been most judicious and humane and until very lately he had always been on very good terms with the prisoners under his charge. It is but justice also to mention that whether the firing did or did not commence by his order... he was one of the first to endeavour to make it cease, and that in my opinion (though not a decided one) no regular order to fire was ever given by anyone. On the contrary I rather conceive the firing to have commenced from the accidental discharge of one musket, or from someone without authority calling fire, perhaps even the prisoners themselves who appear from the evidence to have done so, little expecting to be taken at their word'.

The Inquiry also noted that:

'...this firing was to an extent justifiable in a military point of view in order to intimidate the prisoners and compel them to thereby desist from all acts of violence and to retire as they were ordered from a situation in which the responsibility of the Agent and the military could not permit them with safety to remain.'.

With regard to the shots fired after the prisoners had fled to their prison yards they had this to say: *'the firing continued evidently as a result of individual irritation'*. With the troops getting out of hand there were too few officers to restrain them; most of the officers were at dinner it will be remembered and it was branded as *'quite indefensible'*.

It was a penetrating effort to establish exactly what happened but once again Captain Shortland was cleared of blame and it was the Inquiry's belief he had acted with justifiable intent in every respect. Mr. King had a private opinion however, which he confided to Mr. John Quincey Adams, the American Ambassador to Britain, to whom he wrote:

'...whether the order to fire came from Captain Shortland I yet confess myself unable to form any satisfactory opinion, though the balance of my mind is that he did give such an order'.

He then goes on to praise the Agent in glowing terms:

'...his anxiety and exertions to stop it after it had continued for some little time are fully proved, and his general conduct as far as we could with propriety enter into such details, appears to have been characterised with great fairness and even kindness in the light in which he stood towards the prisoners'.

Of the prisoners themselves he said:

'...they made no complaint whatsoever as to their provisions and general mode of living and treatment in the prison'.

This last aspect of the affair seems to have been overlooked in some accounts – after all it was Captain Shortland who admitted Americans to the market immediately he took office and afterwards showed some compassion to Simeon Hayes and his companions in the 'Black Hole' (probably against instructions). As for Mr. King, his final comments to Mr. Adams were:

'I cannot conclude, Sir, without expressing my high sense of the impartiality and manly firmness with which this enquiry has been conducted on the part of Mr. Larpent, nor without mentioning that every facility was afforded to us in its prosecution as well as by the Military Officers here at the prison, and by the Magistrates in the vicinity'.

The families of the men who were killed or wounded were offered compensation by the British Government, but the Americans politely declined the offer. It was suggested that repatriation was speeded up by the British in order to get important witnesses home from whence they would disperse and probably be untraceable should yet another investigation be made. After two Inquiries it is difficult to believe this, yet it is a fact that only six days after the tragedy Captain Shortland was ordered to prepare 200 men for release – it had been agreed the British should pay for the Cartels, and would negotiate recovery of the cost from any post-war settlement.

Summary

Was it a mutiny? Surely not when thousands of prisoners had already returned to their prisons and only the stragglers remained to be accounted for.

Was it an escape attempt? Again unlikely and for the same reasons. In both cases it was the ringing of the alarm bell that brought the men back out to see what was going on.

Was it a riot? This is a more accurate description of what took place.

Was Captain Shortland the black-hearted villain the Americans viewed him as? A complicated character who showed the prisoners sympathetic consideration to begin with but whose temper often got the better of him.

Who really shouted 'Fire!'? Captain Shortland, a frightened soldier or maybe a defiant American?

These questions remain unresolved to this day – it all depends on whose side you are on and how you view the evidence. It was summed up rather neatly in a television documentary about the incident in which the commentator remarked: *'the Americans blamed Captain Shortland, the British blamed no-one – it just happened'*.

'...we used every endeavour to ascertain, if there was the least prospect of identifying any of the soldiers who had been guilty of the particular outrages... or of tracing any particular death... to the firing of any particular individual, but without success, and all hopes of bringing the Offenders to punishment seem to be at an end.

In conclusion, We the Undersigned, have only to add, that whilst we lament, as we do most deeply, the unfortunate Transaction which has been the subject if this Inquiry, We find ourselves totally unable to suggest any steps to be taken as to those parts of it which seem most to call for Redress and Punishment.

    Francis Seymour Larpent
    Char. King
    Plymouth April 26th. 1815.'

No-one was to be punished.

THE DEPOT'S FINAL CHAPTER – A MISCELLANY

The first Americans leave for home

On 20th April 1815, the first batch of Americans to be repatriated marched out of the Depot for home. It was a profoundly emotive departure so soon after the massacre. There were 249 of them, all of whom had been among the first to be sent to Dartmoor. They displayed a large white flag they had made and on it was depicted the Goddess of Liberty with the slogan *'Columbia weeps and we Remember'*. They felt they'd had a raw deal throughout their captivity and Dartmoor was remembered as an infamous place. All of them were poorly clothed – some were barefooted, no clothing having been issued for nearly a year. It was therefore a sad procession that passed out under the archway to freedom but once outside the walls their joy could no longer be contained. There was an outburst of prolonged cheering which came ringing back to the ears of their countrymen still inside the Depot, who returned their cheers over and over until they were out of earshot. At Cattedown (Plymouth) they embarked on a Swedish ship the 'Maria Christiana' exactly forty days after the Treaty of Ghent was ratified. Charles Andrews was on board still recording his everyday experiences. His narrative stands today as probably the most prolific and truthful (as he saw it) description of prison life at Dartmoor Depot. His writings were endorsed by more than sixty of his fellow prisoners, mostly ships' captains who added their signatures in confirmation of his account being entirely accurate.

Benjamin Palmer was released on 17th. April by which time there was a brisk trade in the selling of their turn for release by desperate men who either needed the money very badly or who had nothing to go home to. He bought a black man's turn (Charles Carrol) for two pounds. The money was deposited with a turnkey on the understanding it would be handed over only when he got clear of the Depot, otherwise it would be handed back to him. In the eight days since the first Americans left someone had evidently made an effort to clothe them because shoes were issued to those without them for the march to Plymouth. By this time hundreds of relatives had congregated at Cattedown hoping to meet with, or at least receive news of their loved ones. Benjamin Palmer was among those who, whilst waiting to embark, were besieged by groups of anxious people clamouring for information and plying them with food and drink. When the time came to board the Cartel they discovered they were to share the voyage home with several officers who had been living on parole at Ashburton. They had little liking for them (the officers had an easy time of it compared to the prisoners at the Depot they thought). With drink flowing freely fighting broke out, resulting in a number of men being taken off the ship to await another Cartel. Benjamin Palmer's final comment on them is illuminating and contemptuous of *'...the Ashburton Gentry, most of whom has made the girls sorry they ever saw them'*.

After Waterloo the French come again to Dartmoor

On his return from Elba in March 1815 Napoleon resumed his position in France, formed a government and raised an army. With all of Europe opposed to him he assumed personal command of the French forces against the combined might of Britain and her allies. His army now comprised approximately 74,000 men, mostly volunteers and veterans, the latter termed the 'Grand Moustaches' by the British soldiers. He was confronted by the Duke of Wellington who commanded a mixed force (including Belgian and Dutch contingents) numbering 67,000 men, of whom only 24,000 were British (the victorious Peninsula Army was sent to fight in America after the fall of France in 1814 and had not yet returned). The Prussian Marshal Blucher brought 52,300 men to the battle. The countryside of Flanders was where the once mighty Bonaparte was to be finally crushed. The Battle of Waterloo was fought on 18th June 1815, the culmination of two lesser engagements at Ligny and Quatre Bras. The victorious Duke admitted afterwards it was a 'damned close run thing', a reference to the timely appearance of the Prussian Army at a critical moment in the fight.

Three weeks later more than 4,000 prisoners from those battlefields arrived at Dartmoor Depot. The roles of the French and American prisoners were now reversed; this time it was the Americans who were leaving and they repaid the compliment they owed the French by handing over their various artefacts – market paraphernalia, tools etc. Several of the Frenchmen had been at Dartmoor before and had collected bits of wood and other odds and ends at the roadside with which to make articles to sell at market. They were a sorry sight having been hustled into captivity straight from battle in uniforms torn and caked in mud, many of them suffering from wounds which had received only the briefest of attention. Blood soaked bandages and pained expressions typified the survivors of a once magnificent army.

The French on the long trek to Dartmoor Prison. From a painting by Paul Deacon. (Reproduced by courtesy of Mr.J.Langton, 'Plume of Feathers', Princetown. Image prepared by Cinnabar, Okehampton).

Napoleon capitulates

This time their stay was a brief one. Napoleon, after many deliberations during which he considered surrendering to the European Powers and the United States in turn, finally plumped for Britain as the place where he could expect the most generous terms. He sent a letter from Rochefort to the Prince Regent, an extract of which reads:

'13th. July 1815

....having been exposed to the factions which distract my country and to the enmity of the greatest Powers of Europe, I have ended my political career, and I come, like Thermistocles, to throw myself on the hospitality of the British people. I put myself under the protection of their laws, which I claim from Your Royal Highness, as the most powerful, the most constant, and the most generous of my enemies'.

This eloquent plea was never answered. On the 15th. July he gave himself up to Captain Maitland of the seventy four gun 'Bellerophon' anchored off Rochefort, accompanied by five Generals, four Lt. Colonels, and four Captains. The French wars were at an end once and for all.

The last of the Yankees depart

At Dartmoor all the Americans had left for home – by 14th. July everyone was aboard their Cartel, the last to go being the 'Rough Alleys' and the Negroes. Rough and ready they may have been but their hearts must have rejoiced at the thought of home. Earlier that month one of them had written: *'...the sweet smile of content was easily perceived on the countenance of all the prison – Moll and Sue is all the talk now'*, which is almost certainly an understatement. Some of the Cartels were taken over by their passengers in mid- Atlantic with the object of landing at ports more convenient to them, especially the black men who did not want to be returned to the Southern States to end their days in slavery. The masters of the vessels concerned were given signed certificates absolving them from responsibility for the change in destination. Charles Andrews recorded the wording of the certificate which was handed to the master of his Cartel:

'We, the undersigned, citizens of the United States of America, do hereby certify that on the second day of June 1815 at twelve meridian, being in Lat. 40.30 Long. 69.30 by mutual agreement of majority of prisoners now on board the Cartel 'Maria Christiana' bound for Norfolk, did take possession of her and directed her for the port of New York'.

The Americans left behind a record of constant umbrage against authority and unrelenting rancour at the alleged injustices they suffered. In a way this was no bad thing for men imprisoned indefinitely, and in many cases wrongfully (those who had been illegally impressed by the Royal Navy for example and who later 'declared themselves'). They were determined to defend their country's independence and to 'bend the knee' to no man, a proud ideal that saved many of the prisoners from hopelessness and death.

The end for Bonaparte

The French prisoners languished on the moor while their master and idol was brought first to Torbay and then to Plymouth where he was confined on board the 'Bellerophon' at anchor in the Sound until his fate was decided. He had pledged to be a model prisoner if the British would agree to maintain him in the style he was used to and might reasonably expect, but because he had returned from exile and caused more bloodshed, the British were taking no chances. To have kept him in Britain would have been an embarrassment they felt. Finally, after considering the Cape of Good Hope as a possible place of banishment, it was decided instead to send him into exile for life on the remote Atlantic island of St. Helena. Napoleon was dismayed when he was told what his fate was to be. He had supposed he would obtain an honourable agreement with the British whereby he would live in relative comfort, together with his retinue in self-imposed exile. Instead he was transferred early in August 1815 to another Royal Navy ship, the 'Northumberland', for the long voyage into oblivion. He died on St. Helena on 5th. May 1821. He had stated a preference for burial in France near the River Seine; otherwise, if the British should dictate he remain on the island (which they did) he chose the Valley of Geranium, since renamed the Valley of the Tomb, as his last resting place. Here he was laid to rest until 1840 when he was exhumed and brought home to Paris where his wish to lie beside the Seine was honoured. His tomb is now a National Monument.

The men he once commanded were now released from Dartmoor and by December most of them had left for France, leaving only a few sick men and the remnants of the garrison behind. By February 1816 everyone had gone home and the mighty gates of the once great bastion slammed shut, leaving the birds to nest in the cocklofts and the ghosts of more than 1500 prisoners who had died there.

Sir Thomas Tyrwhitt

Prince Town's halcyon days were now at an end and the town went into decline despite further endeavour by the stalwart Sir Thomas. One of his major accomplishments was the formation of a railway company which built a horse-drawn tramway from Plymouth to the Dartmoor quarries. It was afterwards extended to the centre of the Princetown, terminating at the present day 'Railway Inn' in an area known as 'The Wharf'. The line was intended to transport granite and products of the moorland farms to Plymouth, bringing back timber, building materials, etc. in the hope of encouraging further development. There was little interest however, and the line closed a few years later.

Sir Thomas never married and died on 24th February 1823 at 71 years of age.

On the north wall of the Church of St. Michael and All Angels at Princetown, there is a Memorial Tablet in his honour which reads:

'Sir Thomas Tyrwhitt, Knt.,
Late of Tor Royal, Lord Warden of the Stannaries,
And many years Usher of Black Rod,
Died Feb. 24th. 1833
Aged 71
His name and memory are inseparable from all the Great Works on Dartmoor, and
cannot cease to be Honoured in this District'.

On the tablet, which is of Italian marble, are represented the Baton of the Order of the Garter and the Tyrwhitt family Crest.

Daniel Asher Alexander, Architect

The man who designed Dartmoor Depot and supervised the building of it afterwards made his home in Exeter and went on to design the huge prison at Maidstone in Kent. He died at Exeter on 2nd. March 1846 and was buried at Yarmouth, Isle of Wight, at his own request. He knew the place well and had an affection for it – in fact he had previously paid for the church tower to be heightened to act as a guide for boats approaching the harbour entrance. He now rests in the churchyard adjacent to it.

Captain Thomas George Shortland, R.N.

Captain Shortland joined the Royal Navy in 1785 at the age of fourteen. He led an active service life and took part in several actions at sea during which he earned the admiration of his superiors as an able Commander and a firm disciplinarian. He served as a Lieutenant on one of the ships that made up the first convict convoy to Botany Bay and lived ashore there for some time as an assistant administrator.

   He took up his appointment as Agent at Dartmoor in December 1813 and remained there until its closure. In April 1816 he was made Captain Superintendent at Plymouth, a position he held for three years. In 1825 Thomas Shortland went to Jamaica as Resident Commissioner and died there in 1827, twelve years after the 'massacre' he is remembered for.

Dr. George MaGrath, Surgeon, R.N.

Dr. MaGrath was a man of superior ability. In an age when amputations were performed without anaesthetics and operations took place under primitive conditions using instruments terrifying to behold, Surgeons were not the most popular of men. George MaGrath however was a giant among them.

   When Dartmoor first opened in 1809 he volunteered for service there, but was passed over in favour of Dr. George Dykar, R.N. He remained at Mill Prison until 1813 when he transferred to the Depot. He at once made a good impression and earned the heartfelt thanks and genuine affection of Britain's most troublesome prisoners of war – the Americans. Charles Andrews on his arrival there that same year wrote: *'no pains had been spared to render the hospital convenient and comfortable and much credit is due to whoever organised it'*. So Dr. MaGrath got off to a good start thanks in part to his predecessor Dr. Dykar.

   During the smallpox epidemic of 1813/14, the good doctor battled heroically to alleviate the suffering even though he himself was in poor health at the time. His humane concern was again made apparent when he attended the casualties resulting from the 'massacre' incident. When the Americans were still waiting for their release from Dartmoor he was the subject of a tribute of gratitude and respect written by the prisoner's representatives to the President of the United States, James Madison. They also wrote to their Ambassador in England, Mr. John Quincy Adams. A narrative such as this cannot allow their gesture to go unrecorded and the following are extracts from the two letters (taken from *A Prisoner's Memoires* by Charles Andrews):

'Dartmoor Prison, March 28 1815
To His Excellency James Madison.
Honoured and Respected Sir:
   Dr. George MaGrath, principle of the medical department for the American prisoners of war

in England. It is impossible for us to speak of this gentleman in terms that will do justice to his superior professional science and unwearied exertions in combatting a succession of diseases of the most malignant character which prevailed amongst the prisoners.

Dr. MaGrath's time and attention were fully occupied in the hospital and in the vaccinating of prisoners. From his exertions his health became seriously impaired but totally regardless of himself he persevered and was the means of rescuing many citizens of the United States from the embraces of death. This truly great man's exertions in the cause of suffering have been rarely equalled, but never excelled'.

The letter was signed by fifteen members of the Hospital Committee. Seldom has such praise been heaped upon any man by his country's foes. The following selected passages are taken from a letter even more remarkable, having been written only three days after the infamous 'Prince Town Massacre':

'Dartmoor prison April 9th. 1815

To His Excellency John Q. Adams.
Sir,

Impressed with the sense of duty which we owe to our country, and to ourselves, we respectfully solicit permission to introduce to your Excellency George MaGrath, Esq. M.D., principal of the medical department of this depot. Language is incompetent to delineate the worth and character of this gentleman, prominent in medical science, enriched by every virtue and accomplishment that can dignify and adorn human nature. His professional skill has been peculiarly conspicuous in his successfully combatting a succession of diseases.'
The shooting is then mentioned:

'Language is too impotent to describe Dr. MaGrath's unexampled endeavours to prevent the effusion of blood; regardless of the many dangers by which he was environed, he persevered amidst the heavy and incessant fire of musketry in his humane endeavours to prevent the fatal catastrophe.

His treatment of the unfortunate wounded Americans is superior to all praise, and was such to entitle Dr. MaGrath to the esteem and gratitude of the citizens of the United States. We therefore respectfully and ardently solicit that your Excellency would be pleased to honour Dr. MaGrath with your particular notice and esteem, and to convey these our sentiments to the government of the United States, for we would wish to give all possible publicity to our high sense of Dr. MaGrath and to evince to our country and the world how gratefully we appreciate the essential services we received from that gentleman'.

This letter was signed by nine members of the hospital committee. Dr. MaGrath bought a house in Lockyer Street in Plymouth after the war and for several years ran a successful medical practice in Union Street during which time he gained an illustrious reputation. On the death of this good man a memorial tablet was erected by public subscription in St. Andrew's Church at Plymouth. It survived the World War Two bombing raids when the church was all but destroyed and can be seen today mounted on the wall opposite the main entrance to the church.

MEMORIAL TO DR. GEORGE MAGRATH IN ST ANDREW'S CHURCH, PLYMOUTH.

'Sacred
To the Memory of
SIR GEORGE MAGRATH
Doctor of Medicine. Inspector of Her Majesty's Fleets and Hospital. Commander of the Most Honourable Order of the Bath. Knight of the Royal Guelphic Order of Hanover. Knight of the Order of the Cross of Christ in Portugal. Fellow of the Royal College of Physicians, London, and Honourable Fellow of the Royal Linnia and Geological Societies, and Member of other Learned Bodies.
He was born in the year 1772 and died at Plymouth June 12th. 1837.
A Ripe Scholar and a Skilled Physician he served his Country
by sea and by Land for a quarter of a Century.
A Follower of the Immortal Nelson, his Patron and Friend.
In all things he did his duty.
As an Officer with Zeal.
As a Citizen with Dignity.
And as a Friend with Devotion.
He was distinguished by Nations for his services'.

PRINCETOWN AND ITS CHURCH

The Christian faith was not neglected on the moor. Services were regularly held in barns and buildings set aside for religious purposes at Bairdown and Prince Hall. Baptisms were often performed in the parent's homes. It has been mentioned already that the Prince of Wales had approved the building of a chapel in the district but it was not until the Prisoner of War Depot was up and running that a start was made. It has always been understood that the architect for the Depot (Mr. Daniel Alexander) designed the chapel and the next door parsonage but it is now known that a Mr. Walters, foreman of works at the prison was specifically instructed to draw up the necessary plans and put them into effect (attention was first drawn to this by Elizabeth Stanbrook, the Editor of *Dartmoor Magazine* in the December 1996 issue).

On 10 January 1812 Agent Cotgrave received a letter from the Transport Office, extracts from which read:

'Sir, the Lords Commissioners of the Admiralty having authorized us to erect a Church together with a house for the Clergyman direct you to order Mr. Walters to draw a plan and elevation of the said Church and House which are to be executed upon the plainest and most economical style possible the Church to contain about 5 or 600 people and the House a Parlour, Dining Room, 4 Bedrooms, Kitchen to be built of the moor or granite stone by the assistance of the necessary number of French Prisoners so that the whole may be executed in the course of the summer. It will be noticed that the House will be under the lee of the Church and the back part may be possibly constructed with a Hip Roof as better calculated to resist the prevailing weather'. (It seems everyone had come to appreciate the vagaries of Dartmoor weather).

After much bickering over Mr. Walters' plans and estimates, even sending him plans and drawings of their own as a guideline, the Transport Office wrote to Captain Cotgrave on 19th. March 1812 informing him of their approval and instructing him to proceed with the work in accordance with what they considered the cheapest design.

The Church of St. Michael and All Angels is a unique edifice having been constructed by French prisoners of war who worked up to the time they left for home in 1814. Then the American prisoners took over and completed the task. As far as is known it is the only church in the United Kingdom to have been built by POWs. Dartmoor Chapel as it was first called was more correctly a 'Chapel-at-Ease' to the Church of St. Petrock at Lydford (the largest parish in England within which Prince Town then lay). It also has the distinction of being one of the highest situated churches in the country, although the term 'Church' only came into effect when Prince Town became an Ecclesiastic Parish in its own right in 1912.

Before and after the building of the church the Minister or Curate in Charge for the area was the Rev. James Holman Mason, a well known clergyman in those days affectionately dubbed the 'Bishop of the Moor'. This remarkable man was born in Okehampton and became curate at Lydford in which capacity he travelled many miles over rough moorland roads, often on horseback, in order to conduct services and perform Baptisms. He afterwards joined the 'improvers' on the moor by leasing and enclosing 600 acres of Duchy land near Crockern Tor on the Prince Town to Moretonhampstead road where he built a dwelling called 'Parson's Cottage'. A cottage stands there now and is marked on the Ordnance Survey map as 'Parsons Cottage' but the original little cot was in ruins before the end of the 19th. century. The Rev. Mason and Sir

Thomas Tyrwhitt were firm friends and this probably influenced his appointment as Chaplain to the Prince of Wales and being appointed Vicar of Treneglos and Warbstow in 1804 (both parishes are in North Cornwall) a position he held until 1848. The Prince made him Deputy Rider and Master Forester of Dartmoor and in 1815 he accepted the post of Vicar at Widecombe where he lived and worked until he died in 1860.

When the Chapel-at-Ease at Prince Town opened for the first time on 2nd. January 1814, it was the Rev. Mason who conducted Divine Service, having been appointed 'Incumbent' minister by the Transport Office. This first service was conducted when the chapel was still under construction and it must have been a makeshift affair because on 16th. May (four months later) the Transport Office wrote to Captain Shortland to:

'approve of your causing the window frames of the church to be fitted and glazed and the several works are to be proceeded with as expiditiously as possible _while the prisoners remain_' (Author's underlining – a reference to the cheap labour provided by the French prisoners whose repatriation was imminent. By 20th. June the French had all gone, there was much still to be done and it fell to the Americans to finish the work). There was no pulpit either: another letter dated 13 August 1814 states: 'The Revd Mr. Mason having informed us that a Pulpit and desk now in St. Sitwells Church (St. Sidwell's, Exeter) has been offered for sale at the price of £22, we direct you to purchase them, at that price, for the use of the church at Dartmoor'.

It was not until 1st. November 1815 that the burial facility was granted. By then the Americans had gone home and the few remaining French (those captured during the 'Hundred Days') were the sick men in the hospital. Several writers including the Rev. Sabine Baring-Gould have alluded to empty wooden coffins being found years afterwards in the churchyard (doubtful), within the Depot itself (definitely not) and in the prisoners' moorland burial ground (now part of the prison farm). It is known that in the late 1800s and early 1900s when the prison was considerably altered a number of empty coffins were discovered in the farm area. Curiously some of them were found stood on end. The mystery was never solved, but the suggestion it might have been the work of 'resurrectionists' (polite term for body snatchers who made their living by digging up newly buried corpses for sale to schools of surgery) or the result of amazing escapes by prisoners of war from shallow graves, seem unlikely.

The Register of Baptisms for Prince Town provides an insight into the character of the place from 12th. April 1807 onwards. On that day the Rev. Mason made this statement on the first page of the Register:

'Register of Baptisms at the Prison of War on Dartmoor within the Parish of Lydford where Divine service has been performed from Jan. 25th. 1807 under the Sanction of the Bishop of the Diocese by James Holman Mason, Vicar of Treneglos and Warbstow'.

Among the entries we find:

April 12th. 1807 (First entry)	Henry, son of Richard Badcock and Martha his wife, residing at Prince Hall, received his full Baptism.
June 7th. 1807	Arabella, daughter of Daniel Lane, Gent., Surgeon at the Prison of War and Margaret his wife.
May 22nd. 1808	Harriet, daughter of Rose Johnson who was killed in the Trafalgar action, and Martha his wife, born March 29th. 1803.

These Baptisms must have been performed either at the Depot or in private houses before the

Chapel-at-Ease was built. The entry for June 7th. 1807 tells us the Depot was staffed to an extent that justified the presence of a resident surgeon well before it was completed. The construction of the prison and the huge stones which had to be manoeuvred into place must have been a hazardous undertaking and there were probably injuries enough to keep the surgeon busy. Other entries in the register include:

Pin cushion made by French Officer from his uniform material and epaulettes. Given to Mr. Richard Edwards who delivered bread to the prison every day.

April 2nd. 1815   *Charlotte, daughter of Richard Edwards, a Baker living at Prince Town, and Elizabeth his wife, was privately Baptised January 18th 1812.*

Richard Edwards supplied bread to the French officers at the Depot.

Two French prisoners of war taken during the 'Hundred Days' are listed as fathers of infants Baptised in 1815. They were:

September 3rd. 1815   *Peter Dartmoor, son of Pierre Joseph Tollat, a French prisoner, Sergt. in the 26th. Regt. and Catherine Elizabeth Eidam, his wife.*

November 19th. 1815   *Catherine Elizabeth, daughter of Pascal Pucket, Sergt. of the 25th. Regt. in the service of France, a prisoner at Dartmoor, and Hellena his wife.*

Up to the end of the year 1815 the entries mention fathers who pioneered the Prince Town and Two Bridges area and whose occupations included:

Moor stone mason	*John Jeffry*
Blacksmith	*John Halfyard, James Rowe*
Carpenter	*Nicholas Eden*
Canal man	*Peter Germon*
Miner	*Benjamin Gill*
Tailor and Turnkey at the Prison	*John Tozer*
Butcher	*John Dunning*
Prince Town Brewery	*William Robins*
Interpreter at Dartmoor Depot	*John Moore*
Weaver	*Thomas Wright*
Steward at the Prison of War	*John Arnold*
Carter at the Prison of War	*George Challacombe*
Slater at the Prison of War	*William May*
Innkeeper	*John Ellis*
Turnpikeman	*John Hannaford*

Also mentioned are a Cordwainer of the Derby Militia, a Bandsman of the South Devon Militia, and other Militiamen belonging to the West Essex (1810), East Kent (1810), Royal Cheshire (1813), Monaghan (1813), and the 12th. Regiment of Foot.

The Church of St. Michaels and All Angels, Princetown. Built by French and American prisoners of war. From a painting by Paul Deacon.

The American Memorial Window, Princetown Parish Church.

What a colourful picture they represent of Prince Town's past! There was even a *'Sailor, residing at the prison'* – one wonders how that came about. Nearly all the above-mentioned names are familiar today in the vicinity of Dartmoor and its borders.

The church has had more than its fair share of misfortune. The bells that should have been installed never arrived. Peace came in 1815 just when they were due and they were diverted to the Dockyard Church of St. Nicholas at Plymouth which was destroyed by enemy air raids during World War Two. In 1868 the church was completely gutted by fire and nearly all the internal fittings put in by the Americans were destroyed. Some renovations were carried out in 1899, but because of financial restraints the work was so badly done that by 1905 the East wall was in danger of collapse. The wall and the East window had to be rebuilt and it was then the Pastor, the Rev. Heathcote-Smith, made an appeal to the American people for help, suggesting this might take the form of a memorial window to be inserted in the new wall. On 7th. June 1908 the *New York Herald* published his appeal and the cause was taken up by the National Society of United States Daughters of 1812. Their President, Mrs. Gerry Slade, thought it appropriate to put the matter to the National Board of the Society, as a result of which a Memorial Committee was set up. Mrs. Slade obtained details of the dimensions and arranged for Messrs. Mayer & Co. of Berlin, London, and New York, to prepare and supply the beautiful stained glass window which is there today. Beneath the window proper is an inscription which reads:

'To the Glory of God in Memory of the American Prisoners of War who were detained in the Dartmoor War prison between the years 1809-1815 and who helped to build this church, especially of the 218* above men who died here on behalf of their Country.
Dulce est Pro Patria Mori'.
* Now thought to be 271.

When Mrs. Slade unveiled the window on 3rd. June 1910 the comment was made that credit would not be claimed by the Society alone but would reflect on the American Nation. In 1925 the Society supplied an American flag to hang in the church. In 1982 a second, larger flag was given with the kind assistance of United States Senator the Hon. William V. Roth who, prior to the flag being dispatched, arranged for it to be flown over the Capitol Building in Washington. It now hangs alongside the national flags of France and Great Britain.

There are no rich legacies or endowments to maintain the church and Dartmoor weather has taken its toll. After 180 years the cold and frost and the wet have rotted the floorboards, damaged the stonework, and rendered the tower unsafe. On one occasion the author examined the west (inside) wall of the tower and noted huge patches of green and black algae clinging to its damp surface (a vivid example of what the old prisons must have been like when the French and Americans were in residence). Princes and Governments have in the past donated substantial sums for its upkeep, but because of its exposed location and the winter storms a constant battle has been fought to keep up appearances. The church had to close in 1994 through lack of funds to carry out the necessary repairs. At the time of writing extensive repair work is under way sponsored by the Churches Conservation Trust, a body established by Parliament and the Church of England to preserve churches of historical or architectural interest. On completion its future will be decided.

MORTALITY RATES AND THE PRICE OF VICTORY

The average death rate at Dartmoor Depot was equal to the worst of that aboard the hulks – around four per cent per year. This figure is misleading though because the epidemics that broke out from time to time pushed the average higher than would fairly be expected. In 1809 for example there was the measles outbreak which killed over 460 Frenchmen in just six months (the official figures for the period are shown) and a smallpox epidemic took a heavy toll especially among the Americans. Typhus, commonly known as gaol fever at that time, was prevalent and the cold wet winters were the cause of chest complaints which often developed into pneumonia. The latter was the greater menace because the conditions that led to it were consistent. Some prisoners helped bring about their own demise; for example those who (for whatever reason) did not possess shoes or sufficient clothing in winter. In an account written by Nathaniel Pierce, an American prisoner from Newberryport, he complains continuously about the mist and cold on Dartmoor and mentions the interior of the dormitories where it was too dark to see to read or write even on a fine day. The Chief Surgeon of England blamed the stale humid atmosphere in the prison blocks for the spread of the so-called 'African Pox' which afflicted the Americans in February 1815. The men must have blocked up the windows to stop the draught, something which created an unhealthy, stagnant environment. There was tragedy too. No less than sixty coroners' inquests were held between April and September that year over the bodies of men 'found dying in the prison', 'found hanged', 'found dead', etc.

The French, due to their longer period of imprisonment, suffered by far the greater number of deaths, more than 1200 including a number of suicides, murders and those killed trying to escape. Of the Americans 271 died but as Mr. Ira Dye implies, there may be others. Two boy ratings died – one of them, John Seapatch, was only twelve years old. Most fatalities among the 'Yankees' occurred during the smallpox epidemic and a third of them were coloured men. There was one murder, one suicide and nine men were killed as a result of the 'massacre'.

The calorie yield for the rations, calculated at approximately 2410 calories per day, was below what a young man needed to keep healthy. Prisoners who could not afford to buy extra rations from the daily market often deteriorated the soonest after the ones who wagered their rations and lost. Benjamin Palmer has related how a performance of *Hamlet* was staged in No. 4 block, and refers with grim humour to the ease with which the ghost was portrayed by an inmate whose gaunt and pale features were not so very different 'from the real thing!' At best the basic rations at the Depot kept them alive.

TOTAL NUMBER OF DEATHS AT DARTMOOR DEPOT 1809-1816.

From May 1809 to the end of the year.	149
1810	419
1811	88
1812	142
1813	239
1814	198
1815	220
1816 (Jan. only)	23
Total	1478

Death Toll at Dartmoor Depot 1809-1810.

1809		No. of Prisoners
MAY	Nil	2479
JUNE	9	2471
JULY	9	3059
AUGUST	3	4052
* SEPTEMBER	15	6031
OCTOBER	21	5993
NOVEMBER	29	5940
DECEMBER	63	5675
1810		
JANUARY	131	5741
FEBRUARY	87	5624
MARCH	63	5399
APRIL	28	5352
* MAY	25	5282
JUNE	17	5261
JULY	12	5247
AUGUST	16	5229
SEPTEMBER	11	5209
OCTOBER	9	5399
NOVEMBER	12	5372
DECEMBER	8	5247

* From September 1809 to May 1810 a total of 462 prisoners of war died, mainly from the Measles epidemic

The Price of War

Between 1803 and 1814 the British captured 122,440 prisoners of various nationalities, most of them after 1805 the year of the Trafalgar battle. Out of this colossal number 10,341 died in captivity and 17,607 were exchanged or paroled to France. As we have seen, accommodating such large numbers caused endless problems to the extent that the Duke of Wellington was specifically asked (3rd. February 1811) not to send any more prisoners of war to this country because of the overcrowding. He nevertheless sent 20,000 more between 1811 and 1812 alone.

Dartmoor Depot and the hulks represented the worst of prison life. At first the hulks were used to accommodate prisoners for whom there was no room anywhere ashore; later they became reception centres for newly captured men who were assessed and segregated according to rank, etc. before being sent on parole or to the war prisons. Some prison ships were retained for the confinement of recaptured escapees and troublemakers. In 1814 there were an estimated 72,000 prisoners of war in this country, the largest number at any one time. Dartmoor Depot held more than 9,000 from 1812 until the war with France ended. Overcrowding was a problem as early as Sept. 1809 when, only four months after opening, 6,031 men were detained in accommodation designed for just over 5,000. The following year this figure fell to an acceptable level but by June

1811 the number gradually crept up to 6,577. It will be remembered two extra prison blocks were constructed, using prison labour, but the place was still over full when the Americans began arriving in April 1813 and this remained the case until mid 1814 when the French were repatriated.

Consider the number of each class of prisoner for 16th. June 1812, for which the official total figure stood at 54,517, including many innocents – women, children, ships passengers etc. There were nearly 1600 Danish prisoners on board one of the Plymouth hulks. All of them had to be fed, clothed, housed and guarded. The sick had to be attended to and the highest percentage of these were among the officers on parole (some think it a result of duelling). The cost was colossal, as the official figures reveal:

Sum expended for the maintenance of French prisoners during the war

from 1803 to 1814	£6,799,678 13s. 11d.
Ditto for 1815	£71,995 18s. 00d.
Total	£6,871,674 11s. 11d.

Going on for £7m. was spent by the British with little or no assistance from the French towards the upkeep of their men. There was an enormous difference too in the actual cost of waging the wars – £225m. by France and a colossal £831m. by the British. The difference is partly accounted for by more than £52m. (colloquially referred to at the time as 'Pitt's Gold') which the British paid her Allies to arm and equip their armies in Europe. (Author's note: the figures given vary depending on which sources are consulted).

We have seen in this narrative the noblest of human endeavour and the blackest of deeds, the effects of which linger to this day. Many Americans remember injustices that took place during the War of 1812 for which they cannot forgive us and whilst researching for this book a French correspondent provided the author with some very useful information *without rancour* as he put it. Hopefully the bravery and chivalry will be remembered too.

SIGNIFICANT DATES.

1772	Tavistock–Moretonhampstead–Ashburton road Act passed.
1785	Sir Thomas Tyrwhitt joins 'improvers' and establishes Tor Royal.
18 May 1803	Treaty of Amiens ends – war with France renewed.
1805	Transport Office proposes Prisoner of War Depot in Devonshire.
20 March 1806	Sir Thomas Tyrwhitt lays Dartmoor Prison Foundation Stone.
24 May 1809	First French prisoners arrive at Dartmoor Depot.
November 1809	Outbreak of measles epidemic. Nearly 500 prisoners die during winter.
1812	Two extra prisons completed to cope with overcrowded conditions.
April 1813	First 250 American prisoners arrive from Plymouth hulk 'Hector'.
16 October 1813	Romans removed from Dartmoor to Plymouth hulks.
22 December 1813	Captain I. Cotgrave leaves and is replaced by Captain T. Shortland. Two Americans admitted to daily market to buy tobacco and soap.
Winter 1813/1814	Severe winter. Snow to top of prison walls. Water supply frozen.
February 1814	American Government allows prisoners $1^1/_2$d. per day. Coloured men segregated to No. 4 block. 'King Dick' Crafus rules.
March 1814	American Government allows further 1d. per day. All Americans permitted to attend daily market.
11 April 1814	Napoleon abdicates. French war ends.
20 June 1814	All the French have been repatriated from Dartmoor. Napoleon exiled to Elba. British decide to transfer all American prisoners (except the officers) to Dartmoor.
24 December 1814	Treaty of Ghent. War of 1812 ends.
26 February 1815	Napoleon returns from Elba. War with France resumed – the 'Hundred Days'.
13 March 1815	H.M.Sloop 'Favourite' arrives from the United States with ratification of the Treaty of Ghent.
4 April 1815	The 'bread riot'. Fresh bread issued after confrontation with guards.
6 April 1815	The 'Prince Town Massacre'. Nine Americans die and many are wounded when guards open fire.
19 April 1815	First batch of American prisoners leave for home.
18 June 1815	Battle of Waterloo. Napoleon defeated.
1-4 July 1815	Over 4,000 French prisoners arrive at Dartmoor, many for the second time, straight from the battlefields.
15 July 1815	Napoleon surrenders to Captain Maitland on 'Belepheron' and the French wars finally end.
24 July 1815	Last of the Americans leave for home – coloured men and 'Rough Alleys'.
August 1815	Napoleon leaves for exile on St. Helena.
December 1815	All French prisoners have left Dartmoor except for the sick in the hospital.
February 1816	All prisoners gone. The garrison leave. The gates are locked.

For the next thirty four years the prison remained empty. Various ideas were considered for utilising the prison, including a suggestion that orphans from the streets of London be housed there. Albert, the Prince Consort, thought it a suitable location for the confinement of convicts (transportation was coming to an end and the existing British gaols were full). Both possibilities were rejected. In 1846 the British Patent Naphtha Company leased the place and installed retort stokers for the production of gas and oils from peat. It was a short-lived project and the company went into liquidation shortly afterwards.

In 1850 work commenced, using convict labour, to convert some of the old prison blocks at Dartmoor for use as a penal establishment after all. Despite several threats of closure, because of its remote location and expensive running costs, Dartmoor Prison has survived. Today it still plays an important part in Princetown's economy and the confinement of convicted men. Sir Thomas Tyrwhitt would have approved.

Part Two.

DARTMOOR CONVICT JAIL

CONTENTS

INTRODUCTION

The full story of Dartmoor Prison would fill many volumes and the chances are no one person would have the complete story to tell. A writer has to decide what particular form his account will take – what to leave out and what must be included. Some of the details are unpleasant, offensive even, yet they are recounted here as part of the prison's true story. In this section the author has tried to give a balanced description of what life was and is like in our most notorious jail. In some respects it was far worse then anyone could imagine; on the other hand, as with the war depot, some men viewed the place more kindly and we shall meet one who on the eve of his release openly talked about *coming back*.

There are men in prison who have known no other way of life since their youth and are 'institutionalised' – they cannot cope with everyday life because they have been so long accustomed to having their lives arranged for them. There have been men at Dartmoor, there may be some there now, who should not be in prison at all but in a mental institution. Up until 2001 (when Dartmoor was regraded to Category C) the prison was Category B and has held some of the most vicious thugs and gangsters in Britain as well as men convicted of lesser offences of every kind. Murderers, rapists, child molesters, fraudsters, con-men, burglars, robbers, drug offenders, car thieves, the list is endless and all have to be treated equally in accordance with the Prison Service maxim:

'HER MAJESTY'S PRISON SERVICE PROTECTS THE PUBLIC BY KEEPING IN CUSTODY THOSE COMMITTED BY THE COURTS. OUR DUTY IS TO LOOK AFTER THEM WITH HUMANITY AND TO HELP THEM LIVE LAW ABIDING AND USEFUL LIVES IN CUSTODY AND AFTER RELEASE'.

A tall order indeed as we shall see.

Category A	Those who have the means and support (possibly on the outside) for escape **or** are a threat to the public.
Category B	Are a high escape risk but do not have the means.
Category C	Are not a high escape or security risk but may be 'opportunists'.
Category D	Are no risk whatsoever either of escaping or being a threat to the public.

Aerial view of Dartmoor Prison, 1980s.

A DARTMOOR LYRIC

Give him spasms, give him fits,
Punch his guts out and his wits,
Give him boot and give him spade,
Make the other swines afraid.
Damn the Chief and damn the Gov.,
We have little cause to love
Guard or screw or any cuss
Put by law in charge of us.

Catch the devil in his sin,
Knock him down, and stamp him in.
Time enough some other day
To remember him in his own clay,
When old bloody Moorland Jack's
Pretty pussy claws our backs; *
All together, lads, and damn
Any faint off-standish lamb.

Here he lies, his mother now
Wouldn't know his baby brow,
Quick, you fast arriving screws,
You have not a tick to lose.
Fetch a farm cart, chuck him in it,
He may croak in half a minute,
Drive by Doctor's – Chaplain first,
He's the bloke what's wanted worst.

* *Moorland Jack's 'pretty pussy' – the dreaded cat o' nine tails.*

GOVERNORS OF DARTMOOR PRISON

1809 - 1813	CAPT. COTGRAVE R.N.
1813 - 1816	CAPT. SHORTLAND R.N.
1816 - 1850	CLOSED.
1850 - 1854	CAPT. M. GAMBIER R.N.
1854 - 1864	W. MORRISH.
1864 - 1866	CAPT. G. CLIFTON.
1866 - 1868	CAPT. W. P. STOPFORD.
1868 - 1869	W. PITT-BUTTS.
1869 - 1874	MAJ. F. H. NOOTT.
1876 - 1879	CAPT. W. V. F. HARRIS.
1880 - 1890	CAPT. O. W. EVERY.
1891 - 1892	NO RECORD.
1893 - 1899	CAPT. F. JOHNSON.
1900 - 1902	W. H. O. RUSSELL.
1903 - 1907	B. THOMSON.
1908 - 1910	CAPT. G. H. GUYON.
1911 - 1913	CAPT. G. E. TEMPLE.
1914 - 1919	MAJ. E. R. READE.
1920 - 1921	MAJ. T. F. H. WISDEN.
1922 - 1928	MAJ. F. G. C. M. MORGAN.
1929 - 1930	MAJ. G. F. CLAYTON.
1930 - 1931	MAJ. L. H. MORRIS, M.C., L.L.D.
1931 - 1932	S. J. ROBERTS.
1932 - 1945	MAJ. C. PANNALL, O.B.E., M.C., D.S.O.
1945 - 1955	MAJ. HARVEY.
1955 - 1957	J. RICHARDS.
1957 - 1960	G. B. SMITH.
1960 - 1966	D. G. W. MALONE.
1966 - 1968	P. C. JONES.
1968 - 1974	MAJ. N. A. GOLDING.
1974 - 1981	C. B. HEALD.
1981 - 1982	E. R. E. SKELTON.
1982 - 1985	D. THOMSON.
1985 - 1990	R. J. MAY.
1990 - 1992	R. KENDRICK.
1992 - 1994	J. POWLS.
1994 - 2001	J. LAWRENCE.
2001 -	G. JOHNSON.

HOW AND WHY

During the wars with France the British people suffered great hardship due to food shortages and the introduction of machinery and manufacturing equipment that replaced human labour. The conscription of men by ballot often left their families on the verge of starvation. When the wars ended the Royal Navy and the Army discharged their wartime conscripts, bringing about a surplus of men seeking work. By 1850 social conditions had worsened. In the manufacturing towns, where machines had replaced the old cottage industries, the influx of people seeking employment created huge social problems, especially in London the most overcrowded city of them all. In 1800 the population of London equalled twenty per cent of the total number of people in Britain; by 1850 it had risen to more than half. A brief reminder about life in those times will help explain the savagery of the punishments meted out to lawbreakers in our prisons then and how Dartmoor became the most feared of them all.

Mid 19th. century life has been vividly portrayed by our greatest novelists and observers of whom Charles Dickens and Henry Mayhew are prominent. They tell of poverty in the slums that was equal to if not worse than many 'third world' countries today because of lack of employment. In the so-called 'lodging houses' as many as thirty people of both sexes and all ages shared a single room, with six or seven adults and children sharing a bed, the unlucky ones sleeping on the bare floor. There was no running water and no sanitary arrangement other than overflowing buckets in stinking courtyards littered with heaps of refuse and filth from which there rose a nauseous atmosphere that often led to outbreaks of typhus and cholera. It was not uncommon for corpses to remain where they died for days until the stench became unbearable. Desperate men and women took to scouring the banks of the River Thames at low tide in the hope of finding something which could be salvaged and sold ('mudlarks' they were called); other braver souls invaded the sewers for the same purpose (only the well off had water closets and it was not unknown for lucky scavengers to find items of jewellery and suchlike), risking their lives if, as sometimes happened, they overstayed their time before the waters rose again and trapped them.

Under such conditions crime rocketed among a population who endured a daily struggle simply to stay alive. Child criminals were a widespread feature in the capital and Dickens' account of Fagin teaching children to pick pockets ('dipping' it was called) was all too true. The 'ladies of the town' were never more numerous, some of them young girls literally 'moon-lighting' to supplement their scandalously low wages. For women and men a risky minute or two stealing could be more rewarding than weeks of punishing labour for a pittance, or facing an uncertain future foraging or begging. The London 'rookeries' as they were called were the refuge of every type of criminal, vicious thugs, and perverts; so dangerous were these vast slum areas no policeman would venture into them even in pairs. Recreation among the lower classes then included 'ratting' (cock fighting and bear baiting had long since been outlawed) where large numbers of rats were placed in pits and bets made on which of several dogs could kill the most. Bare knuckle fist fights were popular between strong men who smashed each other to a pulp and were sometimes killed. It was a brutal activity in a brutal age.

The reformers of the period had made progress towards abolishing the most degrading and inhuman methods of dealing with offenders: for example women were no longer flogged, roadside gibbets had disappeared, and a great many death sentences for petty crimes had been repealed. Most significant of all, transportation was coming to an end (the Colonies refused to be a dumping ground for Britain's undesirables any longer) except for Bermuda, Gibraltar, and Western Australia which accepted shiploads of convicts from 1850 until 1868 when transportation finally ceased for good. These changes created two problems – how to make prison life a punishment when the sort of everyday existence just described was a punishment in itself, and what to do with thousands of criminals who could no longer be shipped to the other side of the world. The solution that was decided upon was the setting up of local 'Houses of Correction' for men women and children serving short sentences where retribution was provided by devilish devices like the treadmill from which strong men were often removed weeping with exhaustion; the terrible hand operated equivalent the crank, used mainly for women prisoners; picking oakum (to be described later) and the Silent Rule. The overall result was the eventual release of prisoners enfeebled physically and mentally by the horrors that were inflicted upon them. Transportation was replaced by establishing prisons here at home where long term convicts who would normally

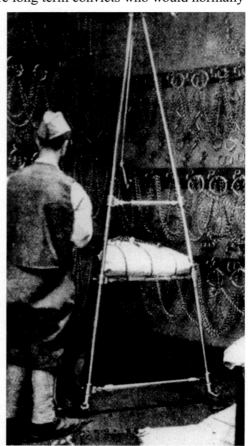

be transported would perform public works similar to what they would have done abroad. These measures gave birth to a number of convict prisons, among them 1848 Portland (quarrying), 1850 Portsmouth (constructing docks and jetties), and 1850 Dartmoor where the severe climatic conditions have already been noted and men were employed quarrying or reclaiming the barren moors for farming. Working in the open under a relentless strict regime was hardship indeed for townspeople, many of whom had never seen the countryside or a farmyard animal, and had no experience of hard manual labour. Not only that but Dartmoor Prison was situated on an exposed site miles from the nearest sizeable town where an uncanny silence prevailed after dark.

Here was no treadmill or crank; there was misery enough breaking rocks and digging ditches, working under armed guards with the threat of a flogging or birching for mutinous behaviour or assaults, supplemented by restricted diet (bread and water) and solitary confinement among many other disciplinary measures. But it was Dartmoor Prison's location, the damp and the cold, the filthy food, the remoteness and illnesses that even affected the warders and their families which made the place a frightening prospect for lawbreakers and prison staff alike. The story begins in 1850 when, after thirty four years, Dartmoor re-opened to receive the first of many thousands of convicts who would live and suffer on 'The Moor'.

The bad old days. Flogging triangle and chain room, Dartmoor Prison. (Courtesy Mrs.Rosie Oxenham).

AN INVALID PRISON

Dartmoor Convict Prison opened on 1st. November 1850. The first task was to convert two of the old French dormitory style prison blocks to the single cell units required for convict inmates. The job was done by artisan prisoners working under civilian contractors who demolished the concrete floors and constructed rows of cast iron cells arranged back to back, separated by corrugated iron partitions. They were situated on landings (referred to as 'wards') four tiers high with a platform around the outside for the guards to patrol between them and the outer stone walls. The floors and platforms for the whole were laid with thick slate slabs laid on an iron framework (Dartmoor Prison Museum has three of the original slabs on display on which an unknown former inmate has painted scenes of the Last Supper). Here is a description of the cells written by Michael Davitt (Irish patriot and a political prisoner) who lived in one of them for five years (1877 to 1882):

'The dimensions are uniform in almost every respect. Length, seven feet exactly (2.13m); width, four feet(1.22m); and height, seven feet one or two inches (2.16m). The sides (or frames) of all are of corrugated iron, and the floor is a slate one. the floors of the three upper tiers of cells form the ceilings of those immediately beneath them. Each ward or tier contains forty two cells, giving a total of 168 for one hall. The sole provision made for ventilating these cells is an opening of two and a half or three inches left at the bottom of each door. There is no opening into external air from any of these cells at Dartmoor, and the air admitted into the hall has to traverse the width of the same to enter the hole under the cell doors.

In the cells on the first three tiers there are about a dozen small perforations for the escape of foul air but on the top ward there were no such perforations – no possible way of escape for foul air except where most of it entered as 'pure' – under the door!'.

Mr. Davitt describes having to sleep on wood planks with his head towards the door in order to breathe, especially in summer and lying full length on the floor with his book under the gap at the bottom of the door to catch sufficient light to read by. The sanitary arrangements consisted of pots in each man's cell which were emptied each morning into tubs; the tubs in turn were emptied every other day and the contents used for manure on the farm. One of the cells he occupied was only twelve foot away from one of these tubs, forcing him to breathe and eat his meals in a stinking environment. He was at last moved to a lower level because his body erupted evil sores through breathing foul air. A number of the iron cells just described were in use until 1908.

Besides the iron boxes which passed for cells two prisoner of war dormitories were re-opened to accommodate the invalid prisoners who constituted the majority of the 1300 inmates. Among them were old men unfit for any kind of work, imbeciles, men with chest complaints, one armed (Davitt was one) and one legged men, and at least one blind man in later years who was able to do basket making. All of them were moved to Dartmoor for the benefit of their health, in the expectation the bracing Dartmoor air would do them good – and to some degree it did, bearing in mind most of them were taken from the convict hulks at Gosport and on the River Thames, or at a later date from the hospital prison at Woking which opened in 1859. The worst of these cases were provided with hospital beds, the rest slept in hammocks just like the prisoners of war all those years before. The invalids were not popular with their guardians because in the main they were incapable of doing the work required of them and were therefore a liability and difficult to manage.

What sort of men were sent to Dartmoor in 1850 and what was the nature of their offences? In many cases they were convicted and sentenced to long terms of imprisonment for crimes which today would be dealt with by social workers or simply warrant a caution. Here is the record of Dartmoor Convict Prison's first inmate:

Inmate no. 1

Adam Prentice aged 43 from Glasgow   10 years for Theft.

Among others were:

Thomas Lake	25	Clerkenwell	7 years	Larceny.
Joshua Lees	22	Stafford	7 years	Stealing a pair of boots.
John Norton	25	Winchester	10 years	Burglary.
John Lewis	22	Ruthin	7 years	Manslaughter.
William Sherry	22	Gt. Yarmouth	7 years	Stealing a sack of 485 herrings.
Henry Hutton	19	Gt. Yarmouth	7 years	Stealing 2 bottles of Porter.
James Hounslow	19	Maidstone	7 years	Bigamy.

It is interesting to note an offence of burglary merited a sentence three years more than for manslaughter and manslaughter was on a par (as far as sentencing went) with stealing a pair of boots. In the years ahead Dartmoor would receive the worst criminals in the land whose deeds repelled and sickened decent people, prompting the then Home Secretary Sir William Joynson-Hicks to comment the place was *'a cesspit of humanity'*.

Convicted men underwent nine months solitary confinement at either Millbank or Pentonville before being moved to a convict prison to commence their sentence proper. There they were expected to spend time in prayer and solitude and reflect on their crimes under the supervision of 'God fearing attendants'. A certain amount of useful work was expected of them also – making hammocks and mats but mainly oakum picking (a job that was done by certain invalid prisoners at Dartmoor). Michael Davitt has written that he enquired of his 'God fearing' warder how he was expected to perform this work having lost an arm, only to be told *'that he had known several blokes with but one hand who managed to pick oakum very well – with their teeth'*. Oakum was used to caulk wooden planks, mainly on boats, and was obtained in prisons by unpicking lengths of old rope, usually tarred and hard as iron. Fingers bled doing this work and to make matters worse the end product, a pile of fluffy strands, was weighed and set against a daily target. Add to this the misery of the Silent System then in force and some understanding may be reached as to how it was inmates went insane or committed suicide. Men went for weeks without saying a word to anyone and saw only their warders or occasionally the chaplain except during exercise (for one hour each day) and in chapel in silent association with one another. When they got to Dartmoor or any convict prison they lived in solitary cells overnight (they still do at Dartmoor) and mixed with their fellow inmates during the day under the strict rule of silence. This rule was relaxed over the years until by 1880 men who had a good behaviour record were permitted to take their exercise (walking in unison one behind the other in circles – known as the 'Fools Parade') with a companion of their choice to whom they could quietly converse. The silent system finally ended in 1950.

Under the directorship of Sir Joshua Jebb, a retired Army Colonel and Chairman of the Directors of Prisons, food was so plentiful, especially bread, that Princetown children were sent to the prison every day to collect what was left over (in some prisons it was thrown away). Good behaviour was rewarded by allowing men to grow their hair and beards (instead of submitting to the 'convict crop' with hair cut as close as the scissors could go), extra letters and association time. After his death in 1863 a stricter regime was applied. Captain Vernon Harris who was Governor from 1876-1879 has recorded the daily routine for Dartmoor convicts at that time:

5.00am	Prisoners rise, wash, clean out cells.
5.50	Breakfast issued.
6.45	Church service (approx. 15mins).
7.00	Parade for labour. The work parties were assembled and counted as they marched off.
11.10	Stop work. Dinner after being counted back and searched.
1.10pm	Parade for labour.
5.15	Stop work. Counted back and searched before returning to cells for supper. Convicts attended classes in the evening to receive tuition in reading and writing. The educated ones read their library books*.
7.45	Return to cells.
7.55pm	Lights out.

* Rev. Rickards, former Dartmoor Prison chaplain and a kindly understanding man, recalled there were several prisoners who educated themselves to a high standard through reading library books – especially languages. On the other hand he remembered one man who put in a request for '*Les Miserable*' because he felt it would cheer him up! Mr. Rickards put several of his own books at their disposal. Basil Thomson remembered a man whose hobby was learning languages and took to handing in requests written in Latin; on one occasion he asked for a book on Sanskrit having already acquainted himself with the rudiments of French, German, Italian and Spanish. He stated it was his intention to go on to study Arabic and Chinese.

There were changes in other directions as well. The food allowance was reduced to prevent wastage, causing hardship for the outdoor workers who were always hungry despite the fact they got more to eat than those employed in the prison workshops (the latter often threw them some of their bread or 'toke' as they called it and risked being punished for it). Prison food was never appetising anyway and by all accounts never matched the descriptions of it. In 1864 prisoners on public works received a daily ration of 28 ounces of bread and one pound of potatoes every day except Sunday when no hard labour was done. Breakfast consisted of a pint of gruel or 'skilly' as it was called (1 pint of water with 2 ounces of oatmeal) and bread; for supper at night a pint of cocoa with bread – if there was any left from the ration. For dinner at mid-day the pattern was this:

Monday	*5 ounces mutton and its liquor flavoured with onions and thickened with left over bread.*
Tuesday	*1 pint soup made from 9 ounces shin of beef, 4 ounces vegetables, 2 ounces pearl barley, flavoured and thickened as for Monday.*
Wednesday	*Same as for Monday.*
Thursday	*1 pound suet pudding only.*
Friday	*5 ounces beef (weighed after cooking, no bone) flavoured etc. as for Monday.*
Saturday	*Same as Friday.*
Sunday	*5 ounces of cheese only (because no work was done that day).*

More than one convict afterwards described the rotten potatoes, filthy carrots and stinking meat they got on their plates, often with beetles and grubs, even in the bread. The men were always hungry, particularly the younger ones who worked out in the open, and there are accounts of ravenous convicts eating boot oil, grass, candles (even though they were impregnated with a highly offensive odour in an effort to prevent them being eaten) and offal picked from the rubbish carts. If caught they faced reporting and punishment. It was on this food and drink that the fit ones laboured at quarrying, breaking stones with hammers and digging trenches to drain the bogs, often up to their knees in water. Boulders were removed from the peat soil by gangs of men pulling on ropes like beasts and broken up for building hedges.

We can already see how Dartmoor's foul reputation was in the making. The Government made this clear to nine convicted Fenians (The Irish Republican Brotherhood who fought for their country's Independence) by declaring:

'...they were sent to Dartmoor to show that the Government is resolved in administering justice with vigour, and putting in force the full power of the law'. (Bell's Weekly Messenger 1865).

Two Victorian Warders. Photo shows Warder Waycott of Princetown (left) with seated colleague.
(Courtesy of Miss Greta Waycott and the late Clifford Waycott, Princetown).

120

Civil Guard manning the main gate Dartmoor Prison. (Courtesy Mrs. Rosie Oxenham).

Convicts hauling boulders from the bogs 1870s. (Courtesy Dartmoor Prison Museum).

EARLY DAYS ON THE MOOR

The first convict prison Governor at Dartmoor was Captain M.Gambier, R.N. He and nearly all the Governors who succeeded him lived in what was the Agent's house to the right of Dartmoor prison's main entrance. It had a drawing room, dining room, kitchen, and four or five bedrooms together with a small strip of land for a kitchen garden. His salary was £500 per annum and the house and garden were allowed to him in lieu of a lodging allowance of £52 per annum. The Deputy Governor, Medical Officer and Steward also enjoyed rent free accommodation situated to the left of the main entrance. The rest of the prison staff included:

2 Principal Warders
6 Warders
8 Assistant Warders
1 Schoolmaster
1 Clerk
1 Cook

Prison security was provided by the 1st. Battalion The King's Own Royal Regiment (4th. of Foot) who marched to Princetown to take up their duties on 1st. November 1850. The detachment consisted of one subaltern (Ensign Jasper Hall); two sergeants; one drummer; forty rank and file; a total of forty four men. Their duties were to provide armed escorts to the outside work parties, the internal supervision being the responsibility of the turnkeys or warders. Several different units served on the moor until 20th. April 1854 when the military guard was replaced by a civil guard made up of army pensioners and comprised two sergeants; two corporals; and thirty six privates. These older men were found to be ineffective and on 4th. June 1857 their places were taken by younger, fit recruits, most of whom had military experience. The guards were armed with muskets and bayonets up to 1868 when these were exchanged for Snider carbines and instructors were sent from the Plymouth Garrison to teach them how to use them. At a still later date the civil guard was disbanded and armed warders took their place. By the 1930s the Snider rifles were only carried on night patrols or in case of escape and were discontinued altogether after 1954.

The soldiers lived in the old prisoner of war hospital to begin with because the Barracks were occupied by Princetown workers and their families who paid a rent to the Duchy of Cornwall and the local Agent Mr.J.Barrington was instructed not to evict them until they had somewhere else to go. By 1852 the whole of the barracks were occupied by the military and subordinate prison employees. Life was hard for them; the only recreation was to be found in the pubs and for the families there was nothing. Their quarters were often damp and very cold in winter, the cause of much illness and misery to the extent that during the first couple of years several warders resigned their posts for the sake of their wives and children, offering to take up employment anywhere except at Dartmoor. One replacement warder resigned on arrival saying he would not do one hours duty in such a place. Drunkenness also became a problem and a number of men were dismissed for neglect of duty because of it.

In February 1853 a severe blizzard struck Princetown and convict parties were put to work clearing the roads. It was a hopeless task and in the terrible cold the guards were permitted to stand sideways to the wind. It was a mistake because a prisoner named Brown took advantage of their restricted vision to make off over the moor. A day or two later he was found by a farmer in an outbuilding and handed over to the authorities who took him to Tavistock hospital suffering from frostbite. He lost several toes. Two soldiers of the 7th. Royal Fusiliers who were marching to join their unit guarding the prison were not so lucky – they died after being caught in the storm together with a corporal who was sent to look for them. The concern now was for the feeding of the prisoners as it proved impossible for the supply wagons to get through. A wise Governor had already laid in an emergency supply of biscuit and salt pork (navy style); now the Board of Admiralty was asked by the Home Department to authorise the Victualling Officer at the Royal William Yard at Plymouth (the victualling store for ships of the Royal Navy) to supply two weeks rations for 1,000 men. Eventually, after the prison had endured a spell on reduced diet, several tons of biscuit and almost the same quantity of salt pork was able to be delivered. This was not the last time the prison faced a food crisis because of winter snow; there were to be times when not only the convicts but the residents of the town would be saved from hunger by Dartmoor prison sharing bread with civilians and killing prison farm animals for food.

The Western Flying Post, Yeovil.
Tuesday, January 10th. 1865

A melancholy occurrence took place on Saturday last.

A young married man named Sweeney, who had just been appointed as a Schoolteacher to the Dartmoor Convict Prison had gone into Tavistock on business. He left the town on foot to return to Prince Town soon after eight o' clock in the evening. A heavy snowstorm came on, and a fierce wind blowing at the time, the drifts in some places became many feet deep.

Sweeney took two hours and a quarter to reach the Merrivale Bridge, a distance of some four miles.

There is a Public House at the bridge, and here he stopped for a while and partook of refreshment.

The gale had by that time increased in fury, and the Landlady urged the poor fellow to stop the night, but being anxious to get home to his wife and young children, he refused the proffered hospitality with thanks, and set out for his home.

He never reached it, his dead body being found the following morning, about three quarters of a mile from Prince Town, in a crouching position close by the hedge.

There were several deaths of prisoners from the beginning from sickness ranging from pneumonia and other chest complaints (mainly due to the damp in the stone cells) to diseases related to vitamin deficiencies (because of the poor diet) like diarrhoea and dropsy. Typhus was still a problem at times and in 1890 there was a cholera outbreak. Some convicts were fatally injured in the quarry and a few were shot trying to escape. They were all buried in a plot set aside for them in the graveyard at the church where interment took place in unmarked graves. At one time there were two or three burials a day. In all cases the next of kin were informed as follows: *'I regret to inform you of the death of prisoner (No. and name) which took place on (date). You are at liberty to attend the inquest which will be held in a day or so, also the funeral which will take place shortly.*

Signed (Governor)'. (From the Governor's journal 1853).

CERTIFIED COPY OF AN ENTRY OF DEATH

GIVEN AT THE GENERAL REGISTER OFFICE

Application Number R007611

REGISTRATION DISTRICT Tavistock

1856 DEATH in the Sub-district of Buckland monachorum in the County of Devon

No.	When and where died	Name and surname	Sex	Age	Occupation	Cause of death	Signature, description and residence of informant	When registered	Signature of registrar
90	Tenth September 1856 Dartmoor Prison Lidford	G —— S ——	male	28 yrs	Convict Prisoner No 3467	Dropsy	M.A. Vallack County Coroner Great Torrington Devon	Twenty Ninth September 1856	Richard Toop Registrar

CERTIFIED to be a true copy of an entry in the certified copy of a Register of Deaths in the District above mentioned.

Given at the GENERAL REGISTER OFFICE, under the Seal of the said Office, the 19th day of January 1996

CAUTION:- It is an offence to falsify a certificate or to make or knowingly use a false certificate or a copy of a false certificate intending it to be accepted as genuine to the prejudice of any person or to possess a certificate knowing it to be false without lawful authority.

Convict Death Certificate, 1856.

Very few relatives took up this offer bearing in mind the difficulty in getting there (Basil Thomson relates how on one occasion it took his horse drawn carriage over two hours to take him the seven miles from Tavistock to Princetown in a dense fog) and the underprivileged backgrounds of the dead men, it is not surprising only one headstone was ever set up for a convict by his family (it stands in isolation in front of the convicts graveyard and bears the words *'L.D.C. who died February 2nd. 1877. My Jesus Mercy'*). It was not until 1902 that the authorities began supplying small memorial stones inscribed with the dead man's initials and date of death. A large granite memorial cross was made with convict labour the same year and erected in memory of those convicts who died before 1902 and have no known grave. One Governor died in office – Captain Oswald Every succumbed to a bout of pneumonia in 1891 and is buried close by the East window of the church.

Most of the convicts were from the lowest classes of early Victorian Britain and there were unmanageable men to contend with right from the start. For example there were:

Edward Gray from Millbank – conduct stated as *'Very Bad'* and having been reported forty times.

Joseph Crove from Pentonville – conduct stated to be *'Thoroughly Bad'* – punished fifteen times. Removed from 'Warrior' hulk at Woolwich for *'violent and outrageous conduct'* for which corporal punishment and extended sentence had been awarded.

Captain Gambier wrote: *'As these two prisoners appear to be very dangerous characters to be placed in association, especially at such a station as Dartmoor, I have thought it right to submit the matter for your consideration'* (letter to Lt. Col. Sir Joshua Jebb, Chairman of the Directors of Prisons, 4th.March 1854). Apparently this eloquent plea fell on deaf ears because on 10th. March Captain Gambier again wrote to Col. Jebb (evidently after receiving a reply): *'Dartmoor is eminently calculated for reception of incorrigible invalid prisoners provided the Governor is given the necessary powers to deal with them'.*

Before long Dartmoor became a dump for troublesome convicts who would be 'out of sight and out of mind there'. A classic example occurred in 1864 after a mass escape attempt by an outside work party led by a man called Smith. He was accused of attempting to kill a Dartmoor warder (there were many such attempts over the years) having previously attacked and nearly killed another warder. He was sent to Millbank where he stabbed an officer in the neck. After a trial at the Central Criminal Court he was convicted and sent back to Dartmoor! A later Governor (Captain Vernon Harris) commented to an enquirer *'we have the very worst of men here you know, all of whom have not less than five years to serve'.* This state of affairs lasted for another 100 years during which time awkward prisoners (and some inefficient prison officers too) would be threatened with 'a trip over the Alps' if they didn't mend their ways.*

*Princetown was never a popular station and there was always a staffing problem which was solved by compulsory service to make up the requirement. After an officer had done his stint he was free to put in for transfer elsewhere and when the time came (in the 1960s) when they could choose where to reside most of them promptly left for Plymouth or Tavistock.

Having noted the Governor's rate of pay it may interest the reader to learn what other staff salaries were at that time:

23rd March 1853

D.Mackenzie	Farm Bailiff	£100	0s per annum
M.Lineham	Principle Warder	£66	0s per annum
J. Henderson	Warder	£56	5s per annum
J. Mitchell	Asst. Warder	£52	0s per annum
S.Head	Baker	£58	15s per annum

Warders in charge of the work gangs received an extra 10d per working day.

By 1866 the staff had expanded to include:

Prison Chaplain	£320	0s
Chief Warder	£155	0s
Engineer (for gas works)	£122	4s*
Stoker	£52	12s
Messenger	£26	6s plus £5 14s for cleaning the arms.

*The old Naphtha Company retort stokers were recommissioned to begin with for lighting the prison (each cell had a tiny gas light situated in an enclosed aperture which could only be lit and extinguished from the outside and provided just enough light for the warders to ensure the occupant was alright). Later a modern gas plant with gasometers was constructed outside the prison walls. In addition to lighting the prison and heating the hot water system, the plant supplied gas for lighting the administration staff accommodation and the terraced houses the warders afterwards occupied. Interestingly, the Jubilee Lamp, erected in the centre of Princetown to commemorate Queen Victoria's Golden Jubilee, was also lit by the prison gas supply, but not a single house or business establishment in Princetown ever benefitted. The gas plant was superseded by a central coal and then oil fired boiler house which in turn gave way to individual computer controlled mains gas units in 1999.

Life at Dartmoor in those early days called for a particularly tough character which is why the majority of prison warders at that time were either ex-servicemen or recruits from the mining communities. Even so, as we have seen, some of them could not face the harsh conditions on the moor, and for the majority of the convicts it must have been a nightmarish experience. There were exceptions though. One elderly convict occupied a cell on the top landing of one of the newly constructed prison blocks and was visited by Governor Basil Thomson who had noticed his record and the fact he had been at Dartmoor for three years and not been reported once. He asked if there was anything he wanted. *'No, sir'* he replied *'I am very happy. I've got the work I like* (stone dressing) *and the cell I like'*. He didn't make use of the library *'I don't read well and in any case the light is not good enough for reading'*. As his cell was eighty foot from the ground on the most unpopular landing and exposed to the full fury of Dartmoor's frequent winter gales, the Governor offered to move him to a better cell. *'Why no sir'* he said confidentially *'you see, I am a sailorman and there's nothing I like better than to walk up and down my cell and hear the wind howling – it makes me think I am at sea again'*. (*The Criminal*)

Convict headstones in Princetown Churchyard.

A multi-storey modern prison block at Dartmoor.

NINETEENTH CENTURY CONVICT LIFE

In March 1853 Governor Gambier penned a memorandum to G.H.Fowler, Esq. of Prince Hall, Dartmoor, inviting him to tender for supplying milk to the prison (between ten and twelve gallons per day at 6d. per gallon). He noted there was nobody else in the district capable of supplying it or offering to. By May 1862 things had changed. Sufficient land had been cleared and drained to support fifty four dairy cows on the newly established and profitable prison farm. A Dairy* had been built with a Dairywoman in attendance (the only female member of staff and on a mere £26 a year) assisted by fifteen convicts who supplied more than twenty five gallons of milk daily for the prison out of which over twenty two pounds of butter per week was made, the surplus being sold to the staff.

*Now the home of the Dartmoor Prison Museum.

The farm is a feature of the prison which has not received the attention which is its due. For one hundred years or more it provided useful and rewarding work for convict work parties for whom it was a popular and sought after occupation. Those who were successful came to love the animals they cared for. An extreme example at a much later date was David Davies, a Welshman who was a regular 'guest' at Dartmoor and is remembered now as the 'Dartmoor Shepherd' on account of him taking such great care of his flock to the extent many of the sheep and lambs had names to which they responded when called. Davies was a compulsive church and chapel offertory box robber but not a successful one it must be said because he always seemed to get caught and sent back to the moor. On one occasion Mr. Winston Churchill, the then Home Secretary, visited Dartmoor accompanied by Mr. David Lloyd George who conversed with Davies in Welsh. Churchill thought he deserved another chance and was influential in obtaining an early release for him, but the Shepherd, as always, was soon reunited with his beloved flock. On one occasion, on the eve of his discharge, he was overheard giving instruction to a warder how best to care for the new born lambs *'until he came back'*!

Dartmoor Prison Farm was famous for the horses they bred (mainly Clydesdales for carting) and the quality of their cattle and pigs. Those which were surplus to requirements were sold at Princetown Fair each year, always at a profit. In the 1860s there were more than 300 men employed in the farm gangs out of which twenty or so who had good records were detailed to care for the animals. The others dug trenches, cleared stones and repaired hedges – all winter work. In the summer they cut and dried turf for fuel to heat and light the prison but in very wet weather they returned to their winter routine (a separate gang were at work reclaiming the virgin moor). A valued bonus for them was being allowed to keep the field mice they caught as pets, much to the envy of other inmates, and to prevent them being stolen the owners carried them inside their shirts at all times. They were treasured possessions, a companion to come home to after the toil of the day and many hours of innocent amusement were passed in their cells teaching the little creatures tricks like climbing cardboard ladders and riding on miniature swings.

There were over one hundred acres of reclaimed land sown with grass for haymaking; thirty acres set aside for growing swedes, carrots and turnips to feed the cattle and pigs; cabbages, celery and onions were also produced. This was only made possible by the huge quantity of manual labour available and heavy manuring. All the sewage from the prison was collected in

Convicts in the fields under armed guard 1882

Convict collecting turnips for feeding cattle.

carts and dumped in a cesspool where, after draining, the solid material was mixed with farm manure for enriching the farmlands. There was another ingredient added to the mix: crushed meat bones from the kitchens (produced by those who could not perform hard manual work but who must have fervently wished that they could). This task was carried out in the 'bone shed', a building twenty foot by ten with a sunken floor so that the workers were on a level with the surface of the pool outside. In this reeking dusty atmosphere the men broke up and crushed the bones to a powder with hammers, hot dusty smelly work at the best of times but killing toil in summer heat. Later on a steam driven crusher was installed, reducing the number of men required but creating an enormous quantity of dust for those who operated it. The bones, some of which still had remnants of meat adhering to them, had more often than not been lying in a putrefying heap outside for days or weeks. Michael Davitt was one who was assigned to this job for a while and as a result suffered from weak heart and lungs for the rest of his life.

The prison quarry (Herne Hole) was extensively worked by convicts under warder supervision well into the following century. It was backbreaking work extracting granite boulders from the cliff face and breaking them up into pieces to be dressed for building additional prison blocks or simply breaking the stone to smaller pieces for road making, repair work, etc. Some stone breaking was carried out inside the prison walls in corrugated iron open fronted sheds, hammering stones to very small pieces for making concrete during renovations and building extra prison blocks. One man afterwards wrote how in winter he and his companions had to clear the snow from their stone seats as well as the piles of stones they worked on facing the biting wind and wore cloth bags over their hands to prevent them getting chilblains. The cold weather encouraged men to keep working to stay warm whilst the guards could only stamp their feet or beat their arms. Quarry work is recognised as one of the most dangerous occupations there are and Dartmoor had its share of casualties including fatalities through mistakes when placing explosives.

Armed guards patrolled the quarry rim as well as being stationed in the quarry proper, whilst to one side of the entrance, on a knoll reached by stone steps, there was a signal station with a tower from which the sentries could observe the farm area. In case of trouble a gunshot would alert them and assistance would be quickly on the scene on horseback. In time field telephones were laid and it was related by an old warder how their effectiveness was demonstrated to his charges. He deliberately neglected to bring the seeds they were to plant and made a great show of using the new device upon which, within a minute or two, a mounted warder came at the gallop bearing the 'forgotten' items. The 'mounties' were a valuable asset in patrolling the farm perimeters and aiding in escape incidents, remaining in service up to 1976.

Within the prison individual stone cells were constructed inside some of the old prisoner of war blocks (they were always wet and cold – the iron cells were much preferred by inmates) and around 1880 work began on the modern prison when one of them (the present day F wing) was refurbished. Further alterations and additions followed and were accomplished either by adding prison buildings to the existing 'French' prisons, or demolishing those that had deteriorated and building on the foundations. These are the prison buildings you see now. Again the work was done by convict labour directed by warders and by the time it was finished several men had died or suffered injuries most of them through falling from scaffolding.

Convicts at work in the prison quarry (Courtesy Dartmoor Prison Museum)

All new entrants were examined by the medical officer to be certified fit either for reclamation work or the quarry, at least to begin with. There were some convicts who had never worked in their lives and did not intend to commence doing so at Dartmoor (having been criminals since childhood), giving rise to cases of self-inflicted wounds in order to avoid it. Some men deliberately injured a knee joint for example, causing an infection by inserting copper wire into it and continuing to do so in their cells at night to keep it going; others swallowed pins, ground glass, soap or soda, in fact anything to hand which would incapacitate them. One man died of a lung infection under suspicious circumstances; the post mortem revealed a couple of needles embedded in his lungs and it was presumed he had swallowed them in the hope he would render himself unfit for labour. Some prisoners simply turned up at the hospital and complained of feeling unwell that day. The doctor was no fool, neither was he a 'soft touch' and those he suspected of malingering were prescribed what was called 'number eights' upon which his assistant (with an evil grin) would hand the offender (whose pallor had turned very pale) a handful of harmless but nasty tasting pills which had to be taken there and then. This procedure usually effected an instant cure. More devious individuals feigned paralysis (the notorious fraudster George Bidwell was one) and even blindness in order to avoid labour but were detected and punished and put to work. One 'paralysed' man was ordered to be carried to his place of work by his mates who dumped him without ceremony or sympathy on the stony ground in the quarry and carried him back to his cell when work finished. After some time he too made an apparently miraculous 'recovery'.

For the genuinely incapacitated men and the elderly there was work enough within the prison. The following trades were operating at Dartmoor in 1900:

Making baskets   for the Admiralty and the War Office.
Tailoring   uniforms for prison warders and the Metropolitan Police.
Twine making   for the Post Office. Sewing mail bags began later.
Shoemaking   boots for the warders (not only at Dartmoor but other prisons too), for the Metropolitan Police and for themselves and convicts elsewhere (these had nails hammered in the soles in the form of the 'broad arrow' the convict's trademark and left an imprint wherever he trod. The first thing an escapee did was to throw his boots away).

Picking oakum (hardly a trade but kept the weak and decrepit men occupied).

There were also carpenters, stonemasons, wheelwrights, building workers (for the extensions already mentioned), cooks and bakers. Many a man without an occupation was able to learn at least the rudiments of a trade in preparation for his release and the place resembled the war depot in its heyday – it was a township in its own right and largely self-supporting.

The inmates, coming as they did from every kind of background and every kind of trade and profession, were directed on entry into their appropriate workplaces where they would be of most use. Not all of these 'tradesmen' were what they claimed to be. The crafty ones among the 'old lags' had picked up the fundamentals of their selected occupation on previous visits inside and managed to avoid the outside work, settling down to a relatively cushy life in a prison workshop. They were 'wide boys' who knew the ropes and providing they did their work and gave no trouble were generally left alone.

Cart gang man-hauling prison cart – used for transporting rubbish and manure.

Examples of Prison Slang from the 1870s

QUOD	Prison.
SNIDE	Forged coins ('Snide Pitchers' – Forgers).
COPPER	Informer (modern term = 'grass').
PLANTING THE SWAG	Hiding proceeds of robbery, etc.
TAKING IN THE CROAKER	Fooling the Doctor (to avoid work).
TOKE	Bread (Slingin' the Toke – giving away bread).
HOOKS OR DIPPERS	Pickpockets.
SNATCHERS	Called 'Muggers' today – despised by Hooks.
GOWK	Country Bumpkin.
MAGSMEN	Confidence tricksters, card sharps, etc.
COCKS	Londoners.
LAGGED	Arrested. Period of sentence = a 'Lagging'.
CHOKEY	Three days punishment on bread and water.
SNOUT	Tobacco or cigarette.
CHUCKED UP	Released.

A CONVICT'S CIRCUMSTANCES

'Ticket of Leave'

When the convict prisons first opened the problem of where to put convicted men was becoming critical. The hulks were dreadfully overcrowded, the gaols were full, and it became necessary to release certain prisoners before their allotted time so as to make room for newcomers. There was an outcry from the public and a Penal Servitude Act was passed to solve the problem by reducing the actual time served on a scale of four years penal servitude for seven years transportation, the last three years being passed as free men on 'Ticket of Leave' under police supervision. Prisoners got a small gratuity on release, usually of about £5. It was paid in instalments over five months, providing they reported to the police and wrote every month stating how they were employed together with a certificate signed by a 'respectable person' (failure to do so or the committing of another offence resulted in the offender being returned to prison to complete his sentence). The 'Ticket' system originated in the colonies and was dependant on good behaviour and industry.

In 1864 another Penal Servitude Act fixed the minimum sentence for convicts at seven years with the granting of a 'Ticket' dependant on a number of 'marks' which had to be earned during imprisonment. The 'mark' system was simple and is best explained by the following example:

'A man is sentenced to five years penal servitude from 1st June 1865; his sentence expires on 31st May 1870. The actual number of days in this period, including the leap-year day, are counted and multiplied by six, making a total of 10,956. This represents the number of marks he has to earn to qualify for early release and (at the rate of eight marks per day) can obtain remission of fifteen months or one fourth of his sentence'.

(adapted from *The Criminal* by Basil Thomson).

Copy of George Bidwell's 'Ticket of Leave'. Bidwell was a notorious forger.

The daily quota of marks was awarded by the warder in charge and a man could lose marks for a poor effort that day or for misconduct. The difference now was that early release did not depend on a combination of good conduct and industry – it was felt that as bad behaviour was not tolerated there was no justification in rewarding good behaviour. Industry alone now counted and just as the prisoners of war in the depot looked for their exchange so the convicts were encouraged to work industriously to earn their daily quota of marks.

The 'marks' arrangement was also a way for men to progress to privileged status. By earning good marks for twelve months men passed to another stage, indicated by a badge sewn on their sleeve and being awarded small privileges. In 1938 there were three stages of one year at the end of which, on entering the fourth or 'special' stage those who qualified enjoyed extra association periods, were allowed to smoke, read one newspaper a week, attend extra association and concerts, and have means of recreation in their cell – some of these men were talented artists, model makers, etc. This greatly reduced the level of unruly behaviour as it gave men an incentive to conform in order to gain a little comfort and a shorter term to serve. There were always the brutal types whose often violent behaviour lost them any marks they might have earned. These were the men most likely to attack warders with spades or any tool that came to hand; who incited others to mutiny and organised escapes (not always supported by their colleagues). Some warders were determined to give their charges a hard time which often resulted in desperate prisoners hitting back when they reached the end of their tether or simply running away from an outside work party at the first opportunity. A number the latter were shot at and killed; those who made a getaway were relentlessly hunted down by armed warders and punished.

Punishments

Serious assaults on a warder or fellow prisoner or inciting a mutiny resulted in corporal punishment being inflicted on the offender, either with the terrible cat o' nine tails or the birch rod. This method of keeping the worst offenders under control lasted for more than a century and more than eighty years after it had ceased to be administered in the Army or the Royal Navy (it was finally abolished in British prisons in 1967). The Governor alone did not have the authority to inflict corporal punishment, it had to be approved by higher authority – the Director of Prisons in the 19th. century, then the Board of Visitors or Visiting Committee as they were called, and finally the Home Secretary in later years. They also decided the form the flogging would take i.e. the 'cat' or the birch and the number of strokes to be given. In every case the medical officer certified the prisoner fit to receive this punishment and had to be present in order to stop it if he considered it would injure the prisoner's health. The Governor also attended and recorded the time and the number of strokes administered. The ritual was very exact and merciless.

Prisoners were tied by the wrists and ankles with leather straps to a specially designed metal frame; the holes in the floor to which the frame was fixed can sill be seen at Dartmoor in what used to be the separate cell block, now closed and converted for other uses. When it was later decreed flogging should only take place out of sight and hearing of other prisoners the venue was transferred to the laundry (situated at the centre of the prison as far away as possible from other inmates) and a wooden free-standing frame was substituted. A canvas screen was rigged in later years so that the officer inflicting the punishment could not be seen by the victim and possibly assaulted in a revenge attack afterwards. Sometimes a warder was drafted in from another prison to do the job. Other refinements included a canvas cover with a square cut out of the centre which fitted across the prisoner's back to protect vulnerable body parts (the kidneys etc.) and a leather collar for the neck. The number of lashes with the 'cat' were restricted to a maximum of thirty six and were inflicted only on men over eighteen years old; prisoners under eighteen were always birched, a maximum of eighteen strokes being permitted.

Latterly the officer (the title of Warder was changed to Prison Officer in 1922) who carried out the flogging received an allowance of 2/6d. (25p) and was often chosen from the biggest of them, one of whom had a reputation for ferocity which gave rise to the boast *'blood every time!'*. The 'cat' affected men in different ways – it either broke them bodily and in spirit or it turned them into 'hard-case' rebels; one recipient is recorded as saying to his tormentors at the finish: *'Right, now I'll fight the best man among you!'*. Another man was found hanged in his cell whilst awaiting corporal punishment and the warders found a farewell note which simply said: *'This is the only way out. I cannot face the cat'* (*Dartmoor Prison* by Rufus Endle). The birch was feared and hated the most because it took the form of a thrashing on the bare buttocks, an indignity in itself and very painful and it often lacerated more extensive areas of skin than the 'cat'. The medical officer or his assistant applied thick lint pads spread with zinc ointment mixed with oil to the affected parts as soon as the victim was released and returned to his cell. There are men who still bear the scars on their backs from this treatment – one elderly gentleman on a

Portable flogging frame
(Courtesy Dartmoor Prison Museum).

visit to the prison museum caught sight of the flogging frame and raised his shirt, uncovering a back criss-crossed with striped marks from a prison flogging. *'This is what they did to me but once was enough'* he declared. One medical officer considered it was degrading for all who took part and that it served only to increase hostility in the victim.

In the old days there were other harsh measures available to maintain discipline in places like Dartmoor for minor offences. A man could be deprived of blankets or his mattress leaving him to get what sleep he could on the three wooden planks which was his bed. The best known punishment was solitary confinement in the punishment block or separate cells on a restricted diet for three days at a time of just bread and water – referred to by the 'screws' as the (weight reducing) *'jockey diet'* (this was abolished in 1979).

The Block as it was called was constructed around 1890 on the site of the old war prison bathing pond and had sixty cells on two levels. Small, walled exercise areas were provided outside thus ensuring complete seclusion at all times. Michael Davitt describes how he spent a short time in this infamous place (as it then was) which was referred to by cynics among the convicts of a later era as the 'Tea Garden'. He was constantly awakened by the howling of demented men, the cries of the hungry ones, and the ravings of vicious rogues, all of them traumatised by close solitary confinement. For recaptured escapees there was the yellow clothing they were made to wear which instantly identified them for what they were, and for convicts who tore up their clothes during fits of despair or just plain stress, a canvas suit was issued and worn. Other inmates sometimes lost their reason and became so violent they required several warders to restrain them (it still happens). Mechanical restraints in the 1800s included handcuffs, weighted chains, strait jackets, cross irons, and belts with wrist manacles. The medical officer authorised restraints and could order them to be removed if he saw fit and in any case the type of appliance used and the duration was recorded together with the reason for it being applied (usually to prevent self harm or harm to others). Cross irons and chains were sometimes used as a punishment but this was forbidden in later years.

Specifications for the Cat o' Nine Tails

Handle: To be made from seasoned silver spruce, free from defects of any nature. Finished dimensions to be $19^3/_4$ inches long by $1^1/_4$ inches diameter, contracting in three positions to the following particulars:

1. *Fluted tip to receive the ends of the tails: $^3/_4$ inch diameter for a length of $3^1/_4$ inches from the top to the top end of the handle.*
2. *Middle waist: $^{13}/_{16}$ inch diameter for a length of $2^1/_4$ inches, the lower extremity being $8^3/_4$ inches from the butt.*
3. *Lower waist: 13/16 diameter for a length of 2 inches, the lower extremity being 11/4 inches from the butt.*

Tails: To be nine in number, free ends whipped with trist, flax, cable laid. Each to be 36 inches in length, firmly secured to the fluted ends of the handle in such a position that the free running lengths should be not more nor less than 33 inches, and made from hemp whipcord of the following specification:

3 cord 5 ply; running weight 82 + 2 yards per pound;
$2^1/_2$ turns per inch, folded;
0.1 inches diameter; the line to be evenly doubled, free from faults and
protruding fibres, and of a firm handle.

All woodwork to be completely covered with blue serge. No.4 (T76), sewn with black linen 3-cord thread No. 35 to a tight fit. Subsequently, the full length of the tip and waists mentioned above to be securely bound with fine twine of a good quality. The overall weight of the finished article to be no less than $8^1/_2$ ounces and no more than 9 ounces.

PRISON COMMISSION.

27.8.56

Some General Observations

An Irish 'rebel' sent to Dartmoor after the Easter Rising in 1916 recorded how, on entering the main gate, he spied what seemed to him to be a group of Turkish prisoners of war. To his amazement he recognised one of them – it was Eamonn de Valera (future Prime Minister of the Republic of Ireland) who was already imprisoned there with some of the survivors of the 'Rising'. He had been fooled by their garb which comprised a 'forage cap', short tunic, waistcoat, knickerbockers tucked into woollen socks below the knee, and iron hard leather boots with arrows in the soles. Arrows also adorned the tunic and cap. It was indeed a ridiculous outfit, but a distinctive one which is why it had been adopted and remained so until the 1920s. An escapee's first requirement, besides something to eat, was to break into a home and steal footwear and clothing, a crime which not only merited an appearance before the magistrates after recapture (who invariably awarded them extra time) but gave away their whereabouts to the police and warders searching for them.

Up until the 1990s inmates got a bath once a week in the old bathhouse, a separate utility shared by all the prisoners who were escorted to and fro' across the open yards. The old time convicts who worked outside labouring were permitted extra baths for dirty work and a change of clothing in wet weather. In heavy rain or snow and if visibility was reduced during a Dartmoor fog, the men were returned to their cells. For less

Convict cap uncovered during renovation work 1992.

severe weather conditions prisoners took shelter in barns or any nearby building, otherwise they erected temporary 'windshields' to protect them from the worst of it.

Convicts led an austere existence under a strict management with little or no contact with the world outside, a frugal diet, few visitors, subjected to the very worst of language by villains of every hue, most of whom gloried in their foul deeds or revelled in every opportunity to teach a newcomer how to emulate their crimes. There were no comforts of any kind and God help you if you fell foul of a warder. Bad reports not only resulted in marks being lost, there was invariably a penalty to be paid such as those just described. Those who transgressed were punished swiftly and relentlessly – the place itself was designed to be and was operated as a punitive institution.

Some men learned to live with their plight and even benefited from it in mind and body. One ex-convict recorded how he was put to work digging peat, the kind of task he was not used to and which he thought would kill him. The men dug in line abreast at a fixed depth for a certain distance at a time and the writer was always last to catch up, the others enjoying a rest until he did. He confided his fears to the warder, a kindly type as it happened who not only advised him to stick it for a bit because he's seen several other men just like him, but did not deduct marks for his poor performance. Sure enough in a week or so he was able not only to keep up but became one of the best men in the team. The work and regular routine, the absence of alcohol, and the breezy Dartmoor air transformed many a pale degenerate into a bronzed, physically fit, clear eyed opposite to what he had previously been. Others never relented, hated authority and looked for any opportunity for revenge on the warders or a chance to escape.

Convict work party assembled with tools and ready to move off 1911.
(Courtesy Mr. Brian Jones).

WARDERS, VISITORS AND VIOLENCE

The first warders and their families were pioneers in every sense. Hemmed in on every side by the moors, their only friends and acquaintances were from among their own kind; there was no transport then other than by horseback or carriage, no recreation whatsoever, and damp gloomy quarters to live in. Coming as most of them did from the towns, the quiet of Dartmoor at night and the blackness outside must have affected them greatly. But things gradually changed for the better.

Terraced houses were built for them, labelled by the authorities Block A, B, C, etc. The warders became the better off residents of the town and in time one of the roads where they were lived was dubbed *'Piano Street'* by Princetown families who could not afford that essential item of furniture. A recreation room with a stage for concerts and dances was then provided followed by a reading room with a billiard table, then a sports ground and a National School. These amenities were often shared with the people who lived in the town so everyone benefited, especially the children, but the comment was made by a later generation that *'you was either prison, railway, or village then'* an indication of how Princetown social structures had evolved. The church played its part organising children's outings and sports days, fetes and all the social events associated with church activities at that time, which often seem trivial looking back from our modern age with the magic of world wide television, but which meant all the world to those hardy, lonely folk of long ago.

Governor collects prison pay. Governor Aggett has returned from Plymouth by train with prison wages and is inside the phaeton with an armed Warder. The driver is Warder Samuel Gilbert (also armed). Date: 1920s.

(Courtesy Mrs. Rosie Oxenham) Image prepared by Cinnabar, Okehampton

In 1883 the GWR steam railway opened, connecting Princetown to the Plymouth – Launceston line. It was a boon to the residents of Princetown and for those who ventured out from the city, either for a ramble on the moor or on a visit to 'see the Transports'. The train earned the unofficial title 'Convict Express' because it soon became a more convenient way of transporting prisoners to and from the prison. This had previously been done by a Plymouth contractor called Moreton who had extensive stables in Mount Street, Devonport just up the road from Millbay GWR railway terminus (long since closed) for the main line from Paddington. Mr. Moreton owned horse drawn wagonettes pulled by four horses for transporting convicts to and from the station to Princetown. There were occasions when perhaps a hundred men were moved from Dartmoor and extra wagonettes had to be procured at short notice. On other occasions, either because of the fog on the moors or snow, they missed the train, in which case the convicts were bedded down in the straw loft in the Mount Street stables, with armed warders surrounding the place under the gaze of a curious crowd of onlookers anxious to catch a glimpse of 'Her Majesty's guests'. Supper for them comprised soup, hastily prepared in his wife's wash copper. On one occasion the party stopped on their way to the prison to have some refreshment at Dousland where the local hostelry had prepared a room for them. Hanging from the beams in the passage were a number of hams in the process of being cured and someone was crafty enough to grab one without being seen. The prisoners ate the meal they were given and the ham without being detected, leaving the remains at the feet of the warders who sat at intervals around the same table! The culprit was never discovered (from an article about his father by F. Leslie Moreton in the *Western Morning News* 1930).

With the advent of the railway line to Princetown the number of day trippers increased dramatically. Like all visitors then and now they were interested in the prison and hoped to catch sight of the convict work parties (which were so much more numerous then) and they were rarely disappointed. Until the 1880s visitors enjoyed conducted tours of the prison by prior arrangement, when the messenger who acted as guide received a handsome supplement to his salary by way of gratuities for pointing out to them notorious criminals they'd read about in the newspapers. For some reason it was stopped, probably because groups of as many as twenty were turning up and interfering with their guide's normal duties.

More than one convict has related how, as they boarded the train in London for their journey to the moor, the public often reacted with sympathy seeing them manacled and hustled into compartments with drawn blinds. They often called out some words of encouragement and threw cigarettes to them. In modern times there have been comments made expressing concern for 'those poor fellows' by misguided members of the public. On one occasion an exasperated prison employee could no longer contain himself: *'My dear Madam'* he said *'we are not running a Sunday School here!'.* Mr. Basil Thomson, a former Dartmoor Prison Governor, once commented: *'The cry for reformation of the criminal in prison is an obsession of the later prison reformer who has a mental picture of the prisoners as a single class, ground under the heel of savage disciplinarians. It would be a grievous shock to these well-meaning people if they could hear what the prisoners think of them. They admire their disinterested philanthropy and some of them turn it to their own profit: the others are mildly amused and will afterwards talk of them with a sort of pitying patronage to their disciplinarian keepers with whom they have a complete understanding'.* (From his book *The Criminal*).

A glance at the 'Black Museum' exhibits in the prison museum will illustrate the point: on display are a selection of weapons including hatchets, knives, replica guns made of wood, even a blow pipe capable of killing someone. Every one of these devices has been confiscated either during a routine 'turnover' (unannounced cell search) or taken from prisoners after or during a disturbance. Among weapons with a gruesome reputation were the 'chivs'. These were home made slashing devices, usually a razor blade fixed to a make-shift handle: a razor blade melted into a toothbrush handle or embedded in a piece of soap were methods often used (before disposable razors were introduced officers used to issue numbered razor blades each morning when the men were 'unlocked' and count them when they were handed back after breakfast).

Many a warder in the past has been scarred for life as a result of assault and some have nearly died after being struck by spades, hammers, crowbars and stones or anything else to hand. Others have had to quit the service, unable to carry on because of physical or sometimes mental distress after being assaulted. Governors were not immune to violence either: in 1865 a convict accused of refusing to work carrying turfs appeared before the Governor and threw his boots at him in frustration and resentment. Other Governors, Deputy Governors and at least one Prison Chaplain were assaulted. Major Charles Pannall, the Governor before and during World War Two

'…we are not running a Sunday School…' A vicious weapon confiscated from an inmate when Dartmoor was Category B.

A selection of offensive weapons taken from inmates, some during actual assault incidents when Dartmoor was Category B.
(Both pictures courtesy of Dartmoor Prison Museum).

was attacked at least twice and his face was badly cut with a 'chiv'. The perpetrators were flogged a short time after these incidents occurred but the system failed to stop such things happening altogether. The prisoners who ran amok in the famous Dartmoor Prison mutiny of 1932 (to be described later) were 'out to get the Governor' from the start and some officers narrowly escaped being murdered.

Prisoners often attacked each other and certainly in the past the root cause was associated with tobacco. Smoking or possession of tobacco except for the privileged men was strictly forbidden in the Victorian era and was the cause of more 'reports' by warders than any other offence. Occasionally there would be searches, unexpected ones when for example a work party would be diverted to the Block (leaving a trail of illegal goods discarded along the way) where they were stripped to the skin and every article of clothing examined. Cells were then inspected, mattresses probed and special hooks inserted into vents in the quest for the forbidden article. The only way for a prisoner to obtain tobacco was through what was known as 'trafficking' when a corrupt warder might be persuaded to smuggle some in. A convict would cultivate a relationship with a certain warder and persuade him to post a letter for him; the letter would go to acquaintances at home who would then send a sum of money to the warder's address. After deducting a suitable 'fee' the officer would buy some tobacco and smuggle it in for the recipient in small quantities. This practice was not widespread and is known to have been viewed with contempt by the majority of prison staff; the result of course was that 'baccy' became all the more scarce. Consequently those who possessed the coveted weed gained enormous power over those who would sidle up and offer them any kind of favour for a share of the contraband (the convict grapevine never erred in detecting who was the lucky chap). Some were favoured with a few strands and others were not – hence the fights. It was for this reason, and because of the problems associated with it that Mr. Basil Thomson expressed the view it might be a good thing to allow it on the grounds it could lead to better conduct.

By the 1930s inmates were allowed to buy a limited quantity of tobacco in the canteen by which time they had commenced earning money (it ranged from sixpence to a few shillings and was paid to them in pennies each week) which enabled them to buy small luxuries like jam, sweets, cake, chocolate, etc. A halfpenny a week was retained and saved for them. Every four or five weeks (the men always knew when it was due) they got a paper bag of good things which would include some tobacco, sweets, an orange and an apple. Many a man pledged his bag of 'goodies' against a loan of money, often arranging a deal with several inmates so that when the time came to pay up there was trouble from the ones who were owed and not repaid. The culprit sometimes barricaded himself in his cell to avoid retribution, or refused work and was taken to the Block, anything to keep a distance between himself and them. Eventually he had to face them when he was likely to find broken glass in his food, or perhaps get 'chivved' (slashed with an improvised knife). All through Dartmoor prison history there have been grudge fights or revenge attacks among prisoners, sometimes with weapons such as have been described, having boiling water (laced with syrup to make it stick to the skin) 'accidentally' spilt over them, or an unfortunate fall. These days a favourite trick is to wrap a PP9 battery in a sock and use it as a cosh.

In the past there were two ways of evading retribution from fellow inmates: a debt was cancelled if the man who couldn't pay escaped, the proviso being he had to make it over the wall;

the other method was to ask to be confined in the Block and such requests are sometimes made today and for similar reasons. There have been instances, though rare, of inmates requesting to be moved to what is now called the VPU (vulnerable prisoners unit) where sex offenders are kept separately from other prisoners for their own safety and 'grasses' (informers) take refuge from a possible revenge attack. The drawback here is that once a man joins this class of prisoner he stays in that class even if he is moved to another prison.

A clever piece of modelling in bread, by an inmate, of a Prison Officer in imaginative pose.

Clever work of another kind – an Officer displays a home-made 'rifle' made by inmate when Dartmoor was Category B.

Old style handcuffs with removable screw type key. (Courtesy Dartmoor Prison Museum).

WORLD WAR ONE AND THE 'CONCHIES'

The horrors of trench warfare during World War One are well known and the appalling losses in the early stages of that conflict made it necessary to introduce compulsory conscription. The Military Service Act of 1916 which enforced it also allowed men to apply for exemption on the grounds of hardship, essential occupation, and because of religious faith or moral conviction. It was those who applied for exemption on religious or moral grounds who came to be called 'Conscientious Objectors' and they were in for a hard time. Public opinion generally was against the 'Conchies' who were regarded as trouble makers, unpatriotic shirkers, or revolutionaries. There were such men among them it is true but the majority appear to have been young fellows with religious fervour who simply refused to take part in killing other men for any reason whatsoever. Amongst them were Jews, Quakers, Jehovah's Witnesses, Roman Catholics, Salvationists, Pentecostals and Methodists. Many of the remainder were made up of atheists, agnostics, some communists and a sprinkling of educated philosophers who openly declared they would not take a human life and would rather be shot.

Military Service Tribunals (largely comprised of local dignitaries, tradesmen and retired officers) were set up to consider applications for exemption. Their task was not an easy one as they had to determine who were the genuine objectors and which applicants were using the system to avoid serving. There were applicants who did not belong to the Established Church or any organised religious body and these were very swiftly dealt with:

Question   *'Have you been confirmed?'*
Answer   *'No sir.'*
Question   *'Were you Baptised?'*
Answer   *'No sir.'*
Verdict   *'No church! Not even Baptised! Case dismissed – next!'*

Those who failed the tribunals were sent to France to fight and forty one were sentenced to death for refusing to accept military discipline. More than 16,000 Exemption Certificates were issued however, the recipients either agreeing to perform non-combatant duties at the front (stretcher bearing for example) or work in one of several Labour Camps run by the Home Office, of which Dartmoor Prison was one.

In February 1917 the Directors of the Convict Prisons consented to the whole of Dartmoor Prison being handed over for the duration of the war to the Committee on Employment of Conscientious Objectors. There were a thousand 'conchies' to be accommodated and they began arriving in March, the convict population having been transferred elsewhere. These men were not prisoners and therefore the degree of security could be relaxed: the cell doors had the locks removed and the number of warders were reduced – an unconfirmed figure of only fifty is mentioned in one account. The inmates certainly had an unprecedented amount of freedom and were free to circulate among themselves and outside the prison too in their spare time. They did not wear a uniform either and photos of them taken at the time reveal mostly fine looking young men working or relaxing in their civilian clothes.

The men worked and lived very much as the convicts had done. They were allotted every kind of labour from the kitchens (a sought after job), laundry, farm and quarry to the reclamation work on the moor. They laid a road just outside Princetown still known as 'Conchies Road' and one of the prison fields surrounding the prison farm is still called 'Conchie Field' (they all have names); it was reclaimed from a part of the then open moor by gangs who also broke up the boulders they uncovered and used the stone to build the walls surrounding it. Work was done under unarmed warder supervision but no allowances were made for their special category .

The cells were just as bleak as they always had been and the austerity of the war years meant there was a minimum of heating in winter, making it impossible to dry their clothes properly together with which Dartmoor prison food was at its worst. Potatoes and swedes were the main items in their diet supplemented by suet pudding with black molasses and jam 'roly polies' without any jam. Men's bodies developed mysterious rashes and lumps whilst attacks of dysentery were common – one man died of it at his work in the quarry having (allegedly) been refused hospital treatment. There were many ex-servicemen among the warders who set out to persecute those they regarded as traitors or cowards by making sure those they thought deserved it got the rough, dirty work and heaped verbal abuse on them at every opportunity (warders threw water over them one winter with the comment *'that's what our soldiers at the front have to put up with!'*).

Humiliated 'Conchies' at Dartmoor. The notices read: 'Sweeps – Dido and Fido'. (Courtesy Mr. M. Chamberlain).

The records of individual cases of exemption and the Minute Books of nearly every Tribunal throughout Britain were destroyed in 1921 on Government orders, the result being only two Appeal Tribunals records and some in Scotland survive. The bulk of information therefore concerning these events are only to be found in the diaries and memoirs of those who were there. The public were on the whole unsympathetic towards them, especially when some over zealous men disrupted Sunday services at Princetown Church and Chapels with outbursts of political or revolutionary rhetoric, refused to join in the singing of the National Anthem, and caused offence by singing 'The Red Flag'. At the end of morning worship at the Wesleyan Chapel one Sunday a very angry Princetown resident had had enough; after loudly singing the National Anthem in the aisle he added a few lines of his own consigning the 'conchies' to a very warm place! The Bishop of Exeter felt so strongly about them he wrote to the *Times* accusing them of planning revolution. *'Sacks of letters come and go'* he wrote *'no doubt conveying instructions for those plans of bloodshed which may come at some future time, and bring, according to their view liberty, and to our view ruin to England'*. He was referring to political troublemakers, making it plain he bore the religious objectors no ill will (yet he banned them from the prison Church of England Chapel, prompting the comment from one conscientious objector that *'if we'd been murderers we'd have had free access...'*). Alderman Windeatt, speaking at a public meeting at Totnes was more forthright, declaring the 'conchies' went in and out of the prison as they liked and could buy what they liked in the Princetown shops.

'The Commandant at Totnes hospital had received orders to cut the bread supply to the wounded (soldiers) *to six ounces a day whereas those conscientious gentlemen got nine ounces and could buy as much more as they liked. They wrote blasphemous words at the station and other places in Princetown. They sang 'Keep the Red Flag Flying' and walked out of church when 'God Save the King' was sung or played. One said he had no opinion of the King and that we would be better under a Republic. Yet the Government gave then their railway fares to visit their homes when it cost a soldier 22 shillings to come home to Totnes for a day'*.

Although such behaviour was the mischievous work of a few, much of what Mr. Windeatt said was true and it roused the public to bitter contempt for the objectors as a whole (*'Princetown's Pampered Pets'* the papers cried) but inside the prison there was much suffering bravely borne and regular well attended prayer meetings (one man obtained permission from the Governor and got three days off to walk to Plymouth and back for the purpose of being baptised). No less brave were their wives and families who were scorned by their neighbours and sometimes assaulted in the street. The bias continued after the war ended with many employers refusing point blank to employ them. Whatever one may think of these men, bearing in mind the National fervour prevalent at that time, most of us would concede they possessed a very special brand of courage to stay committed to their beliefs under the most trying circumstances.

'Conchies' trying to get warm. Dartmoor Prison, World War One. (Courtesy Mr. M. Chamberlain).

MUTINY AT DARTMOOR

The build up

The morning of 24th. January 1932 was bright and sunny, the sort of Dartmoor weather that was stimulating and pleasant. It was a tranquil start to the day for Princetown residents preparing for Sunday worship, but before that day ended there was to be terror on a scale never before witnessed either in the town or within the convict prison they lived beside.

Trouble had been brewing for weeks at Dartmoor Prison. The prisoners were surly and discontented, one of the causes being the condition of that most sacred item in a convict's life – the food. For days men had been returning their dinners and more recently refusing their morning porridge because of its watery consistency. The cook had served up satisfactory porridge in the past and could hardly be blamed for the poor quality now; the only conclusion to be drawn was that someone was tampering with it. That was not all. In the period before Christmas weapons had been found as well as ropes and hacksaw blades, all indications that an elaborate escape was being planned. There were 440 inmates in the prison at the time, all confirmed criminals of the worst kind of whom four were ringleaders suspected of creating unrest (possibly as part of the plan). The old time 'lags' had been replaced by a new kind of prisoner – crooks and robbers with cars (the 'motor bandits'), mostly young adventurous men many of whom had seen wartime action. Desperation and daring were their trademarks.

The Governor, Mr. S.N. Roberts, was a stern disciplinarian who had risen from the ranks, having previously governed in turn Swansea, Leeds and Birmingham prisons. He was a veteran of the South African War and in 1909 he joined the prison service as a warder at Wandsworth but went back to his old regiment during World War One as Acting Regimental Sergeant Major. He left the army with the rank of Second Lieutenant having spent the latter part of the war in charge of prisoner of war camps in the North of England. He rejoined the prison service in 1919 and within the year he was promoted to Governor as related. It took some time at Dartmoor for him to win the trust and respect of his officers who had been used to serving under 'officer types', but they accepted him for being fair minded and just. The same cannot be said about his relationship with the prisoners.

One significant change was made under Governor Roberts which upset the convicts and that concerned working practices whereby after three months a man could apply for, and was usually granted, permission to change his occupation. These changes were a welcome relief to inmates facing long sentences, but output suffered in the manufacturing shops and the new Governor decided to allow a change on an annual basis only, which did in fact lead to greater production but it came at a price: it was resented. It was significant too that his predecessors had all been officers or gentlemen (in the oldest sense of that word) whilst he was a 'man's man' so to speak who could give convicts a good talking to in terms they would clearly understand. Yet he could be more than fair when the occasion called for it, as when the complaints about the porridge were found to be justified: instead of being thick and nourishing it was *'like water with grains floating in it'* which was how one inmate described it. Mr. Roberts agreed and on Friday 22nd. January he issued every man with a ration of potatoes, bread and margarine in lieu of porridge.

Critical moments

Further incidents now occurred in swift succession which led ultimately to an eruption of violence. That same Friday, Officer Ernest Birch was set upon by a prisoner who slashed both sides of his face with a 'chiv' made with a razor blade fixed to a piece of wood. So severe was the attack the prison assistant medical officer had to stitch his face where it had been cut right through and where it had just missed his jugular vein. He was detained in the hospital. Governor Roberts attributed the assault to a neurotic prisoner; the medical officer thought he was a psychopath. What upset the other prisoners was the fact that Officer Birch was well liked and they feared the 'screws' would exact their revenge on his attacker in the Block, where he was of course sent. Secondly this same prisoner was popular among them and it is interesting to note that at the height of the trouble which lay ahead the mutineers made for the separate cells to free him.

At midnight on Friday a cautious Governor visited the kitchen and inspected the porridge, finding it to be *'thick and quite good'*. By 8.00am on Saturday it was watery and the suspicion was that it had again been interfered with, possibly by a prisoner helper. When corned beef was given out in lieu it was not well received. The most significant indication of trouble to come took place in the chapel later that morning when the customary short service was held and the weekly news read out. The Governor, who had difficulty getting a hearing, took the unusual step of apologising:

'I am sorry the porridge yesterday was not up to the standard and again today is not as it should be. I have arranged for the Master Cook to come in tonight and cook it himself. I hope this will satisfy you, but I am anxious to see that you get fair play'.

He then left the chapel and the Church Army Chaplain, Captain B.P H. Ball entered the pulpit and announced the hymn number. The choir and some of the men stood but were shouted down by the others and resumed their seats, refusing to take part in any hymn singing that day. Captain Ball bravely sang the hymn by himself.

A critical point had been reached and everyone knew it. The feeling among the staff was that Mr. Roberts had made a grievous error in apologising as the prisoners would regard it as a weakness which they could exploit. He himself must have realised the imminent danger because he telephoned the Home Office just before noon requesting permission to call upon the Devon County Police and Plymouth City Police for assistance if necessary, explaining the unrest and the probable cause. He was advised to call in every available officer for duty over the weekend but to call in the police only as a last resort. Accordingly the Governor telephoned the Chief Constable of Devon (who happened to be his predecessor, Major L. Morris) and Mr. K. Wilson, Chief Constable of Plymouth City Police to arrange for help should the need arise. The Prison Commissioners were so concerned however they at once sent Assistant Commissioner of Prisons Col. G. D .Turner to Dartmoor to *'assist and advise the Governor if he wanted any assistance'*.

The Mutiny

Any trouble at Dartmoor nearly always flared up at Sunday morning service, the reason being there were a minimum number of officers present in chapel. Trouble during the exercise period on the parade grounds prior to the service was rare, partly because there were more officers present and the fact it was a disciplined part of the Sunday routine. Yet this is precisely where the mutiny began.

There had been a lot of shouting during the night and banging of utensils which posed the question of whether it was wise to continue with exercise and chapel. The inmates had seen there were extra officers on duty and were muttering among themselves how *'they were getting windy'*. In one of the prison blocks there was pandemonium already with inmates yelling obscenities and singing *The Red Flag;* consequently it was decided to remove some of them to the Block and that was when another incident occurred which was misunderstood by other prisoners and inflamed the situation further. Two noisy convicts had adjacent cells, one was a known troublemaker, the other a man of limited intelligence who went quietly. The agitated prisoner continued shouting obscenities, challenging the officers *'to come and get him out'*, which Officer George Udy tried to do only to be attacked with a 'chiv'. A scuffle began and the inmate was subdued by a blow from another officer's truncheon after which he was carried to the hospital for treatment to a head wound. The rest of the men, who were still locked up but could hear what was going on, mistakenly thought the 'simple' chap had been struck and were enraged.

Parade ground and Administration Block at Dartmoor before the 1932 Mutiny.
(Courtesy Mrs. Rosie Oxenham). Image prepared by Cinnabar, Okehampton.

It was touch and go whether or not exercise and the chapel service should proceed, but the decision to let it go ahead was made after consultation between Colonel Turner and the Governor. It proved to be an error of judgement for the first serious trouble began on Officer Udy's parade when a convict ringleader called to his mates *'Draw your sticks. Up him boys and kick the ——— out of him!'* adding Udy ought to be kicked to death for knocking out a barmy prisoner (wrongly thinking it was the quiet man who had been hit earlier). The 'sticks' were hidden home made

149

coshes some prisoners had concealed about their persons. With the ringleaders shouting for them to *'come and get the rest of the boys!'* around fifty men broke ranks and followed them to the other parades where other groups broke away and joined them. It was 9.30am. The officers, outnumbered and separated, carried on as best they could returning loyal prisoners to their respective prisons or to a quiet corner of the yards where they remained until order was restored, the 'loyal' convicts being subjected to cat calls and verbal abuse by the rioters (*'come on out you —— blacklegs!'* and so on). Some officers made it to the main gate where they were issued with Snider rifles and buckshot with orders to man the outside of the walls to prevent escapes. Others either stood by their posts or tried to find a place to take refuge from a vicious mob estimated to be 150 or more strong. Several officers were attacked and injured.

At the first sign of trouble Officer E. Dowse, who was manning the main gate, telephoned Plymouth City Police on his own initiative and was assured police help would be sent. He also rang Crownhill Barracks to request military help but had difficulty making them understand what was going on. He did not need to worry because Mr .A.K. Wilson, Chief Constable at Plymouth phoned and spoke to the Commanding Officer of the 8th. Infantry Brigade to explain the situation and was promised two companies of infantry with machine guns. A bus load of Plymouth policemen thirty one strong was soon on its way to Princetown.

The Governor was in his office with his Deputy and Col. Turner when they were alerted by the racket outside, followed by the sound of shattered glass as stones were thrown at the windows. Mr. Roberts suggested calling the police but Col. Turner advised they wait. He (Col. Turner) then went out and tried to reason with the rioters only to be assaulted (he had a bowl of porridge tipped over him and was manhandled, losing his watch and some money in the process); he was saved from serious injury by a loyal convict who whisked him away to a cell and locked him in (he had only to slam the door). A ladder top then appeared at the Governor's office window and an angry mob, out to *'get the Governor'* smashed their way in, upon which the Governor and Deputy Governor ran outside, slamming the door in their faces. They managed to get into one of the old French prisons where they hid for the duration of the mutiny, aware they were the prime targets of the mutineers.

Shortly afterwards the administration block was set on fire. The convicts broke into the Records Office and threw out bundles of documents which they lit with stolen matches and threw back in to set the whole place ablaze. It burned until 9.00pm by which time the building was completely gutted and all the prison records were destroyed with it. The prison fire engine was then taken and vandalised – the rioters were after the ladders on it with which to get out over the walls; for some of them escape was the main object of the whole affair.

The prime concern was preventing escapes. The possibility of maddened convicts rampaging through Princetown was the reason those manning the prison perimeter were told to fire at anyone coming over the top of the walls. One of the officers positioned outside the walls described how the top rungs of a ladder appeared followed by a pair of hands, then the face of a prisoner whose eyes widened with surprise when he saw the officers with rifles before disappearing back inside. Other officers had the same experience and the fact that several strange cars were seen in the vicinity before and after the disturbance lends credence to the suggestion that a breakout was at the root of it all. Seven prisoners altogether were shot and wounded, one of them was on the roof of the twine shed and sustained serious injuries from a wound to his neck and from falling to the ground. Those convicts who saw it happen were incensed: *'the bastards have killed one of our men. Come on boys, stop at nothing. Murder the bastards!'*. This is one of the milder battle cries that were heard that day.

The scene in the yards resembled a nightmare: men were screaming abuse, fighting among themselves over food and cigarettes they discovered after breaking into the officers mess, blaring out tunes on stolen instruments belonging to the prison band whilst their mates partnered each other for clumsy 'dancing'. One prisoner was wearing an officer's hat, another a stolen coat, all were in a frenzy of excitement and taunting officers they met. Other men were wandering aimlessly beneath the huge cloud of black smoke rising from the burning administration building, unable to come to terms with their new-found 'freedom'. Weapons were sought and found – hammers from the internal stone sheds, butchers knives taken from the kitchen, iron bars, table legs for clubs (with broken glass embedded in them), and firemen's hatchets taken from the fire engine. The convicts had complete control of the prison and were looking for anyone or anything to attack. The Wesleyan Minister, Rev. Ernest Scholes, was spotted running to the hospital (the nearest haven) with convicts in pursuit; they were after his keys (all chaplains had keys which enabled them to move freely about the prison) especially the master key which would unlock any door (when the mob entered the Church of England Chapel a quick thinking assistant chaplain dropped his keys down one of the organ pipes). Mr. Scholes was overpowered at the hospital entrance and his keys forcibly taken from him before he was dragged safely inside and treated for shock. Having possession of keys enabled convicts to enter any building they wanted: most important to them was gaining entry to the Block which is where they made for, chanting obscene slogans and intent on releasing the worst troublemakers at Dartmoor including those who had attacked the two officers on Friday and Saturday. Two of the officers manning the Block were lucky to get away without serious injury when they arrived. They were saved by one of the original four ringleaders ('Ruby' Sparks). *'Come on let's do the bastards in'* said someone. Sparks intervened saying *'they are not the worst of 'em – let them go'* and to the officers *'go on, beat it whilst you have the chance'*. Both men wasted no time 'beating it'.

All this time yells and screams could be heard in Princetown and women looked at one another with fear in their eyes, wondering about their prison officer husbands' safety. When they saw smoke and flames rising from within the walls and heard shots being fired they were close to panic. Two little girls who lived on farms at Blackabrook were taking a short cut across the prison farm area on their way to Sunday school when the tumult erupted and fled in terror to the nearest farm where one of them lived, the other child being so scared the father took her home in his motor cycle side-car. When the police arrived at 10.50am they were greeted by waving handkerchiefs and tears of relief of women on their doorsteps. Mr .A .K. Wilson their Chief was already there, having sped on ahead by car and two more coach loads of police were on their way from Paignton and Torquay. At Exeter they were on stand-by 'ready to go' and Major Morris was on his way to the prison to help. Because the two Governors and other senior officers were either trapped or in hiding for fear of their lives Mr. Wilson took charge of the situation.

The Mutiny is Quelled

Chief Constable Wilson tried to reason with the mutineers and was greeted with jeers and shouts of *'Why don't you come and get us?'* and so on. Prison officers had the barrels of their rifles aimed at them through the bars of the inner gates and Mr. Wilson, who had thirty one policemen behind him got six prison officers with rifles to accompany him and his men who were about to enter the yards. Turning quietly to them all he said *'it's going to be them or us lads. Draw your sticks* (truncheons) *and show no mercy'*. Drawing his revolver the chief was the first man through the gates heading a charge of thirty eight men against over a hundred armed criminals.

It says much for the discipline and determination of those policemen, armed only with wooden truncheons, that they fought and won a battle with some of the most violent prisoners in Britain wielding weapons that could kill. It was all over in about fifteen minutes. The mutineers made the mistake of breaking up into groups who were more easily subdued; a pitched battle would have been harder to overcome. There were broken limbs and broken heads for the medical officer to mend and some casualties among the policemen but nothing serious. *'These chaps are pretty tough when menacing the weak and defenceless'* remarked one policeman *'but you should hear the squeals when they are on the receiving end'*.

Deputy Governor's office wrecked during the Mutiny.
(Courtesy P.C. Simon Dell, M.B.E., Tavistock).

The Aftermath

The prisoners who took part in the disturbance were stripped and searched before being either returned to their cells or taken to the hospital for treatment to their wounds. The ringleaders and their supporters were confined in the separate cells. Colonel Turner came stumbling up the drive dazed and shocked. Governor Roberts and his Deputy came out of hiding when the police charged in and told their story. There were plenty of stories to tell, among them:

How the rioters broke into the boiler house intent on roughing up the officer in charge and how he was protected by the loyal prisoner helper who hid him behind the boiler and smashed the water level gauge glass (a highly dangerous and brave thing to do), releasing high pressure steam in a roaring, scalding, blinding cloud, causing the intruders to quickly withdraw.

One of the policemen who took part was a plain clothes CID man who had turned up for work that morning and was bundled into the waiting coach with the others.

How a prisoner in the act of munching a sandwich was met by a policeman. "What kind of sandwich have you got there?" he was asked. "It's a ham one" he replied. "Well try making a ham sandwich out of this!" said the copper thumping him on the head with his truncheon.

How several officers were warned by the men who took no part in the riot of approaching dangerous mutineers and protected them from assault. These men were not forgotten when the reports were made, together with some who took part in the rioting yet had the basic decency to stop the others from inflicting harm: they were recommended for leniency at their trial afterwards.

How about one hundred armed soldiers arrived from Crownhill as promised and took up positions outside the gate to prevent a mass escape. Luckily their services were not after all required.

The police from Paignton and Torquay arrived too late to take part in the proceedings. Exeter police were summoned to their headquarters and waited on stand-by but were told to stand down shortly afterwards.

Governor Roberts was moved to Cardiff. Major Morris, who had been a popular Governor (he received several cheery greetings from inmates who remembered him) played a large part in restoring things to normal at Dartmoor. Major Charles Pannall. M.C., D.S.O. (formerly in charge at Camp Hill Borstal Institution, I.O.W.) was specially chosen to be the new Governor and he remained at Dartmoor for the next thirteen years which included the duration of World War Two.

Casualties
Prisoners:
From police truncheons: twenty three and ten more in the prison hospital.
Firearm wounds: seven of whom four were in hospital.
Injuries from fellow prisoners: exact number unknown but two in hospital.
Bruises, minor wounds and some burns: nine prisoners in hospital but several more unreported.

Officers:
Officer Birch (whose face was badly cut) was later transferred to Plymouth hospital.
Four Officers badly hurt and off sick.
About twenty Officers suffered less serious injuries, out of which four had hospital treatment.
The others carried on with their duties.
One Officer was afterwards invalided out of the Service.

Miraculously no-one escaped and no-one was killed.

The Administration Building, Dartmoor Prison – gutted by fire during the 1932 Mutiny. (Courtesy P.C. Simon Dell, M.B.E., Tavistock).

Retribution

For security reasons it had been decided the trial of the mutineers would be held at a Special Assize Court in Princetown where a total of thirty one convicts faced charges of assault, malicious damage, maliciously setting fire to an office with intent to injure, and *'being riotously and tumultuously assembled with others to the disturbance of the public peace, feloniously, unlawfully and with force did demolish, pull down or destroy, or begin to pull down, demolish or destroy, a building devoted to public use, or erected or maintained by public contribution'*. The defendants included a teacher, tailor, song writer, carpenter and engineer.

The Duchy Hall (since demolished but which was situated opposite Princetown Primary School) was converted for courtroom use by erecting a tiered dock with rails to which the prisoners were handcuffed. The Judge's Chair was brought from Exeter and the school made available for the Barristers to change into their robes and whigs.

The proceedings commenced on 23rd. April 1932 before The Right Honourable William Viscount Finlay, K.B.E., one of the Justices of the Kings Bench Division of the High Court of Justice. The Jury sat facing the dock where every defendant could be clearly seen. The results were as follows:

Nine verdicts of 'Not guilty'.

Four found 'Guilty' of riotous assembly. Two were given ten years and two given eight years penal servitude.

Sixteen 'Guilty' of malicious damage. One given six years, two given four years, seven given three years and sentences of twenty one months, twenty months, eighteen months (2), fifteen months and six months penal servitude to the others.

One sent to serve the remainder of his sentence after pleading 'Guilty' to the above.

One 'Guilty of malicious damage and riotous assembly' (ten years penal servitude).

The two men who attacked Officers Birch and Udy were tried separately and with a different Jury. Thomas Davis was found 'Guilty' of inflicting grievous bodily harm to Officer Birch and received twelve years penal servitude. David Brown who was charged with attempting to maliciously wound or cause grievous bodily harm to Officer Udy was found 'Not Guilty'.

Twenty seven 'loyal' convicts had their sentences reduced and eleven were therefore released immediately.

CALENDAR OF PRISONERS

AT THE

ASSIZES

BEFORE

The Right Honourable William Viscount Finlay, K.B.E.,
One of the Justices of the King's Bench Division of the High Court of Justice

HOLDEN AT

P R I N C E T O W N

On Monday, the 25th day of April, 1932.

SAMUEL MANNING MANNING-KIDD, Esq., High Sheriff.

HENRY FORD, Esq., Under Sheriff.

JOHN WILLIAM ST. LAWRANCE LESLIE, Esq., Clerk of Assize.

INDEX.

Beadles, William H.	....	3
Brown, David	....	2
Bullows, Thomas	....	4
Burgess, Harry	....	5
Castor, Anthony	....	6
Conning, Joseph	....	7
Cosgrove, Patrick	....	8
Davis, Thomas	....	1
Del-Mar, James	....	9
Dewhurst, Thomas E.	....	10
Gardner, William	....	11
Garton, George	....	12
Greenhow, Alfred	....	13
Hardy, Herbert	....	14
Hart, Alfred	....	15
Hill, Albert H.	....	16
Horn, James	....	17
Ibbesson, James	....	18
Jackson, otherwise Robb, John	....	19
James, Edward	....	20
Kavanagh, Patrick	....	21
Kendall, Victor	....	22
Mason, William	....	23
Moore, Walter F.	....	24
Muir, Alexander	....	25
Mullins, John	....	26
Roberts, Frederick	....	27
Saxton, Charles A.	....	28
Smith, Frederick	....	29
Sparks, Charles J.	....	30
Stoddart, Harry	....	31
Tappenden, Sidney	....	32
Taylor, Joseph	....	33

(Courtesy Mr. B. Estill, Devon & Cornwall Constabulary Museum, Exeter).

MORE HARD TIMES

When Major Pannall took over the Governorship at Dartmoor prison in 1932 (after the mutiny) there can be no doubt a firm hand was required and here was a man who was capable of delivering it. During his thirteen years in office he showed a great deal of understanding and flexibility but coming as he did from a tough establishment (the Borstals were renowned for troublemakers) and with his wartime military experience, he too could be tough and uncompromising when the situation demanded it.

Despite some of the old customs that still prevailed at Dartmoor, much had changed since the really bad old days. Since the 1920s, for example, the closets in the yards had been modernised so that individual closets with doors and proper facilities had replaced the buckets with wooden cross beams for seats that previously served the convicts needs (prisoners tied their handkerchief to the door handle to indicate it was occupied). 'Slopping out' (the term used for emptying the overnight contents of prisoners' cell pots) continued for another seventy odd years. The Silent Rule was not as rigorously enforced, talking being permitted during exercise or association and as necessary in the workplace, but no idle or prolonged conversations were allowed (the charge would have been *'disobedience of orders by talking after being told to stop'*). By the 1930s the old style convict dress had been discarded to be replaced by more conventional attire (in the 1960s shirts and ties were worn) and the arrow symbol had disappeared from clothes and boots. Some of the other conditions which applied at that time included:

Laundry:	Weekly	Fortnightly	Monthly	Yearly
	Aprons	Pillow slips	Sheets	Blankets
	Dusters	Bolster cases		
	Handkerchiefs	Mattress covers		
	Towels			

Stages: 1st. 2nd. 3rd. and Special Stage (the origin of the term 'Old Stagers').
Each Stage was of one year duration.

Privileges   2nd. 3rd. and Special Stages could attend concerts, lectures, etc.

Association: 2nd.Stage two evenings a week
3rd. Stage three evenings a week.
Special Stage every evening.

Special Stage prisoners were allowed to smoke in a smoking room provided and one paper per week up to 6d. in value, paid for privately. No criminal or unsavoury contents or betting news.

Exercise: After examination by the medical officer, men were graded A or B.
Qualified instructors only.

Grade A   Exercise under supervision from Physical Training Table Card or
War Office P.T. Manual.
Marching and running in lieu of P.T.

Grade B   Must always have the best Instructor
Where no Instructor was available – walking or marching in lieu.

Bathing   Must bath at least once a week.

Going to Bed   Not permitted until specified time.

The characters of those who were sent to Dartmoor had not changed though. The Governor himself was viciously attacked when paying a visit to the Block. Two men, both former Borstal prisoners were awaiting trial for assaulting an officer, and Major Pannall had permitted them to sit outside their cells with the doors open. When he entered the building he was attacked by them, one man leaping on his back without warning and slashing his face with a razor blade they'd managed to conceal. He needed several stitches. Further problems arose when men began refusing meals allegedly because of poor quality. It seems certain from what the Governor wrote at the time that a group of troublemakers were behind it all who hoped to gain a more varied diet and possibly other concessions. Major Pannall was not a man to be trifled with however and in any case it was stated by some of the men that they took part because they were frightened of 'the Gang'. The figures speak for themselves:

5th. June 1939	135 prisoners returned dinner.
6th. June	30 returned breakfast and 60 their dinners.
7th. June	18 returned breakfast and 57 their dinners.
8th. June	80 returned dinners.
9th. June	Returning of meals ceased. (Nothing gained – and they were hungry).

Then the IRA arrived. There had been a nasty incident in Coventry that year when an explosion occurred killing several civilians. Those responsible were caught and tried after which twenty members of the IRA ended up on the Moor. They made trouble from the start, but significantly they were set upon by other prisoners at morning parade after boasting about their 'exploits'. Two of them had to go to hospital after being punched and kicked to an extent that the officers had great difficulty in getting them away from their attackers.

In September a number of military prisoners from Chelmsford arrived and Major Pannall was 'unfavourably impressed with them'. He summoned the senior officers and told them 'that the slightest sign of insubordination must be firmly dealt with, very firmly'. This was repeated to the Officers on parade the next day.

The Governor and his staff then faced problems of another kind on the outbreak of World War Two on 3rd. September 1939. Senior officers were appointed ARP (Air Raid Precaution) Wardens responsible for blacking out the windows at night with black curtains some of which went missing. It should be explained that prisoners who smoked lit their cigarettes with an ingenious home-made device comprising a tin for keeping a piece of burnt rag, a needle or an old razor blade, and a small stone. Striking the metal sharply against the stone produced a spark which, with careful nurturing and blowing, could be coaxed into a glowing ember with which to 'light up' (in later years strands taken from mop heads served the same purpose). No doubt this was the fate of the missing curtains! If compelled to buy matches prisoners learned the art of splitting each matchstick into five or six individual ones.

Gas mask drills were introduced when every inmate was issued with this device and taught how to wear it. Fire drills followed and preparations made in case the prison was hit by a bomb. Several men made applications to join the armed forces and many of them were granted. 'Ruby' Sparks who took a leading part in the 1932 mutiny at Dartmoor was one who was successful and joined the Army. He is remembered today by his old Commanding Officer, Col. F. Theobold of Moretonhampstead, as having all the makings of a good soldier but Sparks got into trouble over forged ration and identity cards as a result of which he was soon back on the Moor. He is better remembered now as the man who holds the 20th. century Dartmoor Prison record for being at large for 170 days after escaping in January 1940, aided by the wartime blackout.

When France was occupied and an invasion of Britain appeared imminent it was decided to transfer prisoners from Parkhurst on the Isle of Wight to the comparative safety of Dartmoor. The 'Princetown Flier' was commandeered for the day of their arrival and all passengers for Princetown that day travelled by special buses provided by the GWR. The newcomers were manacled for the journey and marched from Princetown station between rows of prison officers who lined the route to the prison, under the gaze of large crowds of curious spectators. In the prison blocks they were accommodated three to a cell until more suitable arrangements could be made.

There was further trouble from the IRA prisoners in March 1940 when, after being set to work as a separate group, they refused certain tasks and their ringleader was taken to the Block for punishment. This inflamed the situation and culminated in an incident when, after one Officer went to the canteen to fetch what they'd ordered, his colleague was overpowered, his keys and whistle taken, and he was locked in a cell. The prisoners then barricaded the entrance doors and proceeded to smash up the place. Using the stolen keys, they obtained picks and shovels from the store where they were kept and forced doors from their hinges, broke up slate floors and set light to their bedding. It was 3.30pm before officers finally managed to break in and arrest the culprits who were put in solitary confinement in the Block. There they refused to wear any clothing and for days stayed in their cells with just a towel for covering. Eventually they were split up and sent to other prisons.

Up until the outbreak of war the Governor had made efforts to maintain morale by permitting concerts at regular intervals. A Methodist choir sang at morning service, the Salvation Army band performed, a company performed *The Cat and the Canary* (an unusual choice for a convict prison, being a thriller play), the Palace Theatre (Plymouth) Orchestra gave a performance, followed by the then world famous Geraldo and his band. On 10th. March 1940 inmates were treated to the first film show ever at Dartmoor – the records refer to 'a picture cinematograph'. All these entertainments took place in the Church of England Chapel.

The prison ran like clockwork under Governor Pannall who fully justified the faith placed in him following the mutiny. He made the occasional misjudgement (as when he was cut about the face in the Block) but he evidently showed a generous amount of understanding towards his charges tempered by ruthless retribution towards offenders. As one old hand put it: *'they knew exactly where they stood'.*

From the Governor's journal:

3rd. September 1940 *Prisoner H—— threw tea over the M.O. and Chief Officer.*

4th. September 1940 *A number of prisoners in each hall refused to go to their cells at 12 noon. I ordered large staves to be issued to Officers and I went to the halls. After some demur they went to their cells.*

20th. September *Secretary of State confirmed 12 strokes of the birch on H——. It was carried out at 12.15pm this day.*

8th. November *Officer M—— was assaulted by F—— in B Hall this morning.*

2nd. December *Twelve strokes with the Birch Rod on F—— was approved and inflicted at 12.30 p.m.*

Prison Officers' cap badges. Two patterns for two reigns – H.M. Queen Elizabeth II and H.M. King George VI.
(Courtesy Dartmoor Prison Museum)

Chief Officer's cap badge and epaulettes.
(Courtesy Dartmoor Prison Museum)

Chief Officer's cap badge and cloth epaulettes which replaced the stainless steel type shown above because of injury risk during forcible restraints.
(Courtesy Dartmoor Prison Museum)

26th. February 1941	*The Governor was assaulted by prisoners J—— and McC——. in E Hall.*
10th. March	*12 strokes with the Birch Rod on McC——18 strokes with the cat on J——. Approved and inflicted this day.*
22nd. August	*Officer Gurton was seriously assaulted by K——.*
18th. October	*18 lashes with the Cat o' nine tails was inflicted on K—— at 12.15 p.m. this day.*

On 31st. March 1941 the Governor handed over to his Deputy and went to London to receive the O.B.E. from His Majesty the King. World War Two ended in 1945 and Major Pannall left Dartmoor that same year. In November a number of Borstal inmates arrived and were so troublesome they were transferred back to the Isle of Wight.

The post war years brought no immediate improvements to Dartmoor. It was a period of austerity and struggle to return the country as a whole to normal in the aftermath of the biggest upheaval ever in the history of our island. There was little change in the prison regime and lack of investment made matters worse. The boundary wall was crumbling, wet infiltrated the cells, especially on the top floors of the wings so that some of them became uninhabitable. In the early 1950s one complete wing was demolished, having deteriorated beyond repair and the huge hut that houses the present day gymnasium was built on the foundations.

The old kitchens with gaps in the roof were the refuge of jackdaws and cockroaches; during the war years one of the old 'French' prisons (the very one where Governor Roberts took refuge in the mutiny) was reduced to a single storey building and converted for use as a replacement kitchen. Food for each wing had to be taken in containers on trolleys across the open yards in all weathers. The sanitary arrangement were the same as they had been for decades and the early morning 'slopping out' routine was the most nauseating memory inmates took with them when they left the Moor. Uncertainty and indecision on the part of successive Governments meant that the prison was falling into decay amid rumours that the place would soon be shut down. This state of affairs lasted until the 1990s when severe criticism by the Prison Inspectorate at last compelled the authorities to begin a programme of modernisation.

BAD GUYS AND ESCAPEES

All prisoners are bad guys or they would not be where they are and Dartmoor prison has had more than its share of the worst of them. Some of them were accorded fame and notoriety they did not entirely deserve and such a one was Frank Mitchell, the 'Mad Axeman'. His disappearance from an outside work party on the moor in December 1966 sparked the biggest

Frank Mitchell, the 'Mad Axeman'.
(Courtesy Mirror Syndicates International)

manhunt in Dartmoor Prison's history and dominated the newspaper headlines for weeks. 'Big Frank' (6 ft. tall with a huge physique) was a dangerous individual but contrary to what the public thought at the time (and some still do) the 'Axeman' never killed anyone. He was of limited intelligence and subject to fits of rage terrifying in their ferocity but the prison officers soon learned how to handle him and the old hands who were there at the time will tell you he was generally compliant providing he wasn't provoked. He had one conviction for robbery with violence and was flogged at least twice for assaulting prison officers in other prisons. He was an habitual criminal with convictions for burglary, larceny, office breaking and receiving. When he threatened an elderly couple in their home with an axe whilst on the run after breaking out of Broadmoor the press were quick to allocate him the title for which he is remembered today and which he himself revelled in.

Mitchell vanished without trace. He was given permission during a break from work to feed some ponies a short distance away from the hut the party were using and disappeared. It is now known he was a close associate of the Kray gang and was visited in prison by Charlie Kray. By the time the alarm was raised Mitchell was speeding along the A30 (in the car that rendezvoused with him by arrangement) bound for London where he was harboured by one of the Krays. He was murdered later because allegedly he had become a liability. Nobody was ever charged with his murder and his body was never found.

John George Haigh was a different type. Dapper, debonair, good looking, and an immaculate dresser, Haigh was one of the most cold blooded killers of the 20th. century. He was in Dartmoor after being convicted for fraud and earned the nickname *'Old Corpus Delicti'* (*Corpus Delicti* (Latin) = body of offence) for arguing continuously with his fellow inmates a charge of murder would never be upheld without a body. He was hanged in 1949 after being convicted of what he thought were the perfect murders – disposing of the bodies in a bath of sulphuric acid and simply pulling the plug when they had dissolved. His was not the only such case. A Union Castle Line steward, James Camb, was sentenced to hang for the murder of South African film star Gay

Gibson on the 'Durban Castle' bound for Cape Town. He pushed her body through a porthole into the sea. He was a lucky man because his sentence was suspended during a trial period prior to capital punishment being abolished when his death sentence was commuted to life imprisonment. He too was on the Moor for a time.

The 'Tichborne Claimant' was famous for what he was – a claimant to a fabulously wealthy family fortune. The Tichborne family resided at Tichborne Hall in Hampshire and their only son Roger Charles Doughty Tichborne was their heir. He had set off to see the world and was lost at sea in 1854 when the ship went down with all hands in a storm whilst on a voyage from Rio de Janeiro to New York. His distraught mother never came to terms with his death and advertised world wide for information about him. It arrived from Australia in the form of one Arthur Orton, alias Thomas Castro, son of a Wandsworth butcher and a clever actor claiming to be her son whom she had not seen for several years. Everyone except the mother knew at once he was an impostor even after the family doctor carried out a physical examination and confirmed various birthmarks and defects known to have been those of the missing man (one wonders what the doctor may have been offered). Orton took the family to court over his claim and lost. The result was a trial for him on a charge of perjury that lasted 180 days. Found guilty as charged, Orton was awarded fourteen years Penal Servitude and sent to Dartmoor. There he was revered by many awe-struck inmates and treated with contempt by a few, but maintained his assumed identity to the end. He was released in 1884 and promptly confessed to being a fraudster. Mrs. Moreton, wife of the Mr. Moreton who met prisoners at Plymouth and took them to the prison in wagonettes, believed in him and on hearing one of her husband's passengers had been the famous claimant declared *'he should have had a carriage and pair!'*.

In November 1932 two prisoners, Michael Gaskin and Frederick Amey were helping to repair the roof of one of the prison blocks and awaited their opportunity to abscond. When it came they grabbed the ladder they were using and ran with it to the wall close by the American cemetery, climbed up and over and were gone, disappearing into a Dartmoor mist. They were out for five days, during which time the warders and police were sent on wild goose chases not only on the moor but as far afield as Gunnislake in Cornwall and Chagford on the far side of Dartmoor, following up reports of sightings. Men went for days without shaving or eating properly and were at the end of their tether when the Chief Constable, Major L. Morris, M.C. who was also a former Governor at the prison, decided to shorten the search times and cover a wide area in very quick time by hiring an aeroplane from Haldon (Exeter) airfield. He himself took off with the pilot/owner Mr. W. Parkhouse and together they made several flights, the first time ever a plane was used for this purpose. At one point they saw a white dog in the woods near Lydford apparently excited by something in the bushes nearby. As they could not distinguish anything significant Major Morris thought it must be a rabbit that attracted the animal. In a way it certainly was because the residents on the moor referred to escaped convicts as *'rabbits'* and to *'catch a rabbit'* was to earn the £5 reward for doing so. Amey and Gaskin were hiding in those bushes and were desperately trying to shoo the dog away when the plane appeared. Both men lay low hoping for the best when Amey looked up and said to his comrade *'I bet that's Major Morris in that bloody aircraft!'*. They were recaptured a day or two afterwards just outside Exeter on the railway line they'd been following. Both men were chilled to the bone and developed pneumonia after being returned to prison.

Police road block during convict hunt 1950s. A rare picture of an armed policeman (P.C. Fice) openly displaying his revolver.
(Courtesy P.C. Simon Dell, M.B.E., Tavistock).

Road block during hunt for escaped convict, 1920s. Policeman and Warder work together.
(Courtesy P.C. Simon Dell, M.B.E., Tavistock).

Some escapes have ended in tragedy. One well remembered incident concerned Dennis Stafford and William Joseph Day who absconded on January 25th. 1959 in atrocious weather. The searchers caught sight of them briefly near Burrator then nothing was heard or seen of them until 16th. February when a passer by at Burrator Reservoir caught sight of a body in the lake submerged in several feet of water. It was Day and the true circumstances about his death will never be known, only that he died by drowning. Curiously, he had previously got away from Exeter Prison and was recaptured near Crediton completely submerged in the River Yeo and breathing through a hollow reed. Had he attempted to do the same again when his pursuers got close? As for Stafford, he was linked to a stolen car taken from Yelverton (a prison mitten was found nearby) and was recaptured forty seven days later in the London area. Stafford (who was a handsome man with a reputation as a 'playboy') had escaped from prison before and was recaptured in Port of Spain, Jamaica. After his release he was sentenced to life imprisonment for murder in 1967, a case which was the basis for the film *Get Carter* starring Michael Caine. After being released on licence in 1979 Stafford was in prison twice more and recommended for parole on the second occasion, a decision which was overruled by the Home Secretary. On 28th. May 2002 he was awarded £17,865 in legal costs and more than £10,000 damages by the European Court of Human Rights in Strasbourg for being illegally detained longer than the Parole Board recommendation.

Tragedy of another kind befell prison farm foreman Mr.D.Kennelly on October 1st. 1972 when two inmates, George Peart (serving six years for forgery and theft) and Peter Frost (doing six years for burglary), attacked him in a cowshed before stealing the farm van in order to escape. Mr. Kennelly was bound hand and foot with sisal cord and tape, his wrists tied behind his back and a cloth placed over his head and mouth to prevent him shouting for help. It took him two hours to break free from the water trough he'd been tied to, then (still bound and gagged) he managed to roll across a field to the Rundlestone – Two Bridges road where a passing motorist rescued him. Both prisoners were later arrested in London and returned to Dartmoor. At Bodmin Crown Court they each received a further eighteen months to their sentences for taking a vehicle without consent and causing bodily harm. Mr. Kennelly had hospital treatment for his injuries but left the prison service shortly afterwards, unable to continue because of his experience at the hands of two low category inmates who were due for release the same year.

There have been countless escapes by prisoners on the Moor since Dartmoor opened in 1809. Most of the convict escapers were recaptured and the police prided themselves on doing so before the they got out of the County. Bloodhounds were occasionally used and were 'borrowed' from local owners, one of whom bred them at her kennels at Bratton Clovelly. At one time whenever a convict escaped two police cars were despatched, one to Dartmoor Prison to collect the 'mug shot' of the man concerned and one to Mrs. Blackiston at Bratton Clovelly to fetch a hound, often a dog called Turpin who was known to be a good tracker.

Every trick you ever heard of has been tried by Dartmoor prisoners with escape in mind. Skeleton keys made from wood or bone have been found, ropes with hooks to enable a man to get over the wall, hacksaws and knotted sheets for getting through the barred windows and abseiling to the ground; convicts have torn up the floors, tried digging their way out (the French and American prisoners of war tried this), or just making a run for it.

Bloodhounds getting the scent before tracking escaped convicts from Dartmoor Prison, 1931.
(Courtey P.C. Simon Dell, M.B.E., Tavistock). Image prepared by Cinnabar, Okehampton.

From *The Beat on Western Dartmoor* by Simon Dell, M.B.E.
'November 14th. 1880
Sir,
I have the honour to report for your information that on Friday last, the 12th. instant, a party of convicts working at the quarry at Princetown made an attempt to escape. One convict struck down a warder and a second convict struck down another warder. The two convicts (one named Thomas Bevan and the other Thomas O'Brian) then endeavoured to get off by running out of the quarry, at the same time calling on the other convicts to join. But the warders and guard were prepared and three of the guard fired at the two convicts. Bevan was shot dead and O'Brian was mortally wounded.

> *I have the honour to be Sir,*
> *Your obedient servant*
> *(Signed) William Mitchell. Superintendent.'*

The question is often asked *'why are escapes so few and far between today?'*. The answer is twofold: there are not such desperate criminals at Dartmoor these days with the means of obtaining outside help (Frank Mitchell for example); secondly every escape attempt is examined and any loophole in the defences are sealed. Security now is far greater than it was when Mitchell got away. As a result of the publicity and national concern then, the Mountbatten Enquiry, which had been set up under Lord Louis Mountbatten to investigate the circumstances surrounding the escape of master spy George Blake from Wormwood Scrubs, was extended to Dartmoor and their recommendations were accepted. A security fence was erected inside the boundary wall, security lighting was installed, and radio contact established from a control room in the prison to every officer (the officer in charge of Mitchell's party had to go to a nearby village and use the public call box to report his escape).

This chapter closes with an account of an extremely rare occurrence – murder inside a prison. It happened in the chapel (the old No. 4 block from the War Depot days) which was also the venue for film shows and concerts. The details of this incident reveal the worst of Dartmoor prison 'culture' at that time. Out of 500 inmates twenty two were serving terms of life imprisonment, over 200 had ten to fifteen years to serve and a similar number were serving five and ten years; many of them were murderers and men convicted of violent offences.

On Sunday 11th. June 1961 there was an afternoon film show (*The Blue Lamp*) during which a knife fight took place, the result of which was that one man died on the premises and another two were wounded. The dead man was thirty eight year old Harold Dennis Thirkettle, a native of Hull serving a twelve year sentence for manslaughter who was stabbed by Matthew Nwachukwa, a Nigerian serving ten years for wounding, procuring and living on immoral earnings. The other two were Joseph Lane aged twenty eight, a Yorkshire man serving eight years for manslaughter, and thirty seven year old Thomas Williams, a Welshman with fourteen previous convictions.

The incident occurred during the final part of the film when a disturbance alerted the officers who at once switched on the lights. Nwachukwa was standing on a pew and appeared to be holding other prisoners at bay with his arm raised and a knife in his hand dripping blood. Two officers managed to grab the knife and hustle him away to protect him from a large number of inmates threatening to kill him (he already had a knife wound in his back). Lane and Williams had serious knife wounds. Then Thirkettle was seen being carried by other prisoners who told officers he had also been stabbed and this was found to be the case – three stab wounds to the chest, one of which had penetrated his heart. He died soon afterwards. The weapon came from the prison mat shop and had the word 'grass' scratched on the handle. It had been thrust into Nwachukwa's back and left there; the victim himself had managed to remove it and in a frenzy of fear stabbed all three wounded men sitting behind him in the belief it was one of them who carried out the attack (he had been warned he might be attacked because sex offenders were disliked).

Nwachukwa stood trial for manslaughter at Winchester Assizes, pleading not guilty on the grounds he had acted in self defence, and this was accepted by the Judge and Jury who found him *'Not Guilty'*. No further charges were brought concerning the other two stabbings. Who stabbed Nwachukwa? Dartmoor prisoners would not talk openly about it neither would they give evidence, but police officers heard enough from them *'off the record'* to be convinced it was not the dead man who did it.

'The Mounties' leaving the prison on a typical Dartmoor misty day.
(Courtesy Mr. Brian Jones).

Discharge Party returning 'home' after working clearing the prison leat, the prison's water supply in the 1950s. These prisoners had less than six months left to serve, hence their DP title.
(Courtesy Mr. Brian Jones).

INSTRUCTIONS FOR THE GUIDANCE OF OFFICERS IN THE USE OF FIREARMS.

ESCAPE OR ATTEMPTED ESCAPE.

1. In case of absolute necessity it is lawful to fire at a Felon but not a Misdemeanant if an escape cannot be otherwise prevented.

2. If it becomes necessary to shoot, the first shot should be aimed well above the escaping convict, and if a second shot is required it should be aimed low, so as to avoid the danger of wounding a vital part.

MUTINY OR VIOLENCE.

1. If two or more convicts combine to escape, or perform any act of mutiny or violence which is the legal duty of an officer to prevent, and if force is used or threatened by such convicts in resisting officers in the execution of their duty, and there are reasonable grounds to suppose that the officers may be by such force overpowered, or suffer bodily harm, then it is justifiable to use firearms, if the force used or threatened by such convicts could not be resisted by other means.

2. If in any circumstances a convict gives an officer reasonable grounds for believing himself to be in peril of his life, or bodily harm, the officer is entitled to use firearms if he cannot protect himself by other means.

3. Except in the case of absolute necessity a Warning should always be given before firearms are used, and as far as possible aim should always be taken to avoid wounding a vital part.

GOVERNOR.
H.M.PRISON
DARTMOOR
29 - 5 - 35

'RUBY' SPARKS
Notorious escapee and one of Dartmoor's most colourful characters

John Charles 'Ruby' Sparks, army deserter (two weeks) in 1923 and habitual criminal. Convictions for larceny, garage breaking and other crimes. Escaped from Borstal, Wandsworth and Strangeways prisons as well as from Dartmoor. Sentenced in 1930 for conspiracy, larceny, shop breaking and being an habitual criminal. At Dartmoor from 1931 to 1938 . In 1939 he was back at Dartmoor again. On the outbreak of war he volunteered for the British Army but was soon in trouble and was sent back to the Moor. He escaped in January 1940 and was at large for 170 days, aided by the wartime blackout – an all time record for the 20th. century for Dartmoor prison escapes.

Sparks was a ringleader in the 1932 Dartmoor prison mutiny at which time he was thirty years of age and described as a bookmaker. He was employed on the coal party for the prison boiler house and was seen inciting others to arson; he was afterwards charged with inciting other prisoners to mutiny and arson (he actively assisted, if not instigated, the burning down of the administration block during the mutiny). He also saved a warder from being attacked and probably killed by other inmates. At the subsequent trial of thirty one mutineers he was sentenced to an additional four years penal servitude and would undoubtedly have got a more severe punishment were it not for the fact he did what he did for the warder.

He was dubbed 'Ruby' Sparkes by the underworld after breaking into a Park Lane apartment belonging to a Maharajah and stealing, amongst other things, a quantity of rubies which he afterwards gave away believing they were fakes. In fact they were worth over £40,000. He was only sixteen at the time. His girlfriend was Lilian Goldstein (known to the police and the public as the 'Bobbed Haired Bandit') who drove a Mercedes motor car for Sparks when she accompanied him on 'smash and grab' raids on jewellers shops, the first of the so-called 'car bandits'.

THE LANDLORD PAYS A CALL

In July 1981 H.R.H. Prince Charles, Duke of Cornwall, toured his Duchy Estates which includes the Forest of Dartmoor within which Princetown lies. The visit incorporated an inspection of one of his leasehold possessions, Dartmoor Prison.

After meeting fifty members of staff and their wives at the 'Old Duchy' (now the High Moorland Visitor Centre) the Prince was conducted around the prison by the Governor, Mr. Colin Heald, during which he presented the Imperial Service Medal to a number of staff with long term service records. Prince Charles received a miniature ball and chain made specially for the occasion by Mr. 'Bert' Hancock, instructor in the prison blacksmith shop.

The accompanying photographs were taken by Officer Roy Johnson to record this memorable event.

Dartmoor Prison Governor, Mr Colin Heald (left), introduces the Prince to the Methodist Minister, Rev. L. Smith (right). In uniform is Chief Officer Arthur Rendle who was responsible for security.

On a stroll around the prison farm dairy. A cheerful party is led by Mr. John Higgs, Secretary to the Duchy of Cornwall (carrying stick), followed by Chief Officer A. Rendle, H.R.H. Prince Charles and farm foreman Mr John Kingman (in light clothing) alongside Mr. John Hitchings, Land Steward to the Duchy. The three men at the rear were members of the Royal Protection Squad.

Prison Officer Barry Hicks (left) shaking hands with Prince Charles. Chief Officer Rendle looks on with Governor Mr. C. Heald (right). Senior Officers A. Stoddern (left) and R. McAdams stand to attention far right.

DARTMOOR PRISON RENEWED

(The author gratefully acknowledges the kind assistance of Dartmoor Prison Governor Graham Johnson and Governor Roger Brown in preparing this final chapter).

Closing Dartmoor.

Rumours about closing Dartmoor Prison began in 1864.

From the *Tavistock Gazette* 4th. November 1864: *'Notice of the appointment of a Captain Clifton as Governor of Dartmoor Prison. It is generally believed at Princetown that the Dartmoor prisons will not remain open for more than two more years'*.

The *Western Morning News* July 1891: *'In the Dartmoor prisons a large reduction is being made in the number of convicts. A little over twelve months since there were over 1,000 there; now there are only 462 it is rumoured that the closing of the convict prison there 'ere long is not improbable'*.

2nd.June 1992: *'CLOSE DOWN DARTMOOR!'* were the headlines in the (Plymouth) *Evening Herald* reporting on the Inspection made by H.M. Chief Inspector of Prisons (Judge Stephen Tumim) in June 1991 which condemned the prison as *'an unsanitary outdated dustbin'*. Similar comments were made prior to the 1932 mutiny and during the 1950s and 1960s when the number of escapes reached unprecedented levels.

Following Judge Tumim's inspection, which took place just three months after a serious riot during which one wing was wrecked and an inmate died, several million pounds were spent on refurbishing and modernising. The prison has been transformed. There is a new central heating system, an up to date kitchen, a well equipped gymnasium, an all weather football pitch, and covered passageways to all parts of the prison. Gone are the Snider carbines, the nailed boots and the weekly trek to the bathhouse where prisoners were issued with clean underwear only after bathing; the 'cat' and the birch rod were abolished in 1967, and the 'bread and water' dietary punishments ended in 1979; troublesome inmates are no longer put in straitjackets or padded cells; even the Block has been closed and replaced by a Care and Control Unit situated in one of the wings. Convicted men at Dartmoor still occupy individual cells and take their meals in them, but they smoke at will and talk to their heart's content.

Prison today

Dartmoor is now a Category C (low security) prison and there are three grades of prisoners:

Basic   Non-compliant men who refuse work, are dirty, or badly behaved.

Standard   Represent the majority who observe the rules and give no trouble.

Enhanced   Good workers, trustworthy and orderly.

The privileges which are available are geared to a prisoner's grade, thus encouraging co-operation and improvement. The Prison Service is responsible for inmates' health and well-being whilst in custody which is why matters such as good food and facilities (showers have been installed in the wings) have improved.

The most important aspect of prison life for an inmate is the quality and quantity of the food. The days when they got a pint of 'skilly' for breakfast and a putrid stew for dinner have disappeared for ever. The kitchen staff used to receive bulk deliveries of foodstuffs which they had to manipulate in order to produce palatable meals. Now they order what they actually need for the following week out of a monetary budget they control. Prisoners, including vegetarians, Muslims, etc. choose what they want for lunch and tea a week in advance, one item only from a weekly numbered menu. This reduces waste and is more efficient, but more importantly it ensures the inmates get the necessary vitamins, etc. required for a healthy diet. The traditional porridge is served on request once or twice a week only; the standard breakfast fare consists of toast or bread, margarine, jam, cornflakes (or other cereals in rotation), fresh milk and tea. A typical dinner (mid-day) menu looks like this:

1. Corned beef and fried egg.
2. Fish fingers.
3. Pork luncheon meat and salad H (H denotes Healthy Eating Option).
4. Stuffed peppers.
5. Cheese ploughmans.
   Choice of chips, boiled or jacket potatoes. Peas. Bread roll.

Some items are marked HL which denotes Halal Meat, prepared and cooked Muslim style, and available to everyone who wants it (the Halal cook made a name for himself on one occasion by delivering 276 spicy chicken pieces which was a popular choice that day).

The tea menu is similar to dinner. For supper, items to choose from would include biscuits, crisps or fresh fruit. In addition there is a canteen where prisoners can 'top up' their rations if they wish – there is no money exchanged as everything is kept account of 'on the book'. The stock items are extensive and a short list will illustrate what requirements are met:

Tobacco (most inmates roll their own)	Biscuits
Soft drinks	Stationary and stamps
Sweets	Tinned fish
Beverages	Tinned fruit
Toiletries (of all kinds)	Batteries

All inmates now receive payment of some kind. The highest paid men are those who work on the farm – they earn a maximum of £11 a week. Those doing less demanding work get an average of £7 weekly whilst those without employment receive £2.50 a week. Occupations undertaken by inmates comprise work on the farm, kitchens, laundry, a textile shop (manufacturing items for the Prison Service and the M.O.D., among others), carpenter shop and 'Concrete Creations' which manufacture high quality garden ornaments for sale in the Prison Museum.

Devon County Council Library Services supply library books; six books are allowed at any one time and provision is made for special requests. The men can keep in touch with their families (a common reason in the past for escapes by worried family men) by telephone; they buy prison phone cards. Letters are not restricted nowadays and up to three second class stamps a week are issued; any extra stamps have to be paid for. Prisoners no longer have to wait three years to be permitted a newspaper; eight free papers are issued daily on each landing in rotation after being rubber stamped 'Stage' – a left over from the old days when only Special Stage men got a paper to read. Inmates have the right to purchase any paper or periodical they wish providing it is on sale in an approved newsagent and can pay for it.

An inmate helps prepare a meal in the prison kitchen.

The modern textile shop at Dartmoor Prison. (Sewing mailbags is a thing of the past).

174

Drugs

Drugs are the curse of every jail, indeed of the country as a whole, and they find their way into the prisons by every imaginable (and unimaginable) means. A volume could be written concerning this problem alone, how to prevent it and more significantly how to apply a cure. Dartmoor prison has taken a lead in this direction by setting up a Drugs Rehabilitation Unit where Auricular Acupuncture techniques are having a significant effect on volunteer inmates. A vetting procedure is employed to select genuine applicants who live separately from all other prisoners in the special wing allocated for this project. Random testing (urine) is carried out every week and blood samples are sent for analysis if there is a positive result. (five per cent of **all** inmates provide a mandatory urine sample once a month). The Acupuncture is administered by trained officers and the methods are closely modelled on the famous Lincoln Centre in the Bronx area of New York City where those in need simply walk in from off the street and get free treatment. One Officer has confided to the author that several very young inmates have said to him *'I'm glad I'm in prison Gov, because if I weren't in here I'd be dead'*.

The Chaplaincy is an essential department in every prison. Many a man is admitted to Dartmoor anxious or afraid, perhaps angry and becomes lonely or suicidal. Sometimes they smash up their cells or attack one another or maybe an officer. Some kill themselves. *'Men without hope are dangerous'* is a maxim the chaplains are very much aware of and chaplains offer hope. They are led by a Church of England Chaplain (appointed in accordance with the Prison Act of 1952), but the department is a Multi-Faith one and includes a Roman Catholic, Methodist, Society of Friends (Quakers), Salvation Army, Church Army, a Muslim (Imam), Buddhist, Jehovah Witness, Christian Scientist and Ecumenical Chaplain, not all of whom are full time. Every prisoner is seen by one of these on entry, regardless of religious registration and everyone in solitary confinement or the hospital is visited regularly. Whatever his offence and however desperate a man may feel, a chaplain will always be there to help if he can. An additional service is provided by 'Listeners', officers and inmates specially trained for this important duty by the Samaritans.

Other facilities include a hospital with a full time Medical Officer assisted by trained prison officer nurses; a psychology department; education classes to G.S.E. standard by private contract paid for by the Department of Education; and a Resettlement Unit is being set up in what used to be 'the Block' which has been completely refurbished to provide forty five individual self contained units, entirely separate from the main prison, where selected inmates will prepare for their release under the guidance of the Princes Trust, local Employment Agencies and potential employers.

Compared to the old days an inmate's life now is one of luxury but it has to be remembered that loss of liberty can be a devastating experience. A prisoner has lost his liberty – that is his punishment. He cannot leave his cell until someone unlocks the door; he is told when he can shower, what time he can eat, when he can mix with his fellow inmates, when he can use the gym and go on exercise, in fact every aspect of normal life is restricted though not denied. It can be a dreary existence, each day being much the same, often for years. The onlooker may think he warrants it for whatever he has done and that Dartmoor prisoners are the worst of the bunch anyway and deserve no sympathy. Indeed no compassion was forthcoming when the author once asked a prisoner, a criminal who had been inside several other prisons besides Dartmoor, what his solution might be to the rising crime rate. His answer was short and uncompromising:

'shorter sentences but twice as hard!' was his reply. Dartmoor Prison Governor Graham Johnson takes a more reasoned and constructive view: 'Every prisoner here is somebody's son, brother, husband' he says 'and if you are going to lock a young man up in a stone cell for several hours out of 24 with just a book to read you are asking for trouble; it will not suffice for a man brought up in our modern society. We take the view that prisoners should be encouraged to accept responsibility and that if we treat them with respect they in turn will learn to demonstrate respect for us. It is about whose standards will prevail, ours or theirs. If their behaviour improves they can move through the Incentives and Earned Privileges Scheme (I.E.P.) – for example some of them now have televisions in their cells* (Author's note: they pay £1 per week). This approach is not new or special, it applies in several prisons all over the country. My aim is to give prisoners here the opportunity to improve their literacy and numeracy abilities and provide work experience so they acquire the basic skills which will help them when they are released. Furthermore, I want to attract men from the South West from other prisons so that they can be near to and get support from their families in preparing for their eventual return to the community they belong to'.

So there you have it – there is so sign of closure. Dartmoor Prison may look gloomy and uninviting from the outside but things are improving on the inside and not just because of cosmetic changes. A new approach to prisoners is being initiated by the Prison Service in an effort to prepare them for their eventual return to society as useful citizens. Dartmoor's reputation as a hard prison for hard men is fading, but its history will always attract an interest and hopefully will provide lessons from which we can all learn.

SIGNIFICANT DATES.

November 1850	Dartmoor converted to a Convict Prison.
1853	Penal Servitude Act ends Transportation.
1853	Three Valiant Soldiers die in snowstorm.
1865	Schoolteacher Sweeney dies in snowstorm.
1883	GWR Steam Railway opens connecting Princetown to Plymouth.
1914	Outbreak of World War One.
1917	Convicts transferred and Dartmoor receives over 1000 Conscientious Objectors.
January 1932	Dartmoor Prison mutiny. Army and Police called to restore order.
September 1939	Outbreak of World War Two. Some military prisoners and IRA at Dartmoor.
1945	World War Two ends. Borstal boys at Dartmoor.
1954	Warders disarmed. Snider guns dispensed with.
1967	Corporal punishment abolished in British prisons.
1979	Dietary punishments abolished.
1990	Riots. Prison block extensively damaged.
1994	Complete refurbishment programme in progress.
2001	Dartmoor Prison regraded category C (low risk inmates).

EPILOGUE

'*I walked out of the prison one cold February morning when the outlines of the walls were blurred by a Dartmoor mist; a heavy dew lay about the mossy stones and birds were trilling their morning song. The damp, moisture-laden air muffled my footsteps and I marvelled at the perfect quiet that prevailed in an establishment where hundreds of convicted men lay sleeping. Outside the Old Chapel I stopped, was that a babble of foreign tongues I could hear beyond the doorway? I sensed a restless murmuring within those dark confines where the Romans, 'King Dick' Crafus and the 'Rough Alleys' lived all those years ago, and in my mind I could hear distant drumbeats and heavy boots crunching in unison along the old Military Walkway. Sharp commands broke the brittle early morning stillness I thought, and through the gloom I imagined the shapes of men pulling a cart on which were a number of rough boxes, sliding and jolting as they made their way from the old hospital towards the burial ground outside; pillars of smoke arose from the cookeries and there was a clanging of pots from within where the cooks were already at work; water gurgled in the waterways; it all seemed very real to me.*

My reverie was shattered by the squawking of the jackdaws that throng the prison (which the convicts of long ago said were the reincarnation of old lags) and I walked on. The ancient stone wall curves towards the gateway, undulating in graceful vertical waves, caused by the passage of time and the innumerable repairs it has undergone; but its shape, height, and the encompassing barrier it represents is much the same as it always was. These are the stones that reverberated to the sound of muskets when the Americans were shot down; yells of reproach and the screams of wounded men echo down the years. The way out lies over the very ground where they fell, desperate men who were not criminals, but soldiers and sailors taken in battle amid cannon fire and the waving of standards; then I passed through the gateway where a poor Frenchman cut his own throat after failing to produce his bedding and was refused his release because of it.

Outside the prison, the tower of the Church of St. Michael and all Angels stands tall among the trees, having weathered almost two centuries of Dartmoor storms. It is a monument to the men of America and those who served Napoleon. Stone by stone they built it and hopefully it will survive many more years, a lasting testament to the futility of war and the hope of peace for every nation'. (Anon.)

BIBLIOGRAPHY

History of Plymouth and its Neighbourhood by C.W. Brachen B.A.,F.E.S. (Underhill, Plymouth 1931).

History of Plymouth by John Harris.

British Economic and Social History 1700-1980 by J. Walker M.A., Ph.D. (Macdonald & Evans 1981).

History of the English People in the 19th. Century Vol. 1. by Elie Halevy. (Ernest Bean Ltd. 1924).

English Historical Documents (Douglas & Greenaway). (Gen. Editor David C. Douglas M.A. Eyre Methuen. 1981).

Buildings of England by Bridget Cherry and Nikolaus Pavsner. (Devon Books).

Outside the Law (from Studies in Crime and order 1650-1850). Edited by John Rule (Exeter Papers in Economic History).

The House of Commons 1790-1820 (History of Parliament) Ed. R.G. Thorne 1986 V.

Dictionary of National Biography.

Dictionary of American Biography.

Maritime History of Devon by M.M. Openheim.

Years of Victory 1802-1812 by Arthur Bryant.

Princetown – the Work of Sir Thomas Tyrwhitt and Daniel Alexander (extract from *Regional Architecture of the West of.England*) by Sir Albert E. Richardson and L. Gill

Historical Records of the 1st. Devon Militia by Col. H. Walrond (Longman, Green & Co.).

The Marches of a Militiaman – an Account of Life in the 1st. Devon Militia (Anonymous). (Anon.) P.R.O., Coxside, Plymouth.

The Amateur Military Tradition by Ian W. Beckett (Manchester University Press 1991).

The British Army – a Concise History by Jock Haswell (Book Club Associates, London).

Prisoners of War in Britain 1756-1815 by Francis Abell (H. Milford – Oxford University Press 1914).

French Prisoners Lodges by John T. Thorp (Printed in Leicester by George Gibbons 1900).

Our Brothers the Enemy by Ron Chudley (Published privately).

Napoleon by Vincent Cronin (Harper Colins 1994).

Napoleon – Master of Europe 1805-1807 by Alistair Horne (Weiderfield and Niclolson).

The Emperor's Last Island by Julia Blackburn (Mandarin Books 1991).

The Fall of Napoleon by David Hamilton-Williams (Brockhampton Press 1999).

The Two Sisters by Jules Poulain.

Diary of Benjamin Palmer, Privateersman by B.F. Palmer (1914).

A Prisoner's Memoires or Dartmoor Prison by Charles Andrews (New York 1852).

Description of Dartmoor Prison with an Account of the Massacre at the Prison by a former American prisoner J. Mellish (1815).

Devonshire Characters and Strange Events by Rev. S. Baring-Gould (John Lane the Bodley Head Ltd. 1908).

Princetown Massacre: Footnote to Baring Gould's account by M.G. Dickinson. (Devon and Cornwall Notes & Queries. Vol.6. p.248-9).

Princetown Massacre.   Devon Record Office (Exeter) – Devon Quarter Sessions:
                         Bundle for Michaelmas 1815 - Box 285.
                         Bundle for Exeter 1815 - Box 284.

Article by Reginald Horsman, Distinguished Professor of History at the University of Wisconsin
   – Milwaukee. Author of *The War of 1812* (Knopf. 1969).

The War of 1812 by Donald R. Hickey (University of Illinois Press 1989).

Princetown – its History and its Prisons: Three Articles by H.S. Hill in the *Western Daily
   Mercury* April 1869).

Transactions of the Devonshire Association (various).

High Dartmoor by Eric Hemery.

A Perambulation of Dartmoor by Samuel Rowe.

Home Scenes of Tavistock and its Vicinity by Rachel Evans. 1846.

One Hundred Years on Dartmoor by William Crossing.

Princetown – its Rise and Progress by William Crossing.

The Criminal by Basil Thomson (Hodder & Stoughton, London 1925).

The Story of Dartmoor Prison by Basil Thomson William Heinemann, London, 1907).

Dartmoor Prison by Rufus Endle (Bossiney Books 1979).

Dartmoor Prison by A.J. Rhodes.

Prison on the Moor by Justin Atholl (John Long Ltd.).

The Truth about Dartmoor by G. Dendrickson and F. Thomas (Vistor Gollancz Ltd., 1954).

Princetown and its Prison by Rev. L. Woollacombe.

Dartmoor Prison Past and Present by Capt. Vernon Harris (William Brendon & Sons).

Leaves from a Prison Diary (2 Vols.) by Michael Davitt (Chapman & Hall, London 1885).

Convict Life – Revelations concerning Convicts and Convict Prisons by 'A Ticket of Leave Man'
   (Wyman & Sons 1879).

A Prison Chaplain on Dartmoor by Rev. Clifford Rickards, M.D. (Edward Arnold 1920).

Shades of the Prison House by Stuart Wood (Williams & Norgate, London 1932)

Victorian Prison Lives by Philip Priestley (Methuen, London 1985).

Dartmoor Prison Lyrics by Oliver Davies (Erskine Macdonald 1915).

The Victorian Underworld by Kellow Chesney (History Book Club 1970).

Selected extracts from: *The Western Morning News* Plymouth.
                          Tavistock Gazette.
                          Truemans Exeter Flying Post.
                          The Western Mercury
                          The Times.